Women, Incarcerated

Women, Incarcerated

Narratives from India

Edited by

Mahuya Bandyopadhyay
Rimple Mehta

Orient BlackSwan

WOMEN, INCARCERATED: NARRATIVES FROM INDIA

ORIENT BLACKSWAN PRIVATE LIMITED

Registered Office
3-6-752 Himayatnagar, Hyderabad 500 029, Telangana, India
e-mail: centraloffice@orientblackswan.com

Other Offices
Bengaluru, Chennai, Guwahati, Hyderabad, Kolkata,
Mumbai, New Delhi, Noida, Patna

First published by Orient Blackswan Private Limited 2022

ISBN 978-93-5442-188-4

040934

Typeset in
Dante MT Std 11/13.5 *by*
Le Studio Graphique, Gurgaon 122 007

Printed in India at
Avantika Printers Private Limited, New Delhi 110 020

Published by
Orient Blackswan Private Limited
3-6-752 Himayatnagar, Hyderabad 500 029, Telangana, India
e-mail: info@orientblackswan.com

Contents

Abbreviations

BPRD	Bureau of Police Research and Development
BSF	Border Security Force
CIA	Central Intelligence Agency
CPI-ML	Communist Party of India (Marxist-Leninist)
CrPC	Criminal Procedure Code
CWC	Child Welfare Committee
DINA	Dirección Nacional de Inteligencia, Chile
DLSA	District Legal Services Authority
FMLN	Farabundo Marti National Liberation Front
ICPR	International Centre for Policy Research
IPC	Indian Penal Code
MIR	Movimiento de Izquierda Revolucionaria, Chile
MISA	Maintenance of Internal Security Act 1971
NACJW	National Authority on Custodial Justice to Women
NALSA	National Legal Services Authority
NCL	non-criminal lunatic
NCRB	National Crime Records Bureau
NDPS	Narcotic Drugs and Psychotropic Substances Act, 1985
NGO	non-governmental organisation
OBC	Other Backward Classes
OPD	Out Patient Department
PIL	Public Interest Litigation
PRI	Penal Reform International
PTSD	post-traumatic stress disorder
SC	Scheduled Caste

SFI	Students' Federation of India
SLSA	State Legal Services Authority
SP	Superintendent of Police
ST	Scheduled Tribe
UNODC	United Nations Office on Drugs and Crime

ACKNOWLEDGEMENTS

Researching prisons and prisoners' lives is a challenging journey and we are grateful for the support we have found along the way. This book is a result of the discussions and papers presented at a workshop titled 'Carceral Logics and Social Justice: Women Prisoners in India', held at the Tata Institute of Social Sciences (TISS), Mumbai in March 2018. Clearly, the book has been in the making for a long time now. We have been joined by several friends, colleagues, and well-wishers in formal and informal ways in this movement from idea to fruition.

First, we thank the Tokyo Foundation for Policy Research (Tokyo Foundation) for supporting us through the SYLFF Leadership Initiatives (SLI) award for the project titled 'Carceral Logics and Social Justice: Women Prisoners in India'. Ms Aya Oyamada needs special mention here for instilling faith in our idea, for patiently answering all our questions, and liaising with us on behalf of Tokyo Foundation. The award from Tokyo Foundation supported the workshop, this edited volume, and meetings with activists, scholars, and practitioners in Mumbai, Delhi, and Kolkata with an effort to build a network of individuals and organisations that work in prisons. We are thankful to Joyashree Roy and the JU-SYLFF team at Jadavpur University for guiding us through the process of applying for the SLI award. Uma Chakravarti and Vijay Raghavan are our strengths as we navigate prison worlds and lives. We thank them for egging us on and believing in our ideas.

The workshop focused on issues experienced by women in prisons in India, and we invited participants from different parts of the country to speak on their work with women in prison and how they conceptualised gender justice in prisons. We attempted to initiate a dialogue among activists, scholars, and practitioners working with women in prisons in India, and to that end, the participants varied widely in their professional profiles. We would like to thank Vijay Raghavan, Penelope Tong, Mamta Kumari, Swati Sathe, Upneet Lalli, Uma Chakravarti, Shereen Sadiq, Sadaf Modak, and Sharmila Purkayastha for generating a robust discussion through their presentations. Most of them are also our contributing authors, and this volume would not have been possible without their sustained interest in entering into these difficult dialogues across disciplinary boundaries, and those of academia, administration, and social work practice.

We appreciate the efforts of the chairpersons for the sessions at the workshop—Meena Gopal, Shewli Kumar, Sharon Menezes, Vijay Raghavan, and Shamim Modi—for nuancing the discussions and providing their insights into the issues under discussion. We regret that Ilina Sen is not here with us today to share this moment. We remember, with deep gratitude, her encouraging presence at the workshop, the pertinent questions she raised, and the warmth of her engagement with our work and ideas.

We thank S. Parasuraman and Shalini Bharat for providing support to the workshop in their capacity as Directors of the Tata Institute of Social Sciences. We also extend our gratitude to Surinder Jaswal, Deputy Director, Tata Institute of Social Sciences for the welcome address at the workshop. We thank Ms Tomoko Yamada from Tokyo Foundation for her presence at the workshop and her perceptive comments, which will stay with us as we take our work in new directions.

We acknowledge the contribution of our institutions of current affiliation—the Indian Institute of Technology (Delhi) and Western Sydney University—for fostering a supportive environment that has enabled our work on this book.

The team at Orient BlackSwan has, as always, been exemplary in its support, diligence, and meticulous handling of the work that has gone into making this book. Our special words of gratitude and appreciation go out to Vidya Rao for her encouragement in early conversations with her when the book was just an idea, and to Nilanjana Majumdar and Proteeti Banerjee who have worked on the book, despite very trying times, on personal and professional fronts. We also thank Priya Kuriyan and Samprati Pani—Priya, for her generous acceptance of our request to use her illustration for the cover of the book and Samprati for designing the cover.

And finally, a few words on this partnership of ours. Given the issues of access and limited public interest in issues of prisons and prisoners, working in this field can be isolating. But collaborative work and writing together on such complex issues too are never easy. We are grateful for having forged bonds of a special collaboration between the editors and the contributors, which has lent a humane edge to the otherwise dehumanised spaces and narratives that we deal with in our work. Raya has been a witness to our evolving partnership, and we are grateful to her for bearing with our 'prison talk' and accommodating our time to work on this book with her vacations, school, theatre classes, etc.

The manuscript was completed towards the end of 2019, much before the COVID-19 pandemic became a reality in all our lives. The pandemic has had devastating effects on women in prison and their families. Although this book does not focus on women prisoners' experiences of the pandemic, we hope this will initiate a discussion on the deep-rooted issues that confront women in prisons in India.

Introduction
Carceral Logics, Gender Justice, and Resistance

Mahuya Bandyopadhyay and Rimple Mehta

> *Before I was married, I thought the sound of bangles jangling on my forearms would be delightful. I looked forward to being able to wear bells around my ankles and silver necklaces around my neck, but not anymore, not since I had learned what they represented for the man who gave them. A necklace was no prettier than a piece of rope that ties a goat to a tree depriving it of freedom.*
>
> Devi, et al. 1997, 143

Whether as a gun-slinging criminal, India's bandit queen, or a *Devi*, an incarnation of goddess Durga, Phoolan Devi's life offers insights into the journeys of a woman from her home to the prison and beyond. Marriage at the age of eleven, and rape and abuse by her much older husband for several years before she fled and joined a gang of burglars, was only the beginning of a long and arduous experience of confinement and torture. One of the turning points in her life was her gang-rape by members of an upper-caste rival gang when she was eighteen, which led to her transformation as a gang leader in her own right. She returned to the village, seeking out those who had tortured her. She found two of them, who refused to divulge the whereabouts of the others. She opened fire indiscriminately, killing the two rapists and twenty other villagers. This went down in history as the Behmai massacre, and led to her being labelled a fearless and ruthless killer. In contrast, among many of her people, she was seen as a messiah, a Devi, who helped rape survivors and took from the rich to distribute to the poor.

The ankle bells, bangles, and necklaces, which once appeared as objects of beauty and freedom, were symbolic of Phoolan Devi's experience of confinement as she traversed different institutional sites—home, family, marriage, gang, prison, and State. The ankle bells and necklaces were no different from the handcuffs and ropes. The paradox of being a messiah and a dangerous criminal is embedded in these institutional contexts and their intersections of caste, class, and gender. Phoolan Devi is immortalised as a dangerous criminal through the Behmai massacre. The events that led to her violent act have been invisibilised, and her narrative is silenced.

Phoolan Devi's case represents a broader malaise in the fields of criminology and prison studies in India, wherein the figure of the 'female criminal' or the 'female prisoner' has simultaneously been invisibilised and memorialised. Women's Studies has also paid scant attention to women in prisons in India. The understanding and treatment of the female criminal tend to be expressed in relation to male criminality. When the female criminal or prisoner is written about, she is presented as extraordinary, grotesque, and demonic, one who has not only broken the legal frame but has also transgressed several normative and moral boundaries of social life. The figure of the female deviant is seen to bring dishonour to the family and the wider community. Honour, then, is the crucial context within which female deviance is perceived, not just by the institutions of the family and community but by the criminal justice system as well.

This volume demonstrates how the prison and the State act as extended arms of the domains of family and community in dealing with women deviants/criminals. One of the strategies for upholding the honour of the family is the invisibilisation of the female criminals or deviants, keeping them behind the men as only accomplices. Through this, they are further invisibilised in the criminal justice system. For instance, our fieldwork experience has shown that in instances where men and women are case partners, women were given little information about the progress of their cases and were less likely to be considered for bail than their male case partners. The practice of invisibilisation involves multiple strategies, requiring the complicity of institutions beyond the prison. The nature of this collusion and the roles of these institutions determine whether the female deviant will be completely invisible, partly visible as an accomplice, or memorialised for her extraordinary criminal feats.

To address the paradoxical ways in which the lives of women criminals/prisoners are represented, the chapters focus on both the mundane and the extraordinary aspects of their lives, drawing on experiences from Punjab, West Bengal, Maharashtra, and Uttar Pradesh. Some of the chapters use cases across multiple states in the country. The book is a collaborative effort, bringing together a cohort of researchers, social work practitioners, administrators, and activists, whose work revolves around issues affecting women prisoners. Such collaboration is vital because of the securitised and closed nature of the prison, which makes access not only complicated, but also often impossible. The book narrates the experiences of exclusion, marginalisation, and violence in the lives of women prisoners. It also deals with the collapse and remaking of everyday life, interwoven with women's reflections on the different institutions their lives have traversed. We seek to initiate a dialogue between academics and practitioners who deal with the prison system on an everyday basis. While all the contributions in the volume challenge the invisibilisation/memorialisation paradox, they do so from their disciplinary and practice-oriented locations. This brings in a diversity of theoretical and practical considerations to the understanding of the lives of women prisoners. The chapters focus on unravelling the connections between the intimate institutions of family, marriage and kinship, and the State-run prisons, courts, and police, and comment on the methodological and practical difficulties of working with women prisoners. The perspectives of administrators, social work practitioners, and the disciplinary engagements of sociology, literature, history, and women's studies nuance the understanding of the lives and contexts of women prisoners. For instance, the chapters engage with questions of love and the bonds of solidarity among women prisoners differently. Both Kanupriya Sharma and B. D. Sharma's chapters show how love and solidarities among prisoners enable us to rethink the nature of the prison space as simply and unidimensionally oppressive. B. D. Sharma's chapter shows the practical use of these bonds of solidarity towards a creative endeavour. The production of a play uses this solidarity amongst prisoners, and this reveals its empowering character. The volume engages in several such dialogues between researchers, activists, administrators, and social work practitioners, which are critical in rethinking prisons.

The experiences of women prisoners' marginality, in the context of the invisibilisation/memorialisation paradox, produces a sense of deep disquiet. There are layers of neglect and suppression of voice and a sensationalised interest in and desire to represent the women prisoner or criminal. The marginality of women prisoners is evidenced through everyday practices within the prison system and in terms of State policy. This was particularly evident during the Covid-19 pandemic when the constitutional right to life and health was severely compromised for the prison population. Further, the gendered dimension of women's confinement, both within the home and the prison, were exacerbated during the lockdown on account of the pandemic. The shadow of the 'long lockdown' reveals the inequities of access to space and resources, increased surveillance, and social isolation that put women in vulnerable circumstances. Access to processes of justice during the pandemic, such as access to lawyers, interviews with family, furloughs, and visits to courts, were all further compromised during the lockdown.

The Supreme Court of India mandated that each state form a High-Powered Committee to frame guidelines to decongest prisons. The general guidelines were to ensure interim release of prisoners on bail, based on criteria such as the nature and severity of the offence and the length of the sentence. The issue of decongestion of prisons was seen in terms of security and severity of crime, and was not prisoner-centric. Several states attempted to extend the ambit of these guidelines to include more criteria for the release of prisoners, such as first-time offenders, prisoners who had been granted bail but could not furnish bail bonds, elderly prisoners, and pregnant women (Bansal and Sahni 2021).

Despite this, the criminal justice systems' handling of the cases of Safoora Zargar and Father Stan Swamy[1] stand testimony to the additional repression of prisoners during the pandemic. Safoora Zargar was pregnant when she was arrested under the Unlawful Activities (Prevention) Act, 1967 but was denied bail several times, despite the prevalent health risks to her and her child. This was in direct contravention of the basic constitutional right to life and health and all international guidelines related to women prisoners. The granting of interim release to women prisoners is further complicated when they do not have a safe space to go to; nor are there processes in place to ascertain the provision of safe spaces outside the prison. Women prisoners' experiences of repression and marginality must be seen in the context of their lives in structures and institutions beyond the prison, such as marriage, family, caste, and class. The chapters reveal these connections through the narratives of women prisoners, and provide a perspective that provokes us to rethink the fault-lines between the legal/illegal, civility/criminality, violence/torture, and love, conformity, and resistance.

The volume raises some critical questions. How is the prison as an organisation gendered? In what ways do the threat and the actual use of violence, explicitly or implicitly sexualised, feature in the management, control, and treatment of female prisoners? Is it possible to trace narrative continuities between female prisoners' experience of prison life and their experience outside the prison? Leading from this question, would it be possible to explain the totalising nature and mortifying effects of the prison, and to explore the diminished, somewhat disruptive influences of the exercise of total power? What are the different categories through which the State constructs the identity of the female prisoner/criminal, and how are these identities negotiated with alternate and competing discourses? What do women's narratives and writing reveal about the prison as an institution and about the State's treatment of the 'female prisoner/criminal'? And finally, how do these narratives seek to ascribe 'voice' to women prisoners, reconstructing the image of the female prisoner/criminal and our institutions of correction and control?

Carceral Logics

The chapters unfold the workings of the carceral logic and its impact on the lives of women prisoners. Bourdieu's (1980) conception of practice frames our understanding of this carceral logic. It enables us to present the nuances of everyday prison life without collapsing them into the dualistic categories of 'formal-informal' interaction, 'disciplined-rule breaking' activities, or 'agency-total control' of one group over another. Practice negotiates the form, content, and direction of an event. In prison, the actions of the participants, namely the prisoners, warders, and officers, shape any activity. Viewing everyday prison practice as a combination of the formal properties of the system and the dynamics of the agents participating and interacting in the doing of an event[2] reveals layers of the carceral logic that are both transgressive and aligned to the objective of the State.

The totalising structure of the prison seeks to control the prisoner population. Several homogenising practices produce and sustain this totalising structure. Examples of such methods are the classification of prisoners, a rigid everyday routine, strict regulations over the use of prison space, and spatio-temporal constraints on physical mobility and social interactions. These practices reveal the carceral logic of order, control, discipline, and punishment. For instance, the classification of prisoners according to their crimes, their status as undertrials or convicts, and the number of years served is one of the critical practices through which the specific histories of individual prisoners' pre-prison lives and circumstances of their arrest are erased. While this erasure may be considered essential for the management of the prisoner population, the specific histories of pre-prison conditions and consequent incarceration continue to frame the everyday identities of women in prison. Their attempts to negotiate the everyday are further interrupted through the rigid everyday routine and the controls on prison space. Compulsory participation in the regular head count of prisoners ensured adherence to the strict everyday routine and their inability to access different areas within the prison. Space and time are thus both under surveillance. Bodily autonomy was severely constrained, not just through norms around what to wear and how to present the body, but also through controls on mobility and physical interaction with other 'bodies'. These controls create the normative idea of an ideal prisoner body, ensure ease of governing a population perceived to be socially and criminally deviant, and present an overall image of ordered institutional space. All these practices instate discipline within the prison, among prisoners and staff. Such order and conformity create the image of a humane prison, where the goals of prison management and individual prisoners' trajectories coalesce, obliterating any grounds for disharmony.

The projected sense of order camouflages the threat of violence, its regular occurrence, and the accompanying practices of punishments that compel conformity. Violence in prison takes different forms. First, the rhetoric of retribution, punishment, and deterrence demands a certain level of severity that the system adopts and perpetuates in dealing with offenders. Carrying *lathi*s (long wooden sticks) and using physical force is an acceptable way of managing indiscipline. Second, the scarcity of resources and the lack of adequate infrastructural facilities perpetuate violence in two forms—in the indignity of life for the prisoner and the contestations between prisoners over scarce resources. Everyday activities, such as collecting food, sleeping, using the washroom, and the use of water, could potentially become sites of violent confrontations between prisoners. These conflicts are then managed with the use of further violence. Third, the institutional practice of placing a convict in charge of the rest of the inmates legitimises the use of force by such a prisoner to control other inmates. Intersections of community, caste, and class locations aggravate and complicate the hierarchies amongst prisoners. Further, this practice creates newer hierarchies among prisoners and allows for the use of power by one prisoner over another. These are some of the consequences of prison governance.

Violence gets ingrained in everyday functioning, thereby normalising and legitimising its use. Prisoners respond variously to the homogenising and hegemonic practices of prison management. While they appear to be conforming to the established modes of governance, they are, in fact, continuously attempting to negotiate the conditions of prison life through the everyday re-working of these homogenising practices. These everyday negotiations resonate with Bourdieu's (1980) understanding of practice as spontaneous and fleeting. A sense of urgency and immediacy marks everyday practice as the actor or participant in a particular system reacts to a situation that arises within the system. The practice is a response to the 'matter in hand', and is therefore irreversible. Any change in the system, event or interaction that generates the practice can thus alter the practice itself. Despite the routine, fixed, and repetitive everyday that otherwise marks life in prison, the notion of practice has the potential to reveal the transient and fragmented nature of everyday life in prison. For Bourdieu (ibid.), structures are not universal or unchanging, regardless of social conditions, and practice too is generative.

Prisoners use various strategies in response to the homogenising and hegemonic practices of prison life. These are the collaborative management of subversions, managing the image of the female ward and the female prisoner, fostering relationships of mutual benefit with the prison staff, and using every opportunity of mobility within and outside the prison to experience a sense of self and express bodily desires. These are what Scott (1990) would call the 'hidden transcripts' of prison life, which create new structures of meaning and invert, in seemingly insignificant and temporary ways, the effects of hegemonic power.

Gendering the Prison

Penal policy, through most of the twentieth century, was influenced by the intervention of psychiatry in the correctional sphere and was dominated by the belief that women prisoners are likely to be mentally disturbed or inadequate (Zedner 1991). An instance of this in the Indian context is the *pagol bari* (literally, mad house or mental hospital) in Kolkata, where the perceived socially deviant women were imprisoned.

It is no coincidence that with the rise in mental health rights movements, this *pagol bari* was shut, only to be replaced by a women's prison. Before the implementation of the West Bengal Correctional Services Act 1992, the Presidency Central Jail in Kolkata consisted of wards for male prisoners, a separate ward for female prisoners, and one for 'non-criminal lunatic' (NCL) women. This ward too was referred to as the *pagol bari* or the NCL ward. Women prisoners who showed signs of transgression or inability to cope with life in the female ward were often transferred to the NCL ward, ostensibly for treatment and concerns of safety. The threat of transfer to the NCL ward or to a prison in a remote area was one of the ways of disciplining women. In these practices of isolation, containment, and punishment, the response to social deviance and criminality of the female prisoners obliterates the difference between the two. The remnants of this belief persist, and women's criminality continues to be perceived as the performance of femininity and failings of character.

Spatial organisation and access to space are, then, ways of disciplining the female body within the prison. Such disciplining is accomplished primarily through establishing enclosures for women prisoners as additionally fortified, both in terms of physical location and organisation, and through practices of governing female prisoners. The prison is organised with the male prisoner as the archetype. The female prisoner occupies a marginal position in the organisation of prison practice and management and the logic of the carceral. This marginal position is a continuation from the pre-prison experience of exclusion, patriarchal violence, and invisibilisation, where women are denied a sense of self and their identities are attached to the feminine roles within patriarchal institutions.

Women barely occupy 4–5 per cent of the prison population in India, and as a result, they are often left out of the imagination of the prison as an organisation. The disproportionately high number of male prisoners to female prisoners is one of the justifications for the neglect of women's prisons. In Chapter 6, based on empirical research in two women's prisons in Maharashtra, Yerwada Women's Prison and Mumbai District Women's Prison, Sadaf Modak examines prison structures from a gender perspective. The chapter compares the seemingly gender-neutral term 'prisoner' used in prison policy documents with the lived realities of incarcerated women. The female identity within prison represents not only the legal subject in the criminal justice system, but also the social construction of gender. Through the female inmate, the author attempts to understand the kind of citizen the prison creates by examining aspects like education, work, health, space, children, discipline, and sexuality. Prison emerges as another space that reflects and reproduces gendered structures from society.

The female ward is often referred to as a 'prison within a prison'. Spatially, it is a smaller area carved out within a male prison. This physical structure, isolating female prisoners, is reinforced by other boundary-making and confinement practices applicable to women prisoners especially. The idea of the female prisoners as a vulnerable group, a group the authorities could not take 'any risks with', is evident in the practices of boundary creation and maintenance. Thus, the invisibilisation and marginalisation of the female prisoner is not merely an error of omission, but is integral to the organisation of the prison.

The organisation of the female ward and the provisions of security around it replicate societal stereotypes and gendered norms practised outside the prison for keeping women in control, on the pretext of protecting them. The women inhabit the female ward and are not permitted to traverse the other parts of the prison outside their ward without an escort. Men, however, may be able to seek permission to access different parts of the prison. The organisation of space is one aspect of gendering the prison. The practices adopted to maintain order and discipline further perpetuate gender stereotypes. For instance, during our fieldwork in prisons in Kolkata, we observed that cases where rules were not followed, either by the women prisoners or by the staff, were regarded as 'internal matters'. The prison authorities attempted to resolve such cases from within and took great care to keep out any 'outsiders'. Arbitrary measures were employed to deal with such infractions, putting the women prisoners in an even more vulnerable position. In the absence of any formal complaints, women prisoners were denied access to the rules, directives, and redressal mechanisms prevalent in the broader prison regime. Although these instances were not officially reported, gossip around them was common, both among the male prisoners and the staff. The official silence and the gossip that maligns the women prisoners contribute to their sense of disempowerment.

Our work in prisons in Kolkata has further revealed that when men violate prison rules, the prison staff tends to normalise these infractions. Over time, they appear to legitimise such indiscipline. The dynamics of the relationship between the male prisoners and prison staff indicate the tensions and possibilities of moments where there may be an inversion of power. The caution observed by the prison staff while dealing with the male prisoners is one way in which they try to preserve order in prison. Any show of resistance or perceived deviance on the part of the women prisoners is viewed as antithetical to maintaining order and discipline in prison. Classic works on women prisoners draw a connection between the worlds of women prisoners and their experiences of patriarchy and social and economic marginalisation, as distinct from men, both in prison and in society at large (Giallombardo 1966; Heffernan 1972; Ward and Kassebaum 1965).

The Crime in India report 2016 elucidates that about 20 per cent of the total number of women arrested under Indian Penal Code (IPC) crimes from all age groups were arrested for 'Cruelty by Husband or his Relatives', and 45 per cent for the undefined category of 'Other IPC Crimes'. These two are among the thirty-two types of crime listed in the report. The largest share of women's crimes is either in the realm of the undefined general 'other' category or within the domain of marital and familial circumstances. Empirical work has shown (Bandyopadhyay 2010; Cherukuri 2008; Shankardass 2012) that women's roles in the crimes that they are accused of are not easily discernible. They may become scapegoats in crimes committed by male members of the family or other significant men in their lives. Shankardass (2012), through narratives of women prisoners, presents the processes of 'location, dislocation and relocation' that women go through within institutions of confinement and outside, and shows the nature and extent of gender discrimination in society and its pernicious presence in State institutions of confinement.

How women prisoners deal with life in prison and the continuance of the gendered structures across different spaces is a significant question that emerges from Modak's chapter, and is taken up by Mehta (Chapter 7) and Honawar and Raghavan (Chapter 8). They draw on empirical research among foreign national prisoners and recidivists, respectively, to show how the subversions, resistance, and agency of different types of prisoners shape the prison as an institution. Mehta's work reveals the additional burdens of incarceration faced by the Bangladeshi women prisoners. These Bangladeshi women challenge ideas of space and time in prison through their bodily and emotional experiences. Although they do not express themselves in what would otherwise be considered cognitive coherence, their narratives compel us to reconstruct some of our ideas and beliefs about space and time. In addition, it is important to note that these women crossed the boundaries of their homes and national borders to pursue their aspirations or needs for survival. Their actions were direct infringements of State laws. Significantly, they also violated societal norms pertaining to their roles and responsibilities, especially within the domestic realm.

Women are not considered entirely 'rational' human beings because of the emotive weight of their roles and responsibilities in the domestic realm. Thus, their engagement with political and public issues is perceived to be only at an emotive level, and are seen as justifications to disqualify them from actively participating in public life. The invisibilisation of women in the political sphere also stems from the inability to imagine women as being able to engage in public spaces and with political issues at a cognitive level. Prison life further accentuates this invisibilisation. A prisoner is devoid of political rights, and women prisoners occupy an even lower position in terms of their access to political life. Although women's participation in and contribution to political movements in India has received some attention, their lives in prison as revolutionaries have not been adequately represented in either literature or cinema. In this volume, Chakravarti (Chapter 1) reflects on the narratives of women prisoners that she collected while making a documentary on women political prisoners. The author met, heard, and filmed the voices of women political prisoners across India. Their stories cover the period from Emergency (1975–1977) to the contemporary moment. What do these narratives tell us about incarceration and its disciplinary uses; women's socio-political locations and their negotiations with the public space of the 'political'; and their experiences of incarceration—these questions are central to the chapter.

The chapters in this volume trace the pathways to the crime through the worlds of women's familial and intimate relationships, foregrounding the need to understand the connections between patriarchal social relations, intersections of caste, class, and community, and the experiences of women prisoners. Incarceration and its effects on women's lives and the nature of the prison as an organisation cannot be seen in isolation from women's personal histories. We have argued earlier in this introduction about the homogenising practices of the governance of prisoners, which rest on such an erasure of personal histories. In rethinking prison governance and penal policy, and in attempting to re-design prisons as correctional homes, the homogenising practices and the carceral logic of order and discipline persist. This carceral logic inhibits the inclusion of embodied experience. The chapters in this volume show that the nuances of lived experience must be an integral part of rethinking the prison.

Resistance and Nature of the Political

A scene from the 1960s film *Bandini* of a woman grinding grain at the hand-operated *chakki* (grinder) in a prison is in continuity with the metaphors of home and women's roles as caregivers, central to the depiction of women prisoners. In Chapter 1, Uma Chakravarti begins with this scene, in which Nutan, the lead actress, sings a song of separation from her natal family. While the hero of the film is a revolutionary figure, Nutan remains confined to the portrait of an ordinary prisoner. She is depicted as betrayed by the revolutionary hero and has been convicted for the murder of his wife. Cinema has found it challenging to reverse the image of the revolutionary hero to that of a woman, despite their active involvement in several rights-based movements. For instance, in the Telangana armed struggle of 1946–1949, women were equal participants, but their contributions were invisibilised. Through her on-camera interviews with erstwhile women political prisoners, Chakravarti resurrects the image of the female revolutionary hero, otherwise the domain of men. She opens the space for discussing what constitutes the 'political', and women's association with and depiction of political work.

The depictions of women prisoners' lives, set in different types of prisons in India and marked out by the specific background narratives, at once ordinary and extraordinary, uncover a compelling and emergent ethnography of the prison as a coercive institution. The view of the prison as a coercive institution is expressed through the writings of women prisoners about the gendered forms of control and management of their lives in prison. However, this is only one aspect of everyday prison life. Almost all the chapters bring forth stories of negotiation, resistance, and exemplary courage displayed by the women prisoners. Through this, we present narratives of the nature of the 'political' as it unfolds in women prisoners' lives.

The prison also acts as a repository of the State's mechanism of violence. In Chapter 2, Sharmila Purkayastha examines the invisibilised history of incarceration and torture of women political prisoners in India, and focuses on the experiences of women in left-wing movements. From the perspective of the State, Naxalite and Maoist politics has been outlawed. This has been used to persecute political prisoners in numerous ways—through anti-terror and sedition laws, false cases and prolonged detention periods without bail, and torture. Although there are silences around sexual torture, the chapters clearly indicate the range of women's experiences of embodied violence, such as denial of the right to food, lack of access to health services, and regular beatings. As the narratives in the chapters articulate, it is futile to analyse the experience of torture of women prisoners within the heuristic frame of sexual and non-sexual forms of violence. It also indicates a reluctance to hear and acknowledge women's experiences within the broad spectrum of violence. The chapters show how women prisoners' narratives of their torture and incarceration have resisted such conceptual distinctions. The silences around the sexual nature of torture and details of the embodied violence they narrate are not contradictions; rather, they reveal the deeply gendered and sexual nature of violence in these State institutions of confinement.

Therefore, we argue that women prisoners articulate the feminist idea of reading the political in the personal in multiple ways: through challenging their roles in the intimate institutions, disrupting the conventional dichotomies between the public and private spheres, telling and retelling experiences of embodied violence in spaces of custody and care, and using both the public and the private domains to articulate a discourse of women's rights. An instance of such articulation can be found in women's participation in movements that directly affect their access to land and resources, which has been criminalised, leading to incarceration. These women may have never stepped out of the domestic sphere. Their claims, through protest, to rights connected to disruptions in their everyday make them suspects and amenable to State action. Sundari's incarceration is a case in point. Sundari, a homemaker in a fishing community in Idinthakarai in Tamil Nadu, was one of the key protesters in the movement against the Kudankulam nuclear power plant. She decided to protest the setting up of a nuclear plant near her home after seeing the Fukushima disaster in Japan on television, which involved a major earthquake, a tsunami, and a nuclear accident at the Fukushima Daiichi nuclear power plant. Sundari and other women in the community understood the potential effects of the contamination of the sea and the threat to their livelihoods and homes as a direct consequence of the nuclear power plant. She had close to 350 cases against her, of which twenty-four were for sedition.[3]

Although women political prisoners have been represented as a small segment of this broader history of social and political movements, their testimonies have brought to light their harrowing experiences in police and judicial custody. Women's writing is a powerful form of expression of the otherwise invisibilised political realisation of their participation in revolutionary struggles, and their suppression by the State. Purkayastha reflects on how torture provides the connection between incarceration and women's writing. In Chapter 3, Mahuya Bandyopadhyay also engages with the writings of women prisoners from the 1970s to understand women's engagement with political work and their subsequent treatment in prison. While Purkayastha's work in many ways compels her to make a distinction between the political prisoner and the ordinary prisoner, Bandyopadhyay's work displays continuity between the two. Bandyopadhyay draws on the story of a Bangladeshi woman prisoner in Minakshi Sen's *Jailer Bhitor Jail* (meaning, a prison within a prison), and discusses how the Bangladeshi prisoner and Sen negotiate different institutional spaces—kinship, marriage, family, the judicial system, and prison.

Despite the location of these narratives in two temporal eras of the Naxal movement in Bengal and the contemporary movement, they reveal continuities in practices of incarceration and women prisoners' negotiations with kinship, marriage, family, prison, and the judicial system. These continuities also show us the violent experience of incarceration and the everyday instances of support, collaboration, and resistance by women prisoners.

From the writings and expressions of women prisoners in Bengal, we move to the experiences of women lodged in the District Jail of Aligarh, Uttar Pradesh, in Shereen Sadiq's chapter (Chapter 4). The author presents the nexus between patriarchy, family, and the State in examining the nature of crimes committed by women and their treatment within the prison. She finds that most crimes are linked to family, either *of* a family member or *for* the family. In the former case, their offence chafes at their already tenuous bond with families that consider women expendable. In the latter case, the family is too impoverished, hapless, and unlettered to help her. With no adequate family and social support, accompanied by the seriousness of their offence, women are made to languish in prison for an inexhaustible period. Their stay in prison is marked by the deprivation of several humane considerations. Crimes committed by women may be seen as responses to patriarchal violence and to the circumstances in their private spheres, and analysed as resistance to the controls imposed by the family. When incarcerated, their lives become the site for understanding the nexus between the family, community, and State. Preservation of 'honour' is at the heart of this nexus (Mehta 2018).

The volume argues that resistance is as central to the lives of women prisoners as their experience of loss and marginality. A focus on such resistance challenges the invisibilisation/memorialisation paradox. The second form of resistance that the volume has articulated deals with the practices of subversion in everyday prison life. These are intended as ways of getting better facilities, expressing emotions and bodily desires, creating socially interactive spaces, and asserting a sense of self within the prison. Negotiations and resistance also took place for small material benefits from warders, or amongst themselves for space. Sadaf Modak and Rimple Mehta's chapters (Chapters 6 and 7) discuss how the women prisoners continuously try to make a 'place' of the prison 'space'. Mehta adds another layer to the understanding of prison space by drawing a link between space and time. Her chapter highlights the ways in which women prisoners lose a sense of space and time initially, but gradually appropriate them for everyday survival.

Love is the dominant theme in the lives of the women prisoners who are the voices in Kanupriya Sharma's research in a women's prison in Punjab (Chapter 5), where she conducted ethnographic fieldwork. This chapter narrates the many tales of love of long-term women offenders housed in prison in Punjab. The author draws on the intimate lives of long-term women offenders, exploring the myriad ways in which they resist, manipulate, and negotiate institutional and societal norms to ensure their survival. In this ethnographic study, Sharma finds that women employ their social networks within and outside the prison to form new love alliances with male prisoners, correctional officers, and men outside. Prison staff play critical roles in supporting or disrupting such alliances. The functions they perform are linked to everyday prison practice and may even be incorporated into prison policies and reform, altering, even if partially, the idea of the total institution. In exploring the 'romantic' relationships of women in incarceration, the chapter thus highlights the nature of contemporary prison practices as influenced by the cultural idioms of the outside world, ultimately leading to a significant impact on policy decisions in prison reform.

For the women prisoners in Kanupriya Sharma's research, romantic love is a conduit to finding a sense of self and negotiating the terms of imprisonment. Mehta's work draws on narratives of Bangladeshi women prisoners to show how women prisoners use romantic love to transcend the constrained physical space and temporal boundaries of the prison. This chapter explores, first, how the construction of alternative space-time contexts constitutes their subjectivity and what it means for their survival, and second, dwells on the question of how spatio-temporal settings can be conceived as epistemological questions.

As observed in most of the chapters, strategies of resistance shift between negotiating and manipulating situations for their survival. These strategies may defy gender norms or may appear to conform, but they are covertly embedded in betrayals of established patriarchal notions of honour. Through the worlds of the family, pre-prison life, and the prison, the narratives of women prisoners therefore represent the idea of resisting the disciplinary, sovereign, and self-regulatory bio-power unleashed by the State and its institutions (Burchell and Gordon 1991; Foucault 1980).

The 'recidivists' in Mangala Honawar and Vijay Raghavan's chapter (Chapter 8) forged alliances in prison and set forth an example of how an inversion of power was possible in the prison space. The narratives of the women political prisoners in Chakravarti, Purkayastha, and Bandyopadhyay's chapters extend the idea of solidarity beyond the prison walls. The women political prisoners' response to torture in prison was to forge strong friendships, which sustained them in their lives both in and outside prison. Emotional and physical relationships within the prison and outside, pre-prison identities, and continuing relationships with family and community form an essential part of the women's prison culture (Owen 1998).

Honawar and Raghavan highlight another important epistemological question around the category of 'recidivists' and 'habitual' women offenders. This group is considered dangerous, more likely to commit crimes and less likely to be rehabilitated, and therefore perceived to be deserving extended punishment to protect society from future crimes. The chapter discusses the impact of the criminal justice system on recidivism among women, including their experiences and interactions with the prison system. The findings revealed that the prison staff was involved in labelling and stigmatising women recidivists, and was in no way trying to prevent women from committing further crimes. However, due to their prior experience in incarceration, women recidivists were able to manipulate the prison staff and other inmates to their advantage. The prison also became a ground for women recidivists to socialise with other women and form gangs, and for these women's gangs to recruit other young women and girls to carry on their illegal business outside the prison. The authors delve into some of these complexities and interactions between women and the prison system, which emerged as a contested site for negotiating practices of governance.

Underlying all these stories of resistance and negotiations are the emotional journeys of women prisoners, which include the suppression of emotions and desires central to everyday life in prison. Women prisoners connect emotionally with each other by way of forging solidarities, relationships of benefit, or 'love' engagements. Some of these solidarities continue long after their prison terms are over. Mehta (2018) discusses the role that emotions, especially love, play in alleviating the everyday of women prisoners, and how it enables them to recast themselves in ways that were not imaginable previously within the institutions of marriage and family. Prison, therefore, becomes a space for them to explore different sensualities and sexualities, which were forbidden in their lives outside the prison. This experience, however, comes at the expense of freedom in confinement. The chapters in this volume provide an insight into a variety of emotions, which may not be overtly visible but are pervasive in the narratives of the women prisoners in different parts of the country.

The Everyday and Challenges of Governance

Discipline, safe custody, and creating and maintaining a secure environment are quintessential elements of prison administration and everyday governance. These elements are intricately woven into carefully planned and monitored routines of everyday life, centred around waking up, eating, bathing, etc., recreation, court dates and interviews, and prison labour. The administration strives to maintain a rigid control over time, minimising the opportunity for distinct and individual temporal rhythms to emerge. Further, prison governance also requires spatial management. Which prisoner should be next to whom? How many prisoners can be accommodated in a cell or ward? Which prisoners must be placed in solitary confinement? Prison authorities regularly engage with these questions as they use spatial strategies to control, punish, and reward prisoners. For instance, a new prisoner is likely to get a place in the far end of the ward, close to the toilets. A prisoner may also be punished by being moved to this end of the ward or rewarded by being moved up closer to the entrance. We have shown through several ethnographic instances and narrative insights that precarity, uncertainty, and violence pervade the lives of women prisoners as they traverse different institutional spaces. These may be experienced in the prison similarly, or in heightened ways. Some prisoners may also be able to attenuate the violent and precarious effects through resistance and subversions. As discussed in the earlier sections and detailed in the chapters that follow, we show how prisoners use spatial-temporal strategies to negotiate the hardships of prison life, revealing tales of resistance. However, in these prisoner narratives, precarity and violence are present with an unwavering certainty, marking the prison out as a decisive, forceful institution.

Contrary to such an image, when the prison is presented from the perspective of those who are at the helm of everyday governance, for instance, the administrators, we find the same sense of uncertainty. The chapters in the final segment of the volume engage with questions of governance and challenges of working with the system and set up a dialogue with the narratives presented in the previous sections. Here, administrators, a social worker, and a legal activist from a human rights organisation reflect on the existing policies, laws, and practices of governance in prisons. We argue that their narratives indicate a sense of powerlessness within the structures of the prison to realise some humane practices that they had envisaged. Such powerlessness, articulated from relative positions of power, signals the need to rethink and redesign prison practice. The chapters in this segment thus show the precarious nature of the prison as an organisation.

Upneet Lalli and B. D. Sharma's chapters (Chapters 9 and 11) show the ways in which administrators interpreted policy and law to carve out supportive and empowering spaces for prisoners. While narrating from the vantage point of administrators, they emphasise the roles of those working within the system to initiate and sustain enabling programmes for the prisoners. These may be viewed as one-off experiments with an eye on the larger goal of 'reform'. However, the persistence and pervasiveness of these efforts within a localised context indicate the variety and content of the negotiations collaboratively practised by prisoners and some members of the prison management. Sharma's chapter is unique in this respect, highlighting the potential of creative thinking while working within the prison system. This chapter unravels his journey as an administrator in translating the 'spirit of corrections' in West Bengal prisons. Making full use of the opportunity to carefully observe and hear the problems prisoners experience within the prison, he conceived of culture therapy as a possible pathway to initiating change in the way prisoners are perceived and the way they engage with the prison. The image of the prisoner and the idea of reform are articulated anew through this experiment in culture therapy. Such a vision of prison reform is of particular significance since an administrator working within the constraints of the prison system had initiated the experiment with culture therapy. He deals with concerns around security, order, and discipline in the prison while encouraging prisoners to participate in the process of their reform.

Lalli's chapter draws attention to the structural issues pertaining to women prisoners and prison administration. This connects to the spatial organisation, distribution of material resources, and facilities within the prison, which are geared towards serving the male prisoners. Similarly, the programmes for the reform of prisoners are gendered. In this connection, she argues that there is a need for a more gender-responsive system. Challenges of prison governance are generally articulated in terms of containment, security, and internal discipline. The incorporation of practices of corrections and reform are trapped within these overriding concerns of security. The administrators, however, make a clear shift in reflecting on their everyday challenges of prison governance by evoking the need to address structural constraints, rights-based perspectives, and practices of relative freedom within confined spaces and the possible benefits of such practices in the effective management of prisoners, as well as ensuring their well-being. In Sharma's narrative, we see how women prisoners invert the image of the prisoner as one capable of engaging in cultural activities without disturbing the 'order' and 'discipline' that marks prison life. Sharma's initiative to take prisoners outside the prison walls to perform a play in a public space was a break from the past, where the prisoners in judicial custody went out of the prison only to attend their court hearings or on parole. Lalli and Sharma's interventions and their suggestions, expressed in their writing and through these programmes, provide meaning to the women prisoners' negotiations of the public space and what now becomes the private space of the prison. The challenges to the private-public demarcation are subsumed within the context of what Goffman would call the 'selective legitimation' of certain kinds of negotiations.

These challenges are compounded in the pre-trial detention of women. Madhurima Dhanuka (Chapter 10) examines the excessive and arbitrary pre-trial detention of women as one of the structural problems in Indian prisons. Through her interactions with pre-trial detainees, prison officers, medical officers, and legal aid authorities, the author outlines the debilitating, and often irreversible impact pre-trial detention has on the lives of women and their children.

That pre-trial detainees are among the most vulnerable groups of prisoners is intuitively known. The author describes the extent of their vulnerability, in terms of sexual violence, impoverished lives, stigma, and isolation. For women prisoners, this pre-trial detention is a human rights violation, and an expression of the nexus of related abuses and ill-effects, including torture, corruption, and the spread of disease, stunting economic development and undermining the rule of law. The use of excessive pre-trial detention for women offenders, the challenges they face in securing bail, and their distance from family and other institutions of support further the argument about the patriarchal nexus between intimate institutional spaces of care such as marriage and family and State custodial institutions, such as the prison. In this chapter, the author articulates the unique vulnerabilities of women in pre-trial detention in Indian prisons. Reflecting on case law and existing policy frameworks, the chapter also makes a case for introducing changes with regard to women's imprisonment to ensure a rights-based perspective and address the effects of excessive and arbitrary pre-trial detention.

How do we address this sense of isolation, loss, and irreparable exclusion from society that women prisoners experience? In Chapter 12, Penelope Tong poses this question in terms of a fundamental dilemma in prison governance: How do we reconcile deterrence, custody, and reform and rehabilitation? The author draws on her experiences as a social work practitioner to question the concept of reform and asks, 'Where do we go from here?' She provides an insight into the limitations of how *sudhar aur punarvasan* (reform and rehabilitation) are perceived within criminal justice as they fail to fulfil the stated goals of the prison and are not accountable for the rehabilitation of prisoners. Implicitly, this chapter establishes a dialogue with the way the administrators, Sharma and Lalli, pose the challenges of everyday governance. 'Culture therapy' in Sharma's chapter coincides with the policy-level shift in the conception of the prison as a '*shonghsodhanagar*' or place of reform. The challenges he encounters in implementing this programme also bear out the dilemma between deterrence and reform. Lalli's response to the challenges in governing women prisoners is marked by her recognition of the unique vulnerabilities of women prisoners and the structural dimension of this problem. Simply resolving the deterrence/reform paradox within the system will not necessarily translate into enabling systems for women prisoners. Tong engages with this issue by examining its empirical and philosophical moorings. Although theoretical perspectives may have moved the focus from penal proportionality to social justice, there are still no clearly informed methods to direct a course of action concerning crime and reintegration, both within the prison and in the post-release period. The neglect of social and economic disadvantage, experiences of exploitation, trauma, and exclusion, and their implications for routes in and out of crime continue to be beyond the purview of theoretical ideas of reform, as well as its material articulation in the everyday governance of prisoners' lives.

Conclusion

Generating knowledge and understanding about prisons and prison populations is characterised by the limited accessibility to the field. When authorities grant access to the prison, they expect the researcher or social work practitioner to subscribe to the norms of prison administration and the carceral logic. These constraints impact the knowledge that is produced about the prison. Criminology itself is not a fully developed discipline in the country. Feminist criminology occupies an even more negligible proportion of the research done in this field. One of the noteworthy exceptions to this lack is Shankardass' (2012) book of narratives of women prisoners who experienced a loss of human rights and faced many deprivations based on their gender. Shankardass' writing focused on bringing to light the injustice in women prisoners' lives, both before and after the alleged criminal activity. This volume attempts something similar. Yet we depart from such earlier writings to show how the lives of women prisoners enable different theorisations of the prison, primarily the prison as a space of resistance, of rebuilding everyday life, and even of breaking away from traditional institutions that provide security to the lives of women.

The authors in this volume, given their different locations, represent diversity in terms of perspectives, language, and styles of engaging with the worlds of women prisoners. As editors, our search for and the decision to include different forms of representation of the prison and prisoners' lives was a conscious one. In this form, the book enables insights and is accessible to a wide range of readers interested in understanding the experiences of prisoners in India. Even though the focus is primarily on women prisoners, the chapters in this volume present a broader discussion on aspects of prison conditions, reform, and experiences of incarceration in India.

Within a broader context of a dearth of literature, constraints on the practice of research, and surveillance on the articulation of knowledge around the prison, a dialogue between academics, activists, social workers, and administrators has the potential to resist a hegemonic understanding of the prison. Towards this end, the book makes three significant contributions. First, it foregrounds the narratives of women prisoners and the issues faced by them. It marks a significant departure from existing work on women prisoners in India as it uses the voices of women prisoners to critically reflect on State practices in an institution with minimum civil society interference and initiate a dialogue among researchers, practitioners, activists, and administrators. Second, the volume brings together the different perspectives and experiences of those who have engaged with the prison system in varying capacities. The inputs from multiple disciplines and positions have enabled epistemological discussions as well as paved the way for communicating innovative practice-based strategies. Third, it breaks the barriers of academic writing and publishing as limited to those actively engaged in academia. The volume brings forth the value of listening to different voices emerging from research, practice, and activism about the issues of women prisoners. Such an exercise holds tremendous epistemological relevance as it seeks to challenge the limited nature of knowledge generated within a particular discipline.

Endnotes

1. Father Stan Swamy, a human rights activist, died in prison of a cardiac arrest in July 2021. His applications for bail and requests for a straw to enable him to drink water (Father Stan, as he was known, suffered from Parkinson's Disease, which left him unable to do simple physical tasks such as holding a glass or a cup to drink from) were repeatedly denied.

2. Practice, according to Bourdieu, is located within a system, which Bourdieu refers to as 'habitus'. Habitus may be translated as the set of principles, enduring, yet susceptible to change, that make up a particular structure. These principles and their peculiar arrangement within a structure give rise to certain practices and representations typical to that structure. The practices (means) can be continually moulded in accordance with the set of principles (rules) without really striving towards any specified goals or following established procedures to the letter. In the organisational life of the prison, the formal procedures governing action mould the practices to an extent. Equally significant in the development of practice are the responses to these principles of practice. These representations are not directed towards any predetermined outcomes. It is constituted by the practices that conform to the principles of the structure, and simultaneously takes into account the representations that generate new practices. In that sense, the 'habitus' is collective and generative and individual and social. It is set within certain spatial and temporal boundaries that define its limits. At the same time, it is a product of socially and historically conditioned actions. The actions of the agents are not seen in a vacuum or merely in the context of the situation or event at hand; rather, the agent's actions in an event is shaped by her/his conditioning, which goes beyond the immediacy of the event.

3. See Daga (2019), and https://www.dianuke.org/koodankulam-women-from-prison-tell-everyone-we-are-still-here/ (accessed October 2021).

4. Drawn from the book *Jailer Bhitor Jail* written by Minakshi Sen.

References

Bandyopadhyay, M. 2010. *Everyday Life in a Prison: Confinement, Surveillance and Resistance*. New Delhi: Orient BlackSwan.

Bansal, S., and S. Sahni. 2021. 'Bail, prisons and COVID-19: An Indian perspective'. *Alternative Law Journal* 16 August.

Bourdieu, P. 1980. *The Logic of Practice*. Stanford: Stanford University Press.

Burchell, G., and C. Gordon (eds). 1991. *The Foucault Effect: Studies in Governmentality.* London: Oxford University Press.

Cherukuri, S. 2008. *Women in Prison: An Insight into Captivity and Crime.* New Delhi: Foundation Books.

Daga, Sweta. 2019. 'The women protesting the Kudankulam nuclear plant'. *The Caravan*, 2 July. Available at https://caravanmagazine.in/communities/women-protest-kudankulam-nuclear-plant (accessed October 2021).

Devi, P., P. Rambali, and M. Cuny. 1997. *The Bandit Queen of India: An Indian Woman's Amazing Journey from Peasant to International Legend.* Guilford, CT: Lyon Press.

Foucault, M. 1980. *Power/Knowledge: Selected Interviews and Other Writings 1972–1977.* Brighton: Harvester.

Giallombardo, R. 1966. *Society of Women: A Study of a Women's Prison.* New York: Wiley.

Heffernan, E. 1972. *Making it in Prison: The Square, the Cool and the Life.* New York: John Wiley and Sons, Inc.

Mehta, R. 2018. *Women, Mobility and Incarceration: Love and Recasting of Self across the Bangladesh-India Border.* UK: Routledge.

National Crime Records Bureau. 2016. *Crime in India Report, 2016.* New Delhi: Ministry of Home Affairs, Government of India.

Scott, J. C. 1990. *Domination and the Arts of Resistance: Hidden Transcripts.* New Haven: Yale University Press.

Owen, B. 1998. *In the Mix: Struggle and Survival in a Women's Prison.* New York: SUNY Press.

Shankardass, R. D. 2012. *Of Women 'Inside': Prison Voices from India.* New Delhi: Routledge.

Ward, D. A., and G. G. Kassebaum. 1965. *Women's Prison: Sex and the Social Structure.* Chicago: Aldine.

Zedner, L. 1991. 'Women, Crime and Penal Responses: A Historical Account'. *Crime and Justice* 14, 307–362.

Part I

Narratives of Resistance

Chapter 1

THE DARK NIGHT OF THE SOUL

Survival and Despair in Prison 'Diaries'

UMA CHAKRAVARTI

Sometime in the early 1960s, the film *Bandini*,[1] directed by Bimal Roy, made waves among the cinema-going public as its underlying theme was the incarceration of the heroine, played by Nutan, who killed the wife of the revolutionary hero and was punished for her crime. While the unfolding of the storyline makes us sympathise with the heroine, the most lasting impact of the film is the image of a woman grinding grain at the hand-operated *chakki* as she sings of the *babul* (father) she has been wrenched away from in the prison. '*Ab ke baras bhej bhaiya ko babul*' (father, this year send my brother to see me) resonates with women in particular, perhaps because many women sing as they grind at the *sasural* (marital home) and as they recall the natal home with nostalgia and pain. The song was picturised over several images of individual women, middle-aged and young, standing alone against the jail walls, looking outwards through and beyond the jail bars. The jail house is not associated with women, so it is something of a shock to think about women in jail, whether they are there for violent crimes they may have committed or as 'prisoners of conscience'.

That is why the hero is a revolutionary in *Bandini*. The heroine is an ordinary criminal who has been betrayed by the hero and has murdered his wife in a state of shock. Flipping it around is somewhat unimaginable in cinema, but there have been many revolutionary women who went to jail for the political stands they took in our recent history, so it is surprising that these women have not been the subject of any film,[2] either during the period of anti-colonial struggles or in independent India. However, as someone who has been part of the civil rights movement from the 1970s onwards, it is these women whom I was drawn to and it was their lives that I wanted to explore: women who are or were jailed for their political work. When I launched myself into a filmmaking phase of work, I set about doing oral interviews with a range of women who went to jail in independent India. My starting point was the Telangana armed struggle during the years 1946–1949. A second phase focused on Naxalbari and the Emergency in the late 1960s and 1970s. Then I moved into the present where a range of movements is drawing women into them (who do not, however, feature in this chapter because of space constraints).

Prison diaries will examine some themes that emerge from women's experiences of being in jail, the violence that it entails, and the ways in which women survive their jail time. It will also focus on the solidarities forged in jail among the political prisoners, as well as with other women who are spending time for murders they have committed, or other different crimes such as theft, trafficking, soliciting, and so on. Some women kept a diary while in jail like Snehalata Reddy (1977), and others like Primila Lewis (1978) went on to write about their jail experiences in a realistic mode of recall after they came out of prison. Some women became literary writers who turned their experiences of jail into loosely fictionalised accounts of women who survive their jail time through relationships forged with other women, or with animals that go in and out of jail and make for emotional outlets as the women negotiate the brutalities of jail life, allowing them to negotiate their time in jail (Committee for the Release of Political Prisoners 2013; Kondapalli 2015; Mitra 2004; Sen 1993). In this chapter, I draw from the interviews and writings of women who were incarcerated for their political work and went on to write about women in prison. I focus on the somewhat unexplored space of the jail and what it means to be imprisoned, cut off from the world outside. I will draw from my interviews with over thirty-five women, but in particular, I will focus on five women—Koteswaramma, Khatija Ansari, Rajashri Dasgupta and Minakshi Sen, and Snehalata Reddy—as all of them 'wrote' their prison experiences up in some form, allowing us to share their time in prison. One of the thirty-five women interviewed as part of this research remembered her first night in jail in the following way:

> The most lasting memory that I have of my time in jail was the first night I spent there. I was in solitary confinement as a political prisoner who was in C class as I was not formally educated, unlike all the other women political prisoners who were in a different class as they had degrees; they got food which was different from those of us who were ordinary prisoners. My cell was next to the morgue, and I was all alone. I had smuggled pistols hidden in my clothes from Jaipur to Delhi, and had carried empty shells by train to the Punjab, but never felt the kind of fear I felt that night alone, next to the morgue....[3]

This description of the first night in jail is diametrically opposed to our image of a revolutionary, one who embraces a cause and is willing to take huge risks, facing even death in pursuit of dreams of a better world. I have used it here as a way to enable me to draw an arc in the manner in which women experience prison, what they notice about the physical space of the prison, and how they recall it in later years. What also seems to leave a lasting memory of jail life is what mediates that experience: Were you there alone and away from your revolutionary comrades or in a group? The experience is also mediated by how the world outside regards your work, and by the cause for which you enlisted yourself that led the State to mark you as dangerous, and thus put you away from the rest of society. In my listening experience of the interviews of incarcerated women, these are critical to the way women recall jail time. The experience of being a political prisoner provides a common thread in the narratives of women. I am also writing about the changing political context, which is critical in shaping the experience of being in jail. As a historian, this backdrop of the time and the nature of the State, over broadly thirty years, is crucial in how the prison was experienced by incarcerated women and the way they shared their memories with me.

The Early Postcolonial State: Redefining Freedom

I begin with Koteswaramma, who spent a few months in jail just before Independence. She was part of a larger group of women, all comrades in the communist movement of Andhra/Telangana. As communist revolutionaries regarded as carrying out anti-State work of a special kind, they were different from the men and women who had swarmed the jails as nationalists in the struggle for freedom. Communist revolutionaries did both overground and underground work. During the late 1930s and 1940s, there were large numbers of women in the communist movement that culminated in the Telangana armed struggle just before and after Independence. For her, the time in jail was mediated and humanised by the presence of comrades, all of whom were in jail together. The men were in one part of the prison and the women in another. Koteswaramma, who had something of a stormy life as a wife and mother, all of which came up in her interview with me when she was in her nineties, became a particularly animated narrator when she described her time in jail. She began with an anecdote:

> We were allowed to cook our own meals, and the prison staff gave us rice and other rations. The men sent their share of rations to us from their jail with the message, 'Cook for us too'! The women sent the rations back saying, 'Cook for you too? We haven't come to jail to cook for you! The government has given us a holiday! We will not cook for you.'[4]

The men, who did not know how to cook or, more pertinently, even clean the rations before cooking, then ate food with mud and stones in it. Hearing this, the women relented a little and cleaned the rations for the men, but continued to refuse to cook. Put in their place, the men then learnt how to do so.

The jail was also turned into an extension of female time together. The women were a diverse group in terms of age and backgrounds. Together, they joked, played games, shared experiences, mocked the jail staff, subverted rules in their own way, argued with the jail staff, and even chastised them for delays in providing them with *neem* twigs to clean their teeth. One day a young woman got fed up of the waiting, so she climbed the tree which was next to the compound wall and threw down twigs for the others. The jail staff came running, terrified of the possibility of an escape for which they would be held responsible. The women had a good laugh at the terror of the jail staff.

The female camaraderie was not, however, able to transcend the essential meaning of being in jail. For the women who had left small children at home and had tried to reconcile themselves to their imprisonment, the most poignant moment was when the children came to visit their mothers. Koteswaramma had left a 3- or 4-year-old daughter named Karuna behind when she was in prison. While the child could meet her mother, the prison bars separated them from each other. Karuna cried piteously, wanting to cross the bars and go to her mother, while Koteswaramma wept on the other side, but the rules did not permit the mothers to hold their children. Even the jail staff were moved by this cruelty, but were helpless: '*Amma* (mother), we can't bear it,' they said, but rules were rules, and that was it.[5]

So, jail life was jail life, cut off from home and work. Like now and in times past, the wheels of the law were slow to move. As the days turned into weeks and months, there was no news of when the women would be tried. Fed up with the delays, just a few days before 15 August, the women decided to go on a hunger strike, refusing to eat till the cases came up for hearing. The jail staff tried to seduce them with the goodies they would get to eat on the fifteenth, but the women stayed firm: 'It's not independence for us,' they said, and continued their hunger strike. Finally, the cases moved, the women gave up their hunger strike, and were all released.

Around two years later, Khatija Ansari went to jail as a 16-year-old young activist of the Students' Federation of India (SFI), the student wing of the Communist party.[6] She was a young student trying to matriculate when she was introduced to Kalpana Dutt by way of an Urdu translation of her memoir on the Chittagong Armoury raid. Fired by the account of Kalpana's courage, Khatija became an activist and although she had the support of a brother, Firanghi Mahal, her home which housed people with all sorts of political opinions, was outraged. Khatija rode a bicycle, wore men's clothes to put up posters at night, and was lathi-charged at demonstrations. She had thrown a slipper at the magistrate who had ordered the lathi charge, turning her into something of a heroine. A few weeks later, she was arrested in front of the party office at Lucknow as part of a preventive measure, as the party had given a call for an all-India general strike for 19 February 1949. But when the police discovered that she was a juvenile, they were stumped. She was sent to the juvenile jail inside the main jail; other arrestees, such as the well-known Communist writer Rashid Jahan, and a doctor, were sent to the main jail and released after a couple of months. Khatija was in jail for eleven months as she was held under the Preventive Detention Act, allegedly for being a courier for the party. She was taken straight to prison after her arrest and ironically, it was the magistrate at whom she had thrown her slipper who came to the jail to formalise her incarceration.

Khatija was treated with kindness by the jail authorities. As she entered the jail, she was given dinner, and someone had thoughtfully placed a book beside her *thali*, giving her something to read; it was a copy of *The Discovery of India* by Nehru, but in English, a language she did not know. While Khatija was in jail, she lived and interacted with other jail inmates and carried a vivid memory of the young and older women who were in prison for assorted crimes whose stories she recounts in her unfinished memoir. Some women were there for dowry-related murders (even then) and murders committed for an assortment of reasons. But the story of one young girl made a significant impact on her: a young girl of ten, named Ballia, had come into the jail with a doll in her hand. She had inadvertently pushed the *zamindar's* son into the pond while playing with him, and was charged with murder. When Independence came some years later, most of the inmates were given amnesty and released. Not young Ballia. She stayed in jail as the *zamindar* opposed her release.

While Khatija was in jail, there was a call for a hunger strike by the political detainees. She too joined the strike. Here is an extract from her memoir describing the hunger strike:

> Another important event in my jail life was that of a hunger strike for twelve days. The communist party gave the call for a hunger strike by the jail inmates, against the arrest of an important labour leader Moulana Yusuf of Kanpur. It was the month of March 1949. The trade union wing of the communist party of India had given the call for an All India railway strike. While the big wigs of the party had gone underground, the party sympathisers and grassroots activists like me were being picked up one by one. This was the time when Dr Rashid Jahan and Hajra Apa were rounded up and sent to central jail where I was located. I have no idea how the message reached us inside the jail, and we three gave notices to the jail authority (as per jail rules) to start a hunger strike from a given day. I was totally oblivious about the meaning and the processes involved in a hunger strike excepting those about which I was tutored by my two mentors and what I observed on my own during the period of the strike. Cooked food was put in front of us, and we were supposed to eat at regular timings. After some time it was taken out at the usual timing. The second or third day of the strike, a few male jail officers started coming and talking to my elderly mentors. After 4/5 days of strike, I observed one doctor and a nurse, along with Mrs Koul followed by male jail officers, started visiting us. We were medically checked every morning, perhaps as a matter of routine.

On the fifth or sixth day, a few more officers came into the barrack and had a long conversation with Rashid Jehan and Hajra Begum, and left after whispering something to them. Early next morning, Khatija was taken out to another cell and was asked to lie down on a cot. The doctor examined her and told her very gently that she was not well, and urgently needed to take food. He tried his best to convince Khatija about the urgency of doing so, and said, 'If you refuse, I have no option but to force the food through the nasal tube'. But to make things worse, Khatija spotted her *bête noire*, the magistrate, in the group at her side:

> Amongst the couple of jail staff, I could spot the ADM—Bose Mullick, who had ordered the lathi charge on us in front of Hazratganj police chowki (who was mimicking our slogan shouting and at whom I had hurled my chappal which had hit his face)—and had perhaps never forgiven me for that insult! Here again, he shouted at the jail staff and asked them to hold me back on the bed—somehow I was able to disentangle my left foot from the tight grip and made a hard kick at Bose Mullick. This second insult he never forgot, and at an appropriate time, he tried his best to convince A's elder sister to keep away her brother from this 'extremely dangerous girl'. At the time of our marriage, he happened to be the Registrar of Marriages!

He had mocked her for her soft voice while speaking her marriage vows, saying, 'When you shout slogans your voice is loud, what's happened to it now?' Khatija concludes her account of the jail thus:

> I being the youngest amongst political prisoners at the time was not being taken too seriously. And the prison authorities were a bit indulgent to me. On looking back now, perhaps I was treated like a teenager who had absent-mindedly strayed into the serious milieu of left politics. Alas, that was not true. I had firm roots in national politics through my observation during that particular period—1943–47—the active participation of my family in national politics by courtesy of Gandhiji and other important members of the Congress party.

So, with this background, how did Khatija get arrested and serve a prison time of eleven months when others were set free in a couple of months? During my interview with her, I asked her the question: 'How come you stayed for eleven months when others were freed much earlier?' Khatija replied that she had wondered too, and had come to the conclusion that her extended family conspired to keep her there as a way of getting her off the streets and embarrassing them. She also said that jail was not so bad; the warden was indulgent towards her, playing badminton with her and ensuring that she ate well. She did not mind the jail! Summing up, she said that the real jail was the serious atmosphere in Firanghi Mahal with its elaborate codes: '*Asli jail toh woh tha*' (That was the real jail)!

Whatever Khatija might think, we are reminded that it was the post-Independence State with its promise of freedom from tyranny that was now using the Preventive Detention Act against Khatija. Ironically, her detention order was signed by the UP Governor Sarojini Naidu, who had been a frequent visitor to Firanghi Mahal, which reminds us of the independent State's anxiety to stamp out communism as a threat to their administration (they also regarded the socialists as dangerous). Khatija repeated the communist slogans that had rent the air in 1949, '*Yeh azaadi jhoothi hai, Desh ki janta bhookhi hai!*' (loosely translated as: Such freedom is fake, when the people of the country are starving), during the interview I recorded with her in 2012. At the time Khatija was jailed in 1949, Telangana was in the throes of an armed struggle led by the Communists, with large numbers of peasants who were trying to end the feudal era of economic and social oppression. It was in the interests of the new State to end insurgency and fully integrate the state of Hyderabad into the larger Indian union. But the new State could not successfully stigmatise the communists; those who went to jail in the cause of the people stood for 'real freedom'. Going to prison as a political prisoner was then still linked to idealism and sacrifice, as it was during the anti-colonial struggle. So when Khatija came out of jail, she was regarded as something of a heroine, making an impact on other young girls in college who recalled her status as a firebrand radical who had absolutely no fear of anyone or anything, and who went to jail for her political work.

The Emergence of the Repressive State, 1967–1977

By the mid-1960s, India was in turmoil. The unresolved questions of the post-independent State, particularly the 'land question', could no longer be invisibilised as the slogan of 'land to the tiller' had reared its head in large parts of India, but particularly in West Bengal. There were food riots as shortages of food caused severe distress, leading to raids on grain shops, with even the middle classes being drawn into the agitations because of the scarcity. Poverty and unemployment were endemic across the state of West Bengal. Student unrest was triggered off in Presidency College over the corrupt hostel administration. The resistance was led largely by the non-elite students of the college. The composition of the students had changed in the otherwise elite institution from its pre-independence days. Police-student violence became a striking feature of the area around the college. The revolt at Naxalbari, which had witnessed struggles against the *jotedars* over the exploitative conditions imposed on the tribals in the region, mainly by the sharecroppers, led to repression by the landlord-police nexus, and the struggle took a violent turn.[7]

On 24 May 1967, Shanti Munda and other Adivasi women led an action to seize the land from a landlord in their village. One policeman kicked a pregnant woman in her belly, enraging the women who shot arrows at Sonam Wangdi, the policeman who had kicked the woman, killing him. The next day, the women went to grab the land from another landlord, but this time the police had come armed with guns. They fired upon a procession mainly comprised of Adivasi women, including Shanti Munda. Eleven people were killed: eight women, two children, and one man. Ultimately, Naxalbari gave its name to the movement of peasants and the formation of a new party, the Communist Party of India (Marxist-Leninist) (CPI-ML). This new party propagated an armed insurrection to seize power and create a new society where peasants were given lands that had been denied to them historically, even though it was they who tilled the land. The insurrection was the first stage in the revolution that would usher in a new society, and was heralded as such by a new party, the CPI (ML).

As the movement swept the countryside, it found a special place amongst the youth of Calcutta, who joined the movement in large numbers in the city. The presence of an almost stultifying educational system known for corruption played its role in spawning a violent reaction in the universities and the city as a whole. In the general atmosphere of soul-searching, idealism, and revolutionary fervour, students responded to the call to the youth to give up their classrooms and go to the villages to help with the mobilisation of the masses in the countryside. In the early 1970s, Calcutta became the battleground on which the repressive state unfolded its strategies to reassert control over its discontented people. As political power in West Bengal became highly volatile, the ruling party used 'encounters' as a method of flushing out the mostly young radicals of Calcutta, in which many young people were killed.[8] Cossipore, Baranagar witnessed a bloody night on 12–13 August 1971 when the goons of the Congress party, with the help of the police, killed close to 100 young men during a spell of President's rule (Sen, et al. 1978, Vol 1, 159–162). The violence in Bengal has been the subject of many films. An iconic image of a young man running from his pursuers, intercut with images of piled bodies in an alley in the city, has come to be the stock image of the years 1970–1973 in Calcutta in several films made since the 1970s.[9]

The police also used other techniques to stamp out the movement. Torture to extract information had been used since colonial times, but it assumed sinister proportions during the Naxalite upsurge. The police station at Lalbazar was the site of the systematic use of torture, and thus jail experience is, in a sense, a continuum going back to the police station. That is how it appears in the narration of the women who have written about their jail time or been interviewed about it in recent years. When Minakshi Sen and Rajashri met for the first time, they did so in a prison van. Both had spent almost four weeks in police custody at the Lalbazar police station, being interrogated by the notorious police officer, Runu Guha Niyogi, known for his vicious overseeing and even conducting of torture. (He also appears in Chapter 2, this volume.) The account of their jail experiences and their previous experience of interrogation in Lalbazar was part of their joint interview. Rajashri was a reluctant participant (as she had declined to be part of the film I was trying to make) in the interview, but had done everything she could to facilitate the filming session at her house in 2014. She had arranged for Minakshi to come to Kolkata to talk to me and was somehow drawn into the conversation, unknowingly in a sense, as the filming began. The depth of the friendship between Minakshi, Rajashri, and Krishna Bandhopadhaya was evident to all of us in the film team, so it has become the dominant motif in their account of jail experience when they talked about their time in prison. It is that memory that they claim to have carried with them for the rest of their lives, and that has perhaps helped to heal the wounds of the violence in the police station and the jail itself.

As we settled into the formal session of filming Minakshi and Krishna, with Rajashri sitting at the edge of the threesome, I opened the interview with a question, looking directly at Minakshi and Rajashri: 'So when did the two of you meet? Did you know each other before you went to jail?' Minakshi's response came in a torrent of words: 'We did not know each other before. We met in the van taking us to jail from the police *thana*. Incidentally, we were told later [by others] that we talked non-stop for forty-eight hours. We were inseparable after that….'

Their custody in the Lalbazar police station was also a shared experience, except that they did not know each other then. The authorities also took pains to keep them separate as they were intensively interrogated to extract as much information as they could provide (or as much as the authorities believed they could). Finally, after about four weeks, they were sent to jail, although Rajashri returned from time to time for more interrogation sessions. Further beatings were routine, especially in Rajashri's case, who was repeatedly called back to the thana for her pivotal role in an attempted jailbreak. Whenever Rajashri was called, her new friends in prison would give her their petticoats to wear under her sari so that the layers of cloth somewhat cushioned the beatings. It was a moving and poignant moment of recall about the solidarities between the Naxalite jail inmates, and Rajashri recounted this little detail with a mixture of emotion and humour amid other descriptions. Just a month after I interviewed the three friends, Minakshi died very suddenly after a fall in her house, which put her into a coma. Rajashri was devastated. She spoke movingly at her memorial meeting, which I too attended, recalling the relationship between Minakshi and herself in these words:

> I first met Minakshi at Lalbazar police station in October 1973; she was present in the lock-up where I was confined. I noticed that a thin, tall girl with frizzy hair was looking at me. Whenever I looked at her, she stared back at me. She constantly stood next to me like my *bodyguard*. Initially, I suspected her to be a police person as the atmosphere at that time was very threatening, and I could not trust her. It was only when we were taken to jail together that I was reassured. As we were being taken to jail, Minakshi spoke with a composed passionate voice, 'Do not worry, we will be imprisoned for ten years, ten long years.' I replied, 'Why will we be jailed for ten years?' She said, 'Yes of course, we have been charged for sedition (*deshdroho*), we are against the State—and will we not be punished for a minimum of ten years? It could be that we are detained for twenty years.'
>
> I still recount those days. We were arrested as revolutionaries; we could not even express our fears and anxieties. I portrayed myself as courageous, even though I was terrified at heart, especially since this girl was a stranger to me. In a while I realised that both of us were housed in the same cell, right above the *degree cell*. Our other inmate was Kalpana Bose, who was arrested on a different charge. That is when I got acquainted with her (Kalpana).
>
> That was the beginning of my friendship with Minakshi. Not a single day went by, which I didn't spend with her. She did not leave my side for a moment. I think she resolved to be at my side from the very first day. She would always enquire, 'Why are you so quiet? Are you hurt? Why are you crying? Why aren't you sleeping enough? Why aren't you reading? Why are you reading now? Why aren't you eating?' She taught me about love and friendship. We would stay up so many nights, just to talk. It was all because of Minakshi; she taught me the true meaning of friendship.[10]

Minakshi was so protective of Rajashri because of all that she had suffered in the police station, and also because of the tragic way in which the action that her group had planned ended. Rajashri's comrade husband was shot, as she herself was. Rajashri was in the hospital for ten days, during which time she did not know what had happened to him. By the time Rajashri and Minakshi were sent to jail, everyone knew Rajashri's story. As Minakshi said to me, 'It was our instinct to comfort her. Her body was full of bruises, large black marks where policemen had used their heavy boots on her. And she had suffered so grievously.' As the days in the jail went by, the friendship deepened. Why did they have different views on politics? That was a prelude to trying to understand each other as they spent days and nights figuring out life in all its complexities. And they talked about love. As Rajashri recalled at Minakshi's memorial meeting:

> Revolution is not devoid of love and romance; we spent sleepless nights in jail, discussing love, the variants of love, first love, love in school; about the love that could not prosper under parental control, and about what are our dreams about the future—those stories of love, so many stories of love!

The recounting of jail life—its internal architecture that allowed for segregating its inmates, the lunatic ward amongst the dangerous women, the Division cell for the particularly 'dangerous women'. Some of the cells were regarded as punishment locations to discipline recalcitrant prisoners. But good friendships were forged in these conditions, something Joya Mitra writes about in her prison account, even as the State always separated the women from each other. Joya too wrote while in prison. She made notes of all that was going on and based on her jottings, she was able to recall her jail time when she wrote her book on her years in prison:

> In the cells, we now have Rajashri and Minakshi. Rajashri is still very ill. The doctors at PG Hospital had almost snatched her from the jaws of death. She still has stitches on her head/skull, and both her legs have blue, purple and black marks from innumerable cuts and bruises like a child's drawing with a pencil. Rajashri has an unusual ability to turn any situation into laughter. But she is tough underneath. It is as if, after a long time, we have some fresh air in our cells. At least we have more voices to sing out loud. (Mitra 2004, 154)

Minakshi and Rajashri were part of a larger group of friends; about twenty Naxalite women were in jail together. Kalpana, the senior-most among them, taught the newcomers how to survive jail, what to watch out for, and how to be prepared for an assault upon them at all times. The jail staff had built up a mythology of 'ML women' being like vampires, able to suck the blood of the others in the jail, to prevent the non-political prisoners from bonding with them. The ever-observant Minakshi turned her sensitive eyes and ears to making notes and begin writing some of her jail stories. On one occasion, the camaraderie between the ML women took the form of a fake insurrection with dummy weapons which they created (and then restored to their original everyday use before the premises were searched!); bells rang, the staff scattered in panic, and there was mayhem before the 'insurrection' was put down. The jail staff then organised a correctional lecture for the rebellious women, but Rajashri out-argued the poor young man who came to convert them. He left conceding that Rajashri had a point: the women were *revolutionaries*, not criminals!

On a more sombre note, an unexpected situation occurred when several women protesters were brought into jail following a price rise demonstration in 1974 and released after a day or so. The world outside came to know about the Naxalite girls, and the treatment meted out to them after their arrest and detention. An enquiry committee was constituted to report on the conditions in jail, and the group included Ila Mitra, the heroine of the Tebhaga agitation, who was sexually molested during her time in police custody in 1950 in East Pakistan.[11] She asked many probing questions about Rajashri and Minakshi being tortured in custody, but when Ila Mitra discovered that although they had suffered humiliating torture, they were not subjected to rape, she lost interest in their account. Outraged at this, Rajashri and Minakshi recalled Ila Mitra's disinterest in non-sexual torture, and their feeling of being let down by a senior revolutionary who should have listened to them if the investigating committee was serious about doing something about the torture. Fortunately, the rest of the team did record their testimonies, which were summarised and published in journals and newspapers. The law minister denied the allegations, but Indrajit Gupta, the CPI leader, refuted the law minister and reiterated that

Rajashri and Minakshi had both complained of repeated torture in Lalbazar thana in November 1973, and again in April 1974. He also stated that Rajashri was beaten in such a way that she could not show her bruises to anyone without undressing (APDR 1987, 6–7).

The torture in the police station was very real, but neither Rajashri or Minakshi wanted to dwell on the details. They recalled the tragic time in jail when Asghari Begum, a tuberculosis patient, was placed in the lunatic ward. Asghari would shiver in the cold as she had inadequate clothing and bedding, which the ML women tried to agitate against, demanding that she be looked after. Asghari is the subject of a moving piece of writing in Minakshi's book *Jailer Bhitor Jail*, where she talks about Asghari begging to be taken outside to sit in the sun so that she could warm herself. She died without her simple desire being fulfilled.

Quite unexpectedly, before the filming session could close for the day, Rajashri suddenly began to recall the experience of torture in the police station—not with details of the torture, but of the way the human spirit survives it. She was speaking in collective terms but drawing from the deeply personal experience of torture, which was brutal and humiliating and meant to break her spirit. Rajashri survived that torture, she said, because of the way the rest of the people in police custody reached out to her—ordinary people, the pickpockets, the *hoochwalas* (those who make and sell liquor illicitly), the dregs of society—'saying don't worry, we are there for you'. Or telling her, '*Didi*, your father came', moving Rajashri to tears at the humanity of the people sharing the police station space with her. She never met them again after the interrogation phase in the police station was over, but they have stayed with her as people who gave her the will to live and to not give in to the police who were trying everything possible to break her spirit.

Rajashri also recalled that each time she was taken back to the police station for more interrogation, she would be beaten and thrust back into the cell which she had occupied in April 1974. The cell was shared by another young woman who had been booked for allegedly stealing her mistress's necklace. That young woman could not understand why Rajashri was being beaten; she had never heard of the Naxalites or the 'revolution', but she was shocked to see what the police had done to Rajashri. She would hold Rajashri in her arms each night, lulling her to sleep, covering her bruised body with her unstinting love. It was this love, this human-ness, that sustained Rajashri and made her resolve that come what may, she would not become insane; the police could not break her spirit. She was going to live; she was not going to let the torturers break her spirit. She would survive the torture and the humiliation to live again. And she did. That is what the State was afraid of, she said, concluding her account. It could not break her spirit nor that of others in prison with her. It was that innermost part of their selves that the State could not destroy.

The Emergency State

In the last part of this chapter, I will delineate the contours of the dramatic transformation of the State in India during the period 1975–1977, which suspended civil and political rights by imposing a state of Emergency in the country as a whole on 25 June 1975. The police swooped down on thousands of sleeping workers of various political hues and incarcerated them. There was no recourse to the courts—even Habeas Corpus was suspended following the Jabalpur Additional District Magistrate's judgment, which was upheld by the Supreme Court during the Emergency. The press was gagged, so no one knew what was happening in the country except for the rumours that flew, thick and fast. Since no political demonstrations were permitted, there was no visible opposition to the Emergency, or to the incarceration of thousands of people. It was a time when 'encounters', or cold-blooded killings by the police, became the means by which radical opposition was sought to be stamped out, and no one knew they were happening since the press had been gagged. This was official, unlike the actions of the West Bengal governments during the time of the Naxalbari crackdowns. Ranajit Guha (1978) described the Naxalbari crackdowns as a 'dress rehearsal' for the Emergency. The continuities between the two periods are visible in the complete suspension of rule of law, of the civil rights of citizens, and the absence of recourse to the courts to appeal against the arbitrary actions by the State.[12]

Among those arrested in June 1975 were many women—some well-known and others not so. Many went underground and tried to mobilise some opposition, until they too were tracked down and arrested. Some were drawn into an underground opposition that was regarded as dangerous and became 'activists' for the first time. Among them was the well-known actress and theatre person, Snehalata Reddy. In this segment, I will focus on Snehalata Reddy, partly because she wrote a diary *while* in jail and that allows us to see how she felt in the jail, unlike many other accounts that began in jail but were completed much later. As it stands, it is just a small fragment of her diary that was published in 1977, in part because Snehalata died before the Emergency was lifted. She was on parole due to ill health. Just the day before her parole was to end, Snehalata had a heart attack and suddenly passed away. She was only forty-five then. The diary, as she wrote it, remains unpublished. The short fragments were published in the form of a booklet, and it includes a short write-up by U. R. Ananthamurthy, who was both a friend and a civil rights activist, apart from being a well-known Kannada writer. The account here of Snehalata's incarceration is based on this published fragment, and on interviews with her son and daughter and two young friends who were close to Snehalata before and while she was in jail.

Snehalata and Pattabhi Rama Reddy were part of a social, political, and literary circle in Bangalore which was socialist, and were very deeply influenced by Ram Manohar Lohia. George Fernandes was a friend who was well-known to them. Snehalata had been an actress associated with the theatre, and Pattabhi Rama Reddy was a filmmaker. They were in the process of completing their second film when the Emergency was imposed. Immediately after that George, who had been very active in the railway strike the previous year, went underground and the police set up a hunt for him across India, which was perhaps one of the most sustained hunts for a political figure during the Emergency. He used a disguise, dressing as a tennis-playing Sikh to move around, and had visited Bangalore during this phase of being underground. Snehalata and Pattabhi were involved in the resistance movement, along with many others at the time. It was the Emergency State in pursuit of George Fernandes that swooped down on the Reddy family and took all of them in for interrogation, beginning with Konarak, who was only seventeen at the time and alone at home when the police first came to their house. Perhaps it was Snehalata's maternal concern that led her to strike a 'deal' with the police, saying: 'Leave the rest of them, I will answer all your questions.' The others were then let off. Snehalata spent more than a day in police interrogation, and when that ended, she seems to have thought that she would be released thereafter. Instead, she was sent to jail, charged with different things which shifted during the months of her incarceration, and she was never produced in court. Since there was no recourse to the courts during the Emergency, Snehalata and her family increasingly began to feel trapped. Snehalata wrote her diary as a series of jottings during the phase of increasing isolation and despair. The family desperately tried to get her out of jail, raising money to act as security with great difficulty for a bail bond, asking for parole on medical grounds, but nothing worked. Snehalata stayed in prison for almost seven months, even after the police had finally arrested George. Then, she was suddenly let out on a month's parole. The diary is an account of those days and nights in jail before she was paroled.

The extracts from Snehalata's jottings in an exercise book, published in *A Prison Diary*, dwell only on a few weeks of her time in jail. They begin on 22 July and end on 28 August. The jottings are brief, often dwelling upon the state of her health, her asthma attacks, and her desperate struggles to get proper medical attention. They reveal her lonely nights in jail, her anguish at her condition, and her sense of extreme isolation—she was the only woman political prisoner in the Central Jail, perhaps in all of Karnataka. Early on, she had tried to ask for some interaction with other political prisoners: Bangalore Central Jail had a large number of well-known political figures, including Ramakrishna Hedge, J. H. Patel, and her socialist colleague M. S. Appa Rao, who was a close friend. But the jail authorities denied her permission, saying that it would not be 'safe' for her do so. Thus, she was virtually in solitary confinement, with no acknowledgement that she too was a 'political prisoner' like the other men in the Bangalore Central Jail. Instead, she occupied a single cell with a hole at the rear which acted as the toilet. The sense of isolation was extreme.[13] Snehalata's ordeal had begun with a strip search, which was humiliating and outrageous at the same time. The others in her barrack were C-class prisoners who had to clean rice and ragi all day. This task added to Snehalata's asthma, which she had suffered from since her adolescent years. As the days turned into months with no sign of possible judicial reprieve, Snehalata's state of mind began to take its toll on her health. She could not understand why she was being held, why she was not being given bail, and why she had been abandoned by everyone, even her own family, although they were desperately trying to get her out on bail. Experiencing extreme mental torture, Snehalata's asthma attacks began to recur with increasing frequency. The diary extracts are a record of her state of mind as the days turned to weeks and then months:

> July 22, 1976. Fateful day! Really passed out. In a matter of minutes pulse failed, blanked out many times. Had nothing.
> July 23, 1976. Groggy, weak, blacked out throughout the day. Nothing.
> July 24, 1976. Once or twice blanked out.... Heavy breathing throughout.
> July 25, 1976. Long lonely day—I was within inches of death—I should be dismissed or paroled out of here.

The next day, 26 July, Snehalata wrote a long paragraph about being unable to sleep because of blackouts and backaches. She recorded that her asthma had never been so continuous and severe, and feared she was going to have a nervous breakdown. Then she pleaded: 'I want to go home and be with my people. Please get me out soon.'

Her pleas grew more urgent as she realised that she was going to be in jail for an indefinite period of time, and Konarak, her son, would leave to study music, which she wanted him to do very much. She writes desperately,

> Please get me out of here. The police have admitted they have no case. My serious condition is entirely the responsibility of the jail authorities—they prevented me from going to the hospital in the initial stages. Because they prevented me, I am depressed and panic stricken—having asthma everyday for 3 months is not a joke! Are all of them inhuman?

The following day, the diary entry records her telling the authorities that she will not call for a doctor the next time she has an attack; and when she dies, let it be upon their heads. In any case, it is not a matter of urgency for them, so then let them stew in their own juice. Then she writes: 'Pain, severe in the left back region, heavy breathing, extreme fatigue and blackouts .... No examination has been done to find out how exhausted or worn out I have become. I am so completely dejected.'

Death seems imminent to her: 'Is death so simple, so meaningless?'

After an hour more of struggling to breathe, she writes: 'How strange that death could be like that, or is it just an inkling I perceived not an entire reality?'

After crying so much that her throat hurt, in desperation, she writes to the Superintendent of Police. She describes her asthma attacks and reminds him that her family had informed him about her medical condition and about her asthma attacks when she was first jailed. Then she writes:

> Also, the injustice of my imprisonment has mentally depressed me, and I have weeping fits that do not help. I asked to be sent to the hospital, but after 20 days, I was told that the doctors did not recommend hospitalisation. I went up and down to the Victoria Hospital, and the drama that went on is too depressing...excuses were given. All I needed at that time was a break from my continuous attacks for I was suffering mental anguish, being confined here without knowing why....

But there was no relief. This was the Emergency State, entirely ruled by the diktats of those in power.

Snehalata's daughter filled in more details. She described Snehalata being taken to the hospital, and the Medical Superintendent recommending hospitalisation. He would then telephone the authorities to say that he was admitting her, and ten minutes later, there would be a call from someone higher up in the chain of authority, denying permission for her hospitalisation. Her son recounts that on the other hand, there were blandishments being offered to her; all Snehalata needed to do was to sign a bond to be released, which she refused to do. How could she do that? She only believed in justice and goodness! So she stayed in jail.

The letter to the superintendent also says that she wanted to be with her son and the rest of her family; her son was going away for a long period to study. As there was no case against her, she had thought she would be released; however, that was not happening and so she pleaded to be with her son for a few days at least before he left. Finally, she appealed to the superintendent as a mother: 'You should understand a mother's heart, especially as you all know I have no business to be confined here anymore. My life has been an open book.'

In anger, she hits at the authorities: 'Sometimes I wish I had really done something to deserve my imprisonment.'

But immediately, she pleads: 'Kindly let me out on parole even if nothing else is not possible.... The mental agony is depressing me, and I am very ill.'

She ends with a desperate plea: 'Please help me.'

The pleas did not work. Nothing happened. Snehalata began to feel abandoned by everyone, even her family, who were trying to use all their might to get her out. She was in anguish about not being able to see her son properly before he left. She knew she was missing moments of life with Konarak and wrote: 'Next time I see him he will not be the same. He will be a man.'

Snehalata's entries for 28, 29, 30, 31 July and 1 August are clubbed together. The text that accompanies these entries says: 'In the dark night of the soul, it's always 3 'o'clock in the morning, day after day. These are the days I wanted to die, really die.'

Konarak left without a proper meeting with her, with just an all too brief meeting one evening. Then he was gone. For two days after that, she made anguished entries, writing only the word 'Misery, Oh misery!'

The diary entries cease in the published tract after her son left for his studies, so we do not know what she felt or thought after this point in her incarceration. The gloss on her published tract says that Snehalata's health grew worse and worse. She had two bad spasms which, in hindsight, were believed to have been heart attacks. Suddenly, one day in December, the authorities called the family and asked that Snehalata be taken away on parole. Initially, Snehalata refused, saying she wanted to be released and not paroled. Her family persuaded her to take what was being given—a month of parole—and so she went home, where she tried to blot out the jail, only talking about others still in prison, whom she wrote about in her diary.

As the days went by, depression settled back into her as the parole period drew to a close. Two days before the parole ended, Snehalata's heart gave way; her ordeal had finally ended. In a sense, 'she signed her own release papers', as her daughter put it. Her spirit had remained unbroken despite the days and nights of physical and mental torment, but her body had given way.

At some point earlier on, Snehalata had written in her diary:

> If you think you can break my spirit you are wrong; these acts only make me firmer in my beliefs of truth, humanity and freedom of individuals. My body may suffer humiliation, but the spirit, the human spirit cannot be suppressed for long.

Ironically, Snehalata died the day after elections were unexpectedly announced. Her funeral, in which thousands participated, almost became the beginning of an election campaign. In distant Calcutta, Rajashri describes the time when the election results were announced, late at night, while they were in jail. Someone had managed to smuggle in a transistor, and they all listened to it hidden under a blanket. As the great stalwarts of the Emergency fell one by one, the prisoners shouted with joy. It was a heady moment, even though Rajashri and her compatriots did not believe in electoral democracy. Yet, everyone wanted the Emergency regime to go and as each of the notorious Emergency figures fell one by one, the cries of jubilation grew in intensity.[14] The opposition had, among other issues, promised to restore and return to pre-Emergency democracy. In West Bengal, the release of political prisoners was made an election issue by the Bandi Mukti Andolan, the Committee for the Release of Political Prisoners. Since all shades of political opposition to the ruling regime had been imprisoned during the Emergency, there was widespread middle-class support for the release of all political prisoners for the first—and perhaps the last—time in post-independent India.

In August 1977, Rajashri and Minakshi walked out of jail together. They had both refused to sign a bond admitting their crimes, which would have ensured an earlier release. Many others in their circle had signed such bonds to get out of jail. Rajashri said later:

> I clearly remember that both of us left the jail premises hand in hand. On the one hand, there was so much of excitement about our release—finally, 'we are going out', it meant freedom.
>
> Freedom, what does it mean?
>
> Simultaneously, I was also saddened by the fact that this meant that both of us would part ways. Will we never meet again? Of course, we will. For so long, we have spent so much time together, slept together, woken up together: shared our moments of happiness and despair, gone to court together, what will happen now that we are free?

By Way of a Conclusion

As the heady moments of the elections passed, critical questions about the State during the Emergency and its excesses surfaced. The new government appointed the Shah Commission in 1977 to inquire into the excesses of the Emergency. The issue of the torture of political prisoners in police custody also surfaced, as did the terrible conditions that existed in jail. Other committees, such as the Bhargava Commission in 1969 and the Tarkunde Committee in 1977, were appointed to examine encounter killings, which had spread across India from Bengal to Andhra Pradesh to Kerala during the Telangana movement and the Emergency, a time when no one knew what was happening because of press censorship. In the end, sadly, no one was punished. Some of the torture cases dragged on for years in West Bengal, as Chapter 2 (this volume) shows. The notorious Runu Guha got away as the case against him for the torture of Archana Guha Niyogi dragged on till he was convicted, yet he managed to stay out of jail on appeal against the conviction. He then died of natural causes without the country confronting his excesses and creating structures of accountability to counter the actions of the police acting on behalf of the State (Amnesty International 1994; APDR 1987, 13–15). Far away, a father in Kerala pursued his son's disappearance from a university hostel during the Emergency, knocking on every door from the moment Rajan disappeared to the lifting of the Emergency (Eachara Warrier 2004). Finally, the court stated that the father's Habeas Corpus plea against the police held: the police must produce Rajan (which the police obviously could not do, since they had encountered him). That judgment was cold comfort for the anguished father, who never officially got to know what exactly had happened to his son and who should be held responsible for the cold-blooded killing that was believed to have been his fate.[15] Similarly, no one was held responsible for Rajashri and Minakshi's torture in police custody in West Bengal or Snehalata's mental torture in a prison in Karnataka.

Today, jail conditions continue to be abysmal, torture—both physical and mental—continues as before, and has even intensified. Women are being jailed for their political work with no recourse to judicial relief as there are new draconian laws in place that deny bail, and where the cases drag on for years. That, however, will have to be the subject of another essay. Part one of the telling of my story of women political prisoners is for the moment over.

Endnotes

1. *Bandini*, directed by Bimal Roy, 1963, starring Nutan, Ashok Kumar, and Dharmendra, music by S. D. Burman.

2. In the last two decades, the woman revolutionary has made an appearance in films such as *Hazaaron Khwaishein Aisi* (2003; director, Sudhir Mishra) and *Chakravyuh* (2012; director, Prakash Jha), although the story is never built around her. The true revolutionary in cinema is always a man.

3. Interview with Durga Bhabhi, 18 November 1988. Durga Bhabhi (Durga Devi Vohra) was an associate of Bhagat Singh in the Hindustan Socialist Republican Army and helped him to escape from Lahore to Calcutta in 1927 after he and two associates shot a police officer.

4. Interview with Koteswaramma, Vishakhapatnam.

5. Koteswaramma's description of being in jail as a mother is a contrast to Jawaharlal Nehru's description of being in jail; he says, 'The sounds one misses most in jail are women's voices and children's laughter.' The statement presumes the political prisoner spending time in jail is a man and therefore someone who would experience the jail in very male ways.

6. The account here is based on an interview with Khatija, held in March 2013, and an unpublished memoir of sixty-four pages, which was begun in 2012 but has remained unfinished since then.

7. This summary is based on a number of books and articles that deal with Naxalbari and the movement generated by it in the city of Kolkata in particular. I list here only a few of the resources available: Banerjee (1984); Mukherjee and Yadav (1970); Sen, et al. (1978).

8. Encounters, a form of extra-judicial killings of certain categories of people, such as the Naxalites, by the police in a staged manner became a phenomenon during the Emergency, especially in Andhra Pradesh. When the Emergency was lifted, a committee comprising civil rights activists headed by Justice Tarkunde investigated some of these killings and authored a report titled 'Encounters are Murders'. Since then, encounter killings have spread as a way to eliminate certain categories of people by the police across the country, including those believed to be 'criminals' in the eyes of the State.

9. Three films were directed by Mrinal Sen: *Interview* (1971), *Calcutta 71* (1972), and *Padatik* (1974). He made a fourth film, *Mahaprithibi* (1991), which is less well-known. Later, Gautam Ghose made *Kaalbela* (2009), which also used the iconic scene of a young man being pursued and encountered by the Calcutta Police.

10. Dasgupta (2014); transcript translated by Madhulagna Haldar.

11. For Ila Mitra's statement, reproduced as a pamphlet and circulated in East Pakistan in February 1950, see Bagchi and Dasgupta (2003), 56–58.

12. The lifting of the Emergency in 1977 led to an explosion of books, which are too numerous to cite. I have drawn upon a few, among which three were particularly useful: Desai (1986), Kannabiran (2004), and Selboune (1977). I have also drawn upon my personal archive of reports, pamphlets, and other documents.

13. Coomi Kapoor's book on the Emergency describes the conditions for male political prisoners like Arun Jaitley, who told her that they had a transistor, listened to BBC news, took walks, had oil massages, and played games. Conditions for women political prisoners were always worse, but even Maharani Gayatri Devi could take walks every evening with her son (Kapoor 2013, 42–46). In contrast, Snehalata was prevented from meeting her socialist colleagues, even though they were in the Bangalore Central Jail, virtually a stone's throw away from her barrack. Her anguish was a burden that she carried in a lonely cell all by herself.

14. Interview with Rajashri Dasgupta, 9 February 2012; also see Dasgupta (2000).

15. Rajan's tragic story is the subject of the Malayalam film *Piravi* (1989; director, N. Shaji), a most moving account of a father searching for his missing son. It is a story about political immorality and State brutality, and its tragic consequences for a family where the father waits for the son to return, even as his daughter discovers what happened to her brother who will never come back. It received the National Award.

References

Amnesty International. 1994. 'Archana Guha—16 years Awaiting Justice: The Lack of Speedy and Effective Redress Mechanisms For Torture Victims', March.

Association for Protection of Democratic Rights (APDR). 1987. *When to Remain Silent is a Crime*. Calcutta: APDR.

Bagchi, Jasodhara, and Suboranjan Dasgupta (eds). 2003. *The Trauma and the Triumph: Gender and the Partition in Eastern India*. Kolkata: Stree.

Banerjee, Sumanta. 1984. *India's Simmering Revolution: The Naxalite Uprising*. Delhi: Select Book Service Syndicate.

Committee for the Release of Political Prisoners. 2013. *Paro's Kids and Other Prison Stories*. New Delhi.

Dasgupta, Rajashri. 'Freedom Song'. *The Telegraph*, 25 June.

______. 2014. 'Minakshi ke mone kore' ('Remembering Minakshi'). Memorial Meeting for Minakshi Sen, Kolkata, 29 November.

Desai, A. R. (ed.). 1986. *Violation of Democratic Rights in India*. Bombay: Popular Prakashan.

Eachara Warrier, T. V. 2004. *Memories of a Father*. Translated from Malayalam by Neelan Premji. Hong Kong and Thrissur: Asian Human Rights Commission and Jananeethi.

Guha, Ranajit. 1978. 'Book Review, Calcutta Diary by Ashok Mitra'. *Journal of Peasant Studies* 5 (4), 525–527.

Lewis, Primila. 1978. *Reason Wounded: An Experience of India's Emergency*. London: George Allen & Unwin.

Kannabiran, K. G. 2004. *The Wages of Impunity: Power, Justice and Human Rights*. New Delhi, Orient Longman.

Kapoor, Coomi. 2013. *The Emergency: A Personal History*. New Delhi: Penguin/Viking.

Kondapalli, Koteswaramma. 2015. *The Sharp Knife of Memory*. New Delhi: Zubaan.

Mitra, Joya. 2004. *Killing Days*. New Delhi: Kali For Women.

Mukherjee, Kalyan, and Rajendra Singh Yadav. 1970. *Bhojpur: Naxalism in the Plains of Bihar*. Delhi: Radhakrishna Prakashan.

Reddy, Snehalata. 1977. *A Prison Diary*. Mysore: Human Rights Committee, Karnataka.

Selboune, David. 1977. *An Eye to India: The Unmasking of a Tyranny*. Middlesex: Penguin Books.

Sen, Minakshi. 1993. *Jailer Bhitor Jail*. Kolkata: People's Book Society.

Sen, Samar, Debabrata Panda, and Ashish Lahiri. 1978. *Naxalbari and After: A Frontier Anthology*, 2 volumes. Calcutta: Kathashilpa.

Chapter 2
64 Days in Lalbazar
Anatomy of a Torture Narrative

Sharmila Purkayastha

> *They forced me to lie down on a big table and a few of them held my hands and feet tightly. They covered me with a blanket from below my feet all the way up till my neck. After this, two persons beat me from both sides with great force from my knees to my waist. I don't know how long this continued. When I regained consciousness, I found myself lying on the floor. And the policemen were dousing my face with water. I opened my eyes and saw Runu Guha standing before me, smoking a cigar. I felt the weight of my body and I could not bear the pain, especially in my lower back. Afterwards I understood that the blanket was meant to cover the blood. I could not stand up. I was wordless, dry-eyed and surprised. I could not imagine that they could do this to me. Where were my tears?*[1]
>
> Ghosh (2011, 15)

Malaya Ghosh's horrifying account of police torture in Lalbazar police station in 1974 had to wait for over thirty years before being published. Explaining the delay, Ghosh in her Preface says that she was spurred into revisiting her diary because of the contemporary widespread attacks on people's rights by the duly elected Left Front government, which had promised to respect those rights when it first came to power in 1977. Delineating the betrayal of promises over time, Ghosh makes two related observations. First, she contests the liberal democratic argument about the autonomy of State institutions as she says that the experiential history of the 1970s shows that the police and the judiciary were politicised under the Indian National Congress (henceforth Congress) regime.

Second, she reminds that rulers often forget that the people are the real judge of history. Both reasons are offered as explanations for writing her personal narrative of the sixty-four days in police custody. Published in Bengali in 2011, *Lalbajare 64 Din* (*64 Days in Lalbazar*, henceforth referred to as *64 Days*), a slim booklet of fifty-two pages, remains one of the most powerful accounts of police brutality in the 1970s and recalls Latika Guha's *Narak Prakashya Hok* (*Let Hell be Revealed*, 2001), a torture narrative that bears witness to the horrendous torture that her sister-in-law, Archana Guha, their relative Gauri Chatterji, and she suffered in the same police station, Lalbazar, for twenty-seven days. The torture of Archana Guha, which left her paralysed for life, became well-known as it led to a prolonged court case spanning two decades, and which did not yield any significant punishment.[2] Comparatively speaking, the case of Malaya Ghosh (1936–2016) is less well-known, and for that reason it forms the focus of this chapter.

Writing a torture narrative years after surviving torture carries a risk, the risk of reconstruction. Given that the broader purpose of torture testimonies is to provide information about the torturers and their practices, the question of authenticity becomes paramount. Further, since torture narratives are focused on what Elaine Scarry calls the 'demonstration and magnification of the felt experience of pain' (Scarry 1985, 27), the process of recollection is inscribed in the narrative. Can the recollection of pain be the same as suffering it?

The most well-known of such a 'post' account is Luz Arce's *Inferno: A Story of Terror and Survival in Chile*, which was first published in Spanish in 1993 and in English in 2004. Arce's account of torture by Chile's Dirección Nacional de Inteligencia (DINA), Augusto Pinochet's secret military police, took place twenty years after the coup of 1973. A leftist militant-turned-'collaborator', Arce occupies a controversial place in the history of torture as she both collaborated with and also testified against the DINA in the early 1990s. Notwithstanding the twists and turns in her personal history, her torture narrative remained intact and, while reviewing her account, Jean Franco noted, 'The account of the hours of torture, the filth of detention centres, and the constant harassment, written almost twenty years after the event, time and again rehearses the story of defilement, abjection and revival'(Franco 2013, 176).

A 'post' narrative has the potential of rehearsing the actual event and can well serve the urgent need of revisiting the past and learning from it. As a vital document of the 1970s, Ghosh's work does just that, especially since it is by a woman political detainee.

The 1970s was a remarkable decade, which witnessed numerous liberation struggles and corresponding State repression all across the global South. In India, the period is mostly remembered for the State-imposed Emergency under the then prime minister, Indira Gandhi. However, the unprecedented police excesses committed against the Naxalite movement during the early 1970s in Bengal was, as Ranajit Guha aptly described, a 'dress rehearsal' which 'India as a whole was to experience in the nineteen months of the Emergency proclaimed on 26 June 1975' (Guha 2009, 610). Beginning with Operation Crossbow, launched in June 1967, repression was intensified by the deployment of paramilitary forces in Gopiballavpur and Debra in 1969, and finally by the army's Operation Steeplechase in Birbhum in 1971. The unified command directed by the Centre comprised Siddhartha Shankar Ray, Union Minister in charge of Bengal, along with Ranjit Kumar Gupta as police commissioner and J. F. R. Jacob as army commander, Eastern Command. While Bengal was a test case for armed intervention, the increased strength of civil and armed police throughout the country between 1969 and 1974 suggested an overall intensification of the State machinery (Banerjee 2008, 312).

For women participants, especially among the educated youth, the Naxalite movement provided an avenue for fulfilling their ideological commitment towards the poor. Ghosh, a middle-class and middle-aged schoolteacher, was drawn to the movement primarily because of her husband. She started her political journey by teaching and supervising the health of women and children in a nearby *basti* (slum). She was picked up by the police from inside N. R. S. Hospital, a well-known public hospital in Kolkata, on 30 May 1974, and what followed was the most harrowing time of her life.

The police of West Bengal was particularly trained to liquidate Naxalites through 'encounters', as 'the sole motive was to kill the enemy by any means' (Mukhopadhyay 2006, 16). Not surprisingly, the President awarded Runu Guha Niyogi, the infamous torture specialist, with the police medal for gallantry in 1973, for his astonishing success against the Naxalites. The jails of West Bengal overflowed with Naxalites. The state home minister had informed the state assembly in 1973 that 17,787 persons had been arrested for Naxalite-related offences, even while unofficial estimates suggested a higher figure (Amnesty International 1974, 1612).

Occupying a prominent place within the historiography of the 1970s, *64 Days* bears witness to the repression of the Naxalites. Ghosh was released along with other political prisoners as part of the general amnesty promised by the newly elected Communist Party of India (Marxist) (CPI-M) in 1977. The post-release history has directed attention to the nature of participation in the movement. Women's participation in the movement and in jails was substantially lower, a point that is illustrated amply from within the vast historiography of the movement. Notwithstanding this lowered participation, documenting the gendered history of the movement has underlined the pitfalls of the gendered memory, which has aided in invisibilising the issue further (Sinha Roy 2011, 85–91). For erstwhile women participants, the recovery of their history has prompted their reflections on the patriarchal nature and structure of the movement, especially its lack of concern for equal rights for women (Bandyopadhyay 2008). For feminist researchers, the much-needed focus on women participants has enabled the study of a wide variety of issues, such as the discussion of 'non-metropolitan women activists' (Sinha Roy 2011, 15), the 'politics of interpersonal relations and sexuality' (Roy 2006, 101), the question of caste and gender (Sinha Roy 2016), women's innovative resistance practices in custody (Sen 2014, 119–134), and the testimonial transformation of women's 'traumatic memory' of State violence 'into narrative memory' (Roy 2013, 97). This is by no means an exhaustive account of women's participation within the Naxalite movement, but it is meant to indicate the extremely rich and diverse nature of the feminist field.

This chapter examines the gendered nature of the torture practised by police personnel in the 1970s. Through Ghosh's account, it demonstrates how interrogation via torture was inflicted on women detainees who were not 'dreaded Naxalites', but were related to wanted political activists. The focus is equally on how Ghosh resisted the effects of torture by inventing strategies of survival, strategies which recall and contextualise the Naxalite text within contemporary torture testimonies, especially from Latin America. In the light of recent debates on the generic possibility and limits of testimony in bearing witness and in offering personal healing, the chapter argues for a holistic and inclusive understanding of personal and political justice. It concludes with a reminder that Ghosh's testimony serves a very important role in highlighting the culture of impunity that continues to define our contemporary culture of torture of political detainees. The chapter is divided into three parts: the first examines the power of torture, the second addresses the scope of resistance, and the third revisits the issues of justice.

The Breaking of Bodies and Minds

Torture narratives have no telos other than the end of torture. Even when it is known why the person is being arrested, the act of torture always exceeds the facts of the case. Ghosh's account vividly brings out the peculiar convergence of the body and mind under attack: the fears of being alone, of having no control over one's body, of being under surveillance, and of being the target of threats, intimidation, and attacks. The resultant torture is never wholly mental or only physical; it is a combination of both. The torturer's masculinity remains sheathed in silence as he does not need to announce his intentions or actions. It is his will that bears testimony to what is enacted in the torture chamber. The torture is not just a combination of physical and mental pain; it is deeply gendered and deeply sexual too.

One obvious and salient feature is that the victim is alone with the 'knowledge of being beyond help of family or lawyer, of being totally at the mercy of those whose job is to have no mercy' (Amnesty International 1984, 18). The knowledge of the merciless torturer is not all; the victim/survivor also lacks knowledge about her future. Accordingly, the element of surprise haunts *64 Days* as the author cannot come to terms with the modus operandi of the police: 'What will they again do to me?' (Ghosh 2011, 13); 'Will they take me now again to the Naxal chamber?' (ibid., 27); 'Where are they taking me?' (ibid., 37). Till the very end, the uncertainty remains: 'When I heard that familiar jingling sound meant for unlocking the five padlocks of the central lockup, my body shuddered with fear. Will they again lay their hands on me?' (ibid., 45). And, 'Suddenly it seemed that the police van was near the police "case hospital". I became vigilant. My entire body shuddered in fear. Why here again?' (ibid., 49).

The Body in Pain

This anxiety is linked with the fear of pain, the excruciating pain that is inflicted by the torturer during interrogation. Unlike the male participants, many of whom were well-known and held important organisational positions, women Naxalites were mostly sympathisers, never leaders. Ghosh says that at the time of arrest, there was nothing that could prove that she had impeded or obstructed law and order. Apart from verbal opposition to the political state of affairs prevailing under the Congress regime, she had never resorted to any other form of opposition (Ghosh 2011, 17). She could not answer any 'leading' questions during her numerous torture sessions, not because she was arrogant and resistant—as Runu Guha maintained (ibid., 37)—but because she did not know. Yet, she, like many others, was severely tortured and questioned insistently and was threatened with disgrace. Ghosh notes:

> Runu Guha's interrogation started with the name of one woman. I was told to give information of her whereabouts. Umashankar Lahiri (a police official) gave clear instructions:

> 'If she doesn't divulge the details within the next twenty-four hours, then we will shave half her head and put limestone paste on it and parade her in Lalbazar's courtyard.' The person they were referring to I had never heard of. How could I give information? (ibid., 13)

The threat to parade Ghosh with a half-shaved head covered with limestone paste draws upon degrading forms of customary punishments in which victims are forcibly disfigured and publicly shamed. The fear and humiliation underlying this threat of public disgrace is particularly powerful, given Ghosh's position as a 'respectable' teacher. Her horror stems from the fact that her sense of dignity and conscientiousness has been deliberately broken. When she is first taken to Lalbazar, no effort is made to know from her who she is. Instead, Runu Guha instructs his subordinate to put her on the table, a euphemism for torture. On another day, she is triumphantly told by the officer belonging to the Special Branch that they have 'caught' her. 'Caught' has a laced meaning as it can both suggest her physical arrest and the fact that they have unmasked and caught her out. The 'play' of torture is such that the victim can never relax. While Ghosh struggles to understand the import of 'caught', one of the policemen suddenly snatches a ruler and rains a series of blows on the middle of her head. She falls unconscious. At another point, she says that Runu Guha would take her to the torture chamber without any apparent reason and rain blows on her head.

Ghosh's physical pain is compounded by the surrounding filth and dirt of the lock-up, the torture chamber, ante rooms; the putrid atmosphere furthers her dehumanisation:

> It was three in the afternoon. They had taken me to the torture chamber for an entire hour. Then they left me on a rusted tin cot in a dark and squalid room. I did not have the strength to sit up. To the extent possible, I tried to contract my body and lie on one side. Blood had congealed, and my fingers and toes had turned blue. My entire body was oozing with pus and secretion. Finally, the dam broke and the tears rolled unchecked. I did not have the strength to stop or think. I felt dumbfounded and comatose. (ibid., 16)

Isolated from the world outside, the victim's helplessness adds to the sense of resignation, a sense that pervades Ghosh's mind till the very end: 'Today is the sixty-fourth day; I'm in the control of the Lalbazar police van. My body is exhausted; dirty; the mind is dejected. Lice is crawling in my head and body and my clothes have a putrid vapour about them' (ibid., 49).

Ghosh suffers excruciating pain; pain that leaves her maimed for life. However, more than the aftermath of torture, the immediate fallout was that she was left almost dead. For the torturer, it is imperative that the victim does not die. Even when the body under torture collapses and the wounds break out in pus and purulence, the signs of a wet and rotting body proffer a new routine: the game of medical care. While dressing Ghosh's decaying wounds, the doctor on duty at Lalbazar would say that had she cooperated and confessed, 'told everything', she would not have suffered such pain. The doctor's indirect method of pressuring adds to the torturer's belief in the guilt of the victim. Care without healing ensures that the body in pain remains alive, enough to remind the victim that she is responsible for the suffering. The cumulative effect of physical pain and verbal assault, which alternates between threats and recommendations, is intended to mentally break the victim. She says: 'All my beliefs and convictions are being undermined in the torture chamber by Runu Guha Niyogi and his cohorts, especially constables Aditya and Shankar. And, of course, there's Runu Guha Niyogi's special belief that he alone is the law. Nothing else is' (Ghosh 2011, 27). And, 'I have no desire to know what they will do to me tomorrow' (ibid., 49).

Notably, the torturer never admits to mistakes; instead, he uses cunning to test and trap the victim. After they failed to elicit the information they sought from her, she was asked to solve a Maths question of Class IX by Runu Niyogi's boss. Since she was a Maths teacher and could solve it easily, word spread through Lalbazar that she was an influential intellectual, a political activist. And her torture increased.

In her influential work, Scarry points out how the two-fold process of torture, infliction of pain and the verbal act of interrogation, underlines the monstrous relation between the torturer and his prisoner: as the prisoner's world shrinks and breaks down under the weight of pain, the torturer's world swells and expands (Scarry 1985, 35–36).

Loosely organised around an account of what happened before her arrest till the end of her detention in police custody, the narrative style of *64 Days* both observes and disrupts chronology. It offers a 'past' of the survivor, which chronologically is meant to update the reader on the facts of her life before she was arrested. However, the narration of torture follows a back-and-forth movement, not a day-to-day account. This narrative twist adds to and intensifies the horror of torture. Early on in the text, Ghosh focuses attention on what happened to her on the twenty-seventh day, the worst day of her life in Lalbazar:

> However, the very worst they did on the twenty-seventh day. It was midnight then. Suddenly, with a great rattle, I heard the central lock up's lock being opened. My entire body started shivering. Because of the unending torture, I was already quite ill. What will they again do to me? (Ghosh 2011, 13)

After this, she returns to the events of the first morning somewhere in the middle of the text: 'Last morning, I was completely well, whole and alive. Today, I am disabled. I can't sit up straight. There is tremendous pain in the nether region. My entire body hidden underneath my sari, had swelled up' (ibid., 25).

This is immediately followed by an account of the proceedings in the court, as the police is bound by law (Section 167, Code of Criminal Procedure 1973) to give information about the detainee to the judicial authority within twenty-four hours of arrest and explain why further detention is needed. Predictably, in keeping with police practice, Ghosh is taken to court but not presented before the magistrate, and is returned to the lock-up with judicial permission for fifteen days of interrogation in police custody: 'I returned from court before the day was over. I felt deeply despondent. What kind of judge, I thought? My faith has broken. Will I also lose my will to live?' (Ghosh 2011, 26).

The narrative complexity and the disruption of linearity is not a sign of an 'inauthentic' memory; rather, it shows that the act of recalling is guided by certain definite episodes which override the chronological account. The complexity is preserved in the use of tenses: the intermingling of the past in the present. Besides, each such episode is framed by her wider ruminations over the ruins of the political promises that the new nation had made to its citizens, and by her personal recollections of her home, her past, and her family. Such a framed account of torture magnifies the isolation and humiliation that she is forced to suffer as a person and as a woman.

Sexual Torture

The gendering of torture is crucial to the torturer's success in inflicting pain. Scarry's thesis that pain has 'no referential content' (Scarry 1985, 5) is deeply debatable as gender plays a key role in the torturer's scheme of things. Jean Franco demonstrates in her wide-ranging study of torture in the Southern Cone how 'men were deliberately feminized' (Franco 1992, 107), whilst the 'treatment of women prisoners were rooted in sadistic fantasies' (ibid., 109). Franco further argues that the sense of shame and stigma that was attached to female torture often made it impossible for them to speak of what they had survived. In Ghosh's context, the situation of torture is doubly intolerable as her torturer was not only a police officer who had protection from the State, but he was also a famous police officer who had been awarded by no less than the President of India.

In such a situation, the burden of surviving, witnessing, and narrating torture is wholly on the survivor. It cannot be denied that what Niyogi made Ghosh undergo was part of an elaborate sexual fantasy in which the point of torture was to diminish the identity of Ghosh to nothingness. However, the obliqueness with which sexual torture is treated in Ghosh's narrative illustrates the problem of both writing about and witnessing and suffering torture, especially since the female detainee is always at risk of being raped and sexually violated. Outside of the female lock-up, Ghosh is forever surrounded by men, particularly in the torture chamber. Her first impression of Runu Niyogi is of a cigar-smoking man standing in front of her broken body. In addition to the obvious masculine nature of the torture, Ghosh is often the butt of sexual jokes and mockery. When she is first presented before Runu Niyogi, the police personnel grab her arm and try to wrest her bangle off her wrist; they egg each other on by saying: 'Brother, you've put on the wedding bangle on your wife. Why don't you take off your sister-in-law's bangle?' (Ghosh 2011, 12).

The reference to *boudi* or sister-in-law is part of the extended male joke in which the female detainee is treated with familiarity and laughter. When she is taken to court a second time and is unable to sit up in the police vehicle, the constable jokes and invites her to lie on his thigh (ibid., 32). For Ghosh, the situation is intolerable as she is helpless before multiple mockeries: the crude sexual gesture that the policeman mockingly makes at her; the farce that the police play out by taking her in a vehicle with tinted glass to escape recognition from passers-by; the derision and scorn that they heap on her brother's plea in the court premises; and the charade of justice enacted in court. As Ghosh has rightly observed, the police *is* the law, and violence is instituted and justified by the keepers of the law.

The absence of actual sexual torture, such as rape, in Ghosh's text is strikingly similar to accounts written by other ex-Naxalites such as Joya Mitra, Meenakshi Sen, Mary Tyler, and Latika Guha.[3] Such testimonial silence is unsettling, especially since the torture chamber of Lalbazar with its infamous 'table' practices is well-documented, and its sexual aspect was brought home in a report published in 1974. Based on interviews carried out by members of the women's wing of the Communist Party of India, who were detained in Presidency Jail for participating in an anti-price rise demonstration, the report observed how seven young Naxalite women were subjected to the most heinous form of sexual torture by the anti-Naxal squad at Lalbazar. The report offered an account of how it went:

> [G]irls were stripped naked and made to lie on a table. Then they would begin by burning with cigarette—neck, breast, stomach and other soft private parts not excluded—accompanied by all conceivable humiliation. And after this, if any of the girls refused to speak, an iron ruler would be inserted into her rectum. (Editorial, *EPW* 1974, 1171)

The injured women would be returned to jail and, after a minimal period of recovery, brought back as fresh charges would be levelled against them. The report also observed how these prisoners were denied the right to give evidence in court as they were never produced, but were kept waiting in the police vans. The report concluded by stating that if there was no intervention in the given matter, the said women prisoners would either die or be disabled for life. The report was based on interviews carried out in a short time and the possibility of inaccuracies cannot be denied.[4] Nonetheless, this report was the first of its kind to highlight the fact of sexual torture that the detainees underwent in Lalbazar and demonstrate the phenomenon of 'extreme masculinity', which depends upon the unequal relation between 'all powerful males' and 'subjugated women' (Franco 2013, 15). Contemporary documentation by the Association for the Protection of Democratic Rights (APDR) points to horrifying instances of rapes, sexual assaults, and even deaths (APDR 1999, 131–136).

When placed against the silences of torture accounts, the contemporary record of sexual torture of women activists presents a problem of unevenness in narration and documentation. One way of understanding the unevenness is to recognise that within middle-class survivor accounts, the issue of sexual torture is sanitised not only because such survivors were spared, unlike unprotected proletarian women, rural or urban, but also because the survivors' bourgeois sensibility compelled them to address the issue of torture without admitting to the issue of sexual violence implicit within such torture. Such absences in writing could well suggest that the issue of sexual dishonour was a taboo topic among middle-class women Naxalites—a point noted by Durba Ghosh in her analysis of the accounts of women revolutionaries of the 1930s

(Ghosh 2013, 365). Obviously, this patriarchal silencing and self-censorship evident in postcolonial middle-class women's writings is quite at odds with the documentation done by fact-finding reports. However, an amplification is needed on the subject. Does sexual torture necessarily mean rape? If so, the reticence on the discussion of sexual torture in the Naxalite period makes it difficult to know its extent and aftermath, and testimonial silences could point to an invisibilising of the history of sexual torture.[5] Besides, for survivors, testimonies about sexual violence place an intolerable burden, as evident in Kavita Panjabi's exploration of the fiery Tebhaga leader, Ila Mitra's, contradictory relationship with her public testimony on the sexual torture that she suffered at the hands of the East Pakistan State. Examining the '*very uncertainty about owning her court testimony*', Panjabi notes that Mitra had shown complete confusion over it subsequently (Panjabi 2017, 199–200). Arguing the problem of the 'terrifying indignity' that such violations place on survivors, Panjabi cautions that, 'The political gains of such public testimony have to be weighed against the personal costs of victims' (ibid., 253).[6] Hence, it may be futile to ask why Ghosh refuses to enter the discussion. However, if the subject of sexual torture is expanded beyond rape, then, as Ghosh's account shows, sexual torture was practised in a variety of ways, which did not necessarily culminate in rape. In short, Ghosh's testimony offers ways of reading how physical and mental humiliations were deeply sexual in nature. The interesting part is that Ghosh does not acknowledge it, but the reader recognises it.

Unlike the 1970s, the history of sexual assault that the State perpetrates on proletarian women is much more common among contemporary accounts of torture by women Maoists, especially in Chhattisgarh. The case of Soni Sori, an Adivasi schoolteacher who was arrested on charges of Maoism in 2011, is well-known as she made public her sexual torture at the hands of the state police. Soni's torture was not unusual. There is also the account of the peasant girl, Kawasi Hidme, who was abducted by the state police in 2008 and was gang-raped and tortured to such an extent that her uterus was involuntarily ejected, and her situation became known only because of her interactions with Soni in prison.[7] While it may seem that there are no apparent connections between the 1970s and now, the history and documentation of torture of women political prisoners in the postcolonial period really begins with the repression of women Naxalites in custody.

Resisting Torture

Resistance in torture narratives lies in the survivor's will to survive pain, both physical and mental. Surviving torture is not premised upon heroism or exemplary strength, as the torturer claims power over the victim's entire being. The point is to reclaim the mind, if not the body, through strategies of survival. The will to live instructs the survivor's need to 'know' the unknowable. This and other skills of surviving torture mark the narratives discussed below.

> In prison everything is intended to make you alone, isolated, defeated. Your captors say over and over: 'We are your father, your brother, your family. No one else cares for you'. If for a moment you believe them and forget that your people and the struggle still exist, then you are truly alone. (Díaz 1992, Preface)

These remarkable words open the Preface to Nidia Díaz's *I was Never Alone* (1992), and end the account, too. How could a wounded commander of the Farabundo Marti National Liberation Front (FMLN), captured in combat by the Salvadoran military with the help of the Central Intelligence Agency (CIA) in 1984, interrogated without a break for fifteen days and kept in solitary confinement for six months, not be alone? But that is precisely the point of Díaz's account: not to feel alone. Díaz's story of solitude is a dialogic one. The reader finds that she talks to herself, sings, dances, paints, draws, and composes poems during her imprisonment in a damp and dank room inside the military prison in San Salvador. She recalls her days of freedom and struggle in the mountains amid butterflies, fruit trees, and flowers. When she is blindfolded before her interrogators, she fights back; she questions, retorts, challenges, and refuses to collaborate. When she cannot argue, she petitions the authorities and demands answers as to why, as a prisoner of war, she is not entitled to the rights as laid down in the international protocols, and why she is kept in the military prison and not shifted to Ilipango, the official women's prison. Díaz was released in October 1985, after the president was forced to agree to the demand for the release of thirty-four political prisoners in lieu of his daughter, who had been abducted by the FMLN.

Written a few years earlier, Alicia Partnoy's *The Little School* (1998 [1986]) is a similar testimony, which records Partnoy's efforts to withstand the dehumanisation inflicted on her by the Argentinian junta in the mid-1970s. Partnoy's fate was similar to that of 7,000 others, who were detained and were considered a threat to national security. As she says in her Preface, 'it was estimated that over 30,000 people "disappeared" to detention centres like the Little School' (ibid., 16). Because of international pressure, she was released in 1979, and forced to leave her country. She returned after four years of exile to testify before the Argentinian Commission, which was set up to investigate the forced disappearances. *The Little School* is more than a record of what happened, for, as Jean Franco rightly notes, Partnoy uses her 'imagination to "remake" the world that the torturers are bent on destroying' (Franco 1992, 111). To give one instance from the book: two months into her stay in the Little School, a euphemism for a secret detention camp of the Argentinian military junta, Partnoy records that while she was being brought back from the bathroom, blindfolded, she heard a guard singing a folk song. The lyrics ended with the words, 'treacherous death': 'Since that moment they have called me Death. Maybe that is why every day when I wake up, I say to myself that I, Alicia Partnoy, am still alive' (Partnoy 1998 [1986], 43).

Gladys Díaz, a radio journalist and a prominent member of Movimiento de Izquierda Revolucionaria (MIR), the Marxist revolutionary organisation in Chile, was named as an organiser of the coup of 1973. She was arrested in 1975 along with her *compañero* by the infamous DINA, and was confined in Villa Grimaldi, a secret detention centre near Santiago, for three months. In her account, Díaz says that because she was detained in a very small cell in the 'water tower' of the Villa, she learnt to 'read' the footsteps on the stairs:

> So then, when they would come up the steps, I became able to tell when the footsteps were coming to get you or when the footsteps were bringing you food. The rhythm was different. Since we were blindfolded, the other senses became incredibly sharpened. The steps are coming up and you know that you're going to be tortured again. (Díaz 1998, 82)

Like Partnoy, Díaz's survival and release happened because of international pressure. When the Pinochet regime was forced to close the last prison in 1977, Díaz was considered 'too dangerous' and was compelled to leave Chile and not allowed to enter for a whole decade. The editorial note preceding Díaz's account mentions that after the civilian government was re-established in 1990 and a Truth Commission set up, 'Villa Grimaldi was dedicated as a peace park in memory of the victims of the dictatorship's human rights violation' (ibid., 80).

Unlike the Latin American experiences of secret detention, *64 Days in Lalbazar* ends with the end of Ghosh's detention in police custody and with the beginning of her incarceration in the female ward of Presidency Jail. While Ghosh does not write about her three-year stay under the Maintenance of Internal Security Act 1971 (MISA), she does make one crucial point at the very end of her account: the fact that she was never presented before any judge during her detention period. Ghosh's story is not unusual, as MISA allowed for gross abuse of power and enabled the police to use the Act as a preventive detention legislation for long years. It was a democratically elected government that directed the police attack on the Naxalites, a point that Ghosh makes several times in her account. At the same time, the political promise of liberal democracy ensured that the government could not merely get away. Detention of political prisoners, especially under MISA, gave rise to a civil rights movement, which demanded the release of all political prisoners, and which was primarily led by organisations like Bandi Mukti Committee, the Legal Aid Committee, and the APDR.

Within this history, *64 Days* is an extraordinary testimony of the will to live and to survive torture, and Ghosh exhibits various forms of survival techniques. In the lock-up, Ghosh finds meaning in survival in nature, in the sounds of the birds nesting high up in trees outside, or the open sky, which she glimpses sometimes. Even more eloquent and serene is the early morning tuneful *azaan* from a nearby masjid. She cannot place the direction of the music, but with the break of dawn, the sounds of the muezzin's music bring peace and calm, a feeling that makes the lock-up life bearable. Since Ghosh spent considerable time alone in the lock-up, she had to depend upon her mental resources to resist the terrors of torture. One of the most powerful forms of survival is the power of memory, and Ghosh recalls her past, especially in the initial pages of her account. Born in pre-Partition Bengal, she remembers her happy childhood in a village in Khulna, in present-day Bangladesh, where she spent much of her time near the river bank and at home. Equally, she reminiscences about her school days and the importance given to female education in her village, and the fact that it was the home of the well-known chemist-cum-educator-cum-entrepreneur, Prafulla Chandra Ray. Although she never met him (as P. C. Ray passed away while Ghosh was still very young), she remembers her visits to his household with her father, and its happy warmth and love for music. She recalls how her childish heart was filled with patriotic wonder when she heard 'Vandemataram' for the first time, a wonder that never deserted her. Nonetheless, happiness was interwoven with want and unrest as her childhood coincided with the restless 1940s: with the 1943 Bengal famine, World War II, and Partition. Her subsequent adolescence in a refugee family in Kolkata city acquainted her with economic hardship and austerity, a life which brought on a tumult of questions: 'But why did all this happen? Who was responsible for this disaster? Partition? We did not want it. Who was responsible for tearing asunder the lives of common people like us?' (Ghosh 2011, 2).

However, life carried on and, despite disruption, Ghosh went on to study in college and became a schoolteacher in 1960. She participated in the political agitations preceding the 'spring thunder' of Naxalbari in 1967. Her political development occurred after her marriage, as her husband was a political supporter of the Naxalite movement, who had to go underground to avoid arrest. Apart from a brief mention of a happy marriage, Ghosh maintains a studied silence about her marital life, and her account is interspersed with memories of her natal home, particularly her parents. Significantly, in Ghosh's memory, her strong familial connections, her experiences of growing up both before and after Partition, and her commitment as a teacher infuses in her a sense of belonging with the land and its people. She says: 'The country belongs to all of us. The country is mine. India does not belong to any one special person, like Indira Gandhi or Siddhartha Shankar Ray. It is this feeling which gives me courage' (ibid., 10).

She specifically mentions how in her childhood, the music of '*Bande Mataram*', which she had heard in P. C. Ray's house, effortlessly melded into the river banks of Khulna, which had seen and borne the countless sacrifices of people who wished to free their land. While 'patriotism' is a reductive term to explain her feelings for the motherland, the trajectory of her political life is stamped with a deep love for the land and its people. It gives her courage to bear the trauma: 'Keeping my mother and my neglected land in mind, I'll be able to bear everything. I repeated to myself: do what you want with my body' (ibid., 35).

Ghosh's belief in the motherland is neither nationalist nor jingoist. Towards the end of her account, when she faces Runu Guha for the last time, and when he accuses her of belonging to an unpatriotic movement which worshipped foreigners like Mao and Lenin, she answers: 'The great Mao Tse Tung is celebrated by the working class throughout the world. I respect him deeply because he brought liberation to millions of people in a backward country like China' (ibid., 47).

64 Days makes varied uses of memory as Ghosh's powers of recollection are not merely personal. Her account offers a historical understanding of the times, which also serves as a narrative frame for her resistant account of the corrupt and lawless system. Her reflections help her to recognise how the erosion of rights by the police was hastened under the Congress regime of the 1970s. As a political observer, she uses rhetorical questions to unmask her torturers. 'Within a couple of hours, they've killed millions of living cells in my body. On whose authority?' (ibid., 17). She asks:

> But why? Am I antisocial? Or a politico? Or a regular citizen? What category or classification do I fit in? No matter which category I belong to, where is it said that the State has the power to attack and wound me in various parts of my body? (ibid., 18)

Through her own experience, she notices the complicity of the medical establishment as the doctors who look after police cases do not take their profession seriously. When she is taken to a local nursing home for treatment, she observes how the doctor is less interested in examining her and more involved in extracting a favour from the policeman on duty. Corruption thrives as the liaison between doctors and policemen is mutually beneficial: the doctor gives a 'doctored' report and profits, in turn, from the law-keeper.

Ghosh's lock-up stay acquaints her with other instances of routine corruption, between the police and sex workers. Routinely, a group of female sex workers would be rounded up at night before being presented in front of the magistrate in connection with a 'petty case' (ibid., 23), for which they would be bailed out. On her first night, when she is alone, bruised, and battered in the lock-up, Ghosh is confronted with the sudden arrival of a group of garishly dressed girls, who sing and swear loudly. From them she learns that if the police are properly bribed, the girls are spared. The connections between the police and prostitution confirm how the law-keepers are the law-breakers, as they are both the patrons and inquisitors of the brothels. Ghosh's initial reactions are moralistic as she feels pity and horror at their condition; however, a sobering realisation soon dawns on her about the similarities in their situations. She realises that even though their 'crimes' and lives are different, both she and the girls are detainees and in the control of the police.

Ghosh's reflections on the social fabric of crime and its everyday face are tied to her reactions to the culture of impunity and its fallout. She witnesses the brutality that is visited upon a hapless cyclist and a hand-cart puller, who unintentionally come in the way of the police van. Even though she is constrained by her situation, she protests and tells the constable that a day will come when the people will judge this injustice (ibid., 38). She repeats the same when she is forced to sign documents by Runu Guha at the end of her detention. When a high-ranking officer requests her to 'forget and forgive' him (ibid., 47), she says that even if she forgives, she will not be able to forget. She states that it is impossible to forget how she had to face twelve armed men and was subjected to their power and fury.

Ghosh's political insights enable her to observe a resistant world outside of herself, especially among the female police officials and attendants. After being administered thirty-six penicillin injections by the doctor in the lock-up to help heal her gangrenous wound, which had developed out of her torture, she is taken to a police hospital for treatment. This alone fills Ghosh with a sense of victory as she knows that the police are in trouble and wish to have her healed before sending her to judicial custody. When she is taken to the police hospital for treatment, she finds her room heavily guarded by women constables. Ghosh observes a silent protest among them: 'They didn't say anything. But their behaviour told me that they felt that this dehumanised torture, this injustice was not correct. I felt a silent opposition in them' (ibid., 42).

Ghosh's pursuit of this gendered critique is furthered when she meets her former student, who was a home guard in the hospital, or when she listens to a female sub-inspector's account of why her college-going son feels ashamed of his mother's profession. Her stay in the hospital is rehabilitative, not only medically but also mentally. She knows that Runu Guha's power is not absolute.

64 Days recalls the horrors of police excesses against a woman political detainee and examines the corrupting power of the uniform. It shows how brutal torture was normalised as Ghosh had to spend much of her time alternating between the medical room and the torture chamber. Recalled and written at a later time, the narrative ends where it begins as Ghosh pens a chance meeting at the beginning, which frames the entire narrative. Walking along the Behala-Diamond Harbour Road one afternoon, on her way to a political march which demanded the release of political prisoners, Ghosh noticed a familiar face in uniform. As she is startled out of her reverie and her body contorted with the familiar feeling of dread, pain, and fear, she noticed that the female sub-inspector simultaneously recognised her and started running in the opposite direction. Ghosh asks: 'Why did she start running on seeing me? Was it fear? Or, was it her conscience? That means that there is a faculty called conscience in people' (ibid., 4).

'Healing' and Justice

Over forty years have passed since Ghosh and other political prisoners were released by the West Bengal government, which also ensured that the cases lodged against them were dropped. However, the question remains: Was justice done? The long-drawn legal history of the Archana Guha case well illustrated the lack of any seriousness as far as addressing the 1970s era of torture was concerned. The two commissions of inquiry set up in 1977, the Sharma Sarkar Commission and the Haratosh Chakraborty Commission, failed to function effectively to indict the guilty officials. Additionally, the then Chief Minister Jyoti Basu did not take any action against even the few who were indicted.[8]

Over the years, legal and political studies on the prevalence of torture practices in India have constantly stressed the gap between official denial and the practice of torture in police lock-ups and in secret detention centres. The gap is even more pronounced as a rich jurisprudence has emerged concerning methods of interrogation in consonance with safeguards regarding the life and liberty of a person.[9] Recent studies have shown that the Government of India has been successful in denying the fact of torture by deliberately maintaining no consistent documentation on the subject.[10] The onus of recording torture has, more often than not, fallen on the survivors of torture, and testimonial accounts have offered powerful tools to scholars for addressing the issues of personal and political justice.

Within academic debates, testimonies have provided an avenue in historical research for addressing the issues of trauma and justice. More than historical interviews, feminist studies have shown the complex function that women's testimonies have played in recording political violence and in reconstructing State terror.[11] Given the interrelation between trauma, memory, and history, psychoanalytic studies have stressed the importance of testimonies for studying the proofs of 'recovery', and for understanding the layered memories underlying trauma. However, since testimony as a form depends upon the transformation of the traumatic memory into narrative memory, the imposition of linearity risks the elision of the 'precision and the force that characterises traumatic recall' (Caruth 1995, 153). The narrative ordering disrupts the recovery of the historical truth of trauma and the only way forward, and a challenging one at that, is to learn to listen 'beyond the pathology of individual suffering' (ibid., 156). Testimony is wanting as it distorts historical truth. So, even while the twentieth century is considered the 'age of testimony', debates regarding its efficacy in bearing the burden of witness to traumatic memory or its increasing juridical turn have constrained the power and potential of testimony.[12]

Equally, the close interconnection between trauma and testimony has raised questions regarding the latter's ability to provide scope for personal healing. To address this question, Srila Roy in two essays (2009, 2013) explores the possibilities of testimony in 'listening' to and 'acknowledging' individual pain in an exploration of healing beyond *ressentiment*.[13] In her 2009 essay, which is based on her personal interviews of three ex-Naxalite women—Malaya Ghosh, Latika Guha, and Rajashri Dasgupta—Roy suggests the limited possibilities of the testimonial 'narrative cure' (Roy 2009, 144) in engaging with the problem of individual healing and justice. In her account of Ghosh's testimony, Roy finds 'strong retributive emotions' and an interventionist tone, which can carry 'a danger that the call for justice as revenge could work against the reconciliation and healing in the aftermath of violence, preserving rather than liberating the survivor from victimhood' (ibid., 153). Roy argues that such 'narrative cure is a socially normative and a normalizing one', and believes that this 'domestication or containment of traumatic experience is the inevitable cost of recovering in the shadow of violence and devastation, of being healed' (ibid., 166). In the later essay, she critiques the problem of the testimony where she holds that the genre suffers from 'three structural limitations': *one*, the duality between the individual and the collective, implicit in the act of testimony; *two*, the politics of listening; and *three*, the problem of sharing pain (Roy 2013, 97–110). Recalling the 'gendered complexities of testimonial practice'—the fact that women's testimonies on political violence tend to speak through the language of silence—Roy emphasises the performative function of testimony and contends, via an examination of Latika Guha's account, that such testimonies depend upon an erasure of the self. Roy concludes that only as a 'failed performative' can testimony rupture the fixity of the discourses and reconstitute the subject in pain (ibid., 110).

The observations raised by Roy are relevant as she dwells upon the complexities inherent in the testimonial history of trauma arising out of torture. In her earlier essay (2009), Roy had suggested that a 'different site' is needed for mourning and healing to happen, a site other than that of testimony (ibid., 166). Undoubtedly, other sites of mourning are needed for personal rehabilitation, but Roy's conclusion that Malaya Ghosh's 'retributive' testimony cannot offer personal healing is debatable. Roy's project is particularly contentious as she pits personal rehabilitation against the demand for justice in the testimonies of survivors of State violence. Against the demand for situating torture testimonies specifically within a rehabilitative history of personal healing, it is important to realise that the personal and the political subjecthood of the survivor are deeply entangled and cannot be separated at will. It needs to be remembered that survivors of State violence are targeted victims of legislated violence, or violence that is treated as above the scrutiny of law. Such violence is invisible and stays outside the focus of public attention. Roy overlooks this obvious political fact in her very legalistic definition of 'juridical', while driving a wedge between Ghosh's demand for punishment and individual healing.

Ghosh's demand for punishment for lawless policemen is not retributive as policemen are the custodians of law. Policing the police has been a longstanding demand of the civil rights movement in India. Roy forgets that in demanding punishment, Ghosh exposes the similarities between the infamous Congress regime of the 1970s and its Left successor and that, notwithstanding electoral promises, governments in power believe in a coercive State apparatus. Ghosh's account reminds us of the lack of legislative will in addressing the question of punishment of the guilty men in uniform, and how the matter is conveniently left only for the judiciary to intervene in. Ghosh's account underscores a further problem: that since the investigating agency is also the police, it is unlikely to act against itself.

Since the path of justice, outlined above, is arduous, what are the survivors of State violence expected to do? Exactly as Ghosh does: write testimonies so that people know the nightmare of history that is often silenced. *64 Days* urgently places before us the need for demanding systemic changes, and Ghosh writes with the hope that a collective will for justice will prevail in the future, in a better political system that will not fail the people. After all, as she reminds us in her Preface, the real judge of history are the people.

Endnotes

1. Subsequent references are from this edition. All translations, unless otherwise indicated, are mine.

2. In 1977, Archana Guha's brother, Soumen Guha, filed a petition against the inhuman torture that left Archana paralysed for life. The main accused were the then deputy commissioner of police Ranajit (Runu) Guha Niyogi, constable Santosh Dey, and others. After nineteen years, in 1996, the magistrate convicted the accused for torturing and outraging the modesty of the victims with one year of simple imprisonment and a fine of

Rs 2,000. The accused appealed to the High Court of Calcutta which struck down the sentence on 'technical grounds'. The case was reverted to the lower court in early 2000. For an account of the case in the 1980s, see Dutta (1987). More importantly, see Guha (2001). In 2005, Tapan Bandyopadhyay published a novel, *Lal Shalu*, which was inspired by the legal case following the events of the torture that Archana Guha, Latika Guha, and their relative Gouri Chatterji suffered at the hands of Runu Guha Niyogi in Lalbazar in July 1974. Unlike the legal case, the novel ends with the conviction and punishment of Chinu De Roy, the fictional Niyogi.

3. See Mary Tyler's *My Years in an Indian Prison* (1977), Mitra's *Hannaman* (one who is in the process of being killed; Bengali text (1987) and English translated texts of 2004 and 2010), and Minakshi Sen's two volumes titled *Jailer Bhetor Jail* (*A Jail Inside a Jail*, 1993 and 1994). See also Guha (2001).

4. While corroborative information can be found in Dutta (1991), information provided by one of the prison detainees, Minakshi Sen, suggested otherwise. In a personal interview held on 24 November 2010, Sen said that the report had inaccuracies. There was no underground chamber of torture, and the allegation of rape was false.

5. Interestingly, women participants in their recent accounts of the Naxalite movement have challenged the especially male-centric narrative of the movement. What is interesting is that they have also questioned their historical reticence and have interrogated the issue of sexual violence that women participants faced at the hands of male comrades, a problem that was never acknowledged or corrected. For details, see Bandyopadhyay (2008).

6. Mitra's biographer, Maleka Begum, informed Panjabi that for five decades the testimony had been suppressed and that, when asked, Mitra had looked in bewilderment and said: 'Is this my testimony? Did I say all this in court?' Panjabi wonders why Mitra 'blocked' the memory of the testimony and believes that it could be because of 'the unbearable nature of the torture itself, that could be lived only by blocking it out, or was it the trauma of a complete loss of dignity while narrating it in court? Or both? The answer lies in the fact that Mitra never asked, "Did I endure all this?"' (2017, 253).

7. Since this is a subject by itself—sexual torture of women Maoists—and not the focus of this chapter, some salient studies are noted here. Soni Sori's letters written to the Chief Justice of the Supreme Court in 2011 can be found at https://sonisori.wordpress.com/letters-from-jail/letter-to-the-nation/ (accessed October 2021). For a somewhat controversial account of Soni Sori, see Nandini Sundar's *The Burning Forest: India's War in*

Bastar (2016, 270–276). For further accounts of sexual torture, see Women Against Sexual Violence and State Repression's report, *Bearing Witness: Sexual Violence in South Chhattisgarh* (2017).

8. The report of the Sharma Sarkar Commission was tabled by the chief minister in 1979 in which one police officer and some jail staff were held guilty in a jail murder of 1971; the report of the other commission was tabled in 1980. No action was ever taken against the four officers belonging to the Special Branch (see Dutta 1991, 251). Journalist and ex-participant-cum-detainee, Rajashri Dasgupta, writes: 'Though the LF government had promised to probe the numerous lock-up deaths and political murders in and outside the jails during the turbulent period between 1970 and 1977; neither were any reports published nor was a single police officer punished'(Dasgupta 1990, 245).

9. India's refusal to ratify the United Nations Convention against Torture even after belatedly signing it in 1997 has placed in international question its official stand against torture. Since there is no separate stand-alone law against torture, post-1990s jurisprudence and institutional recommendations, including the 1996 D. K. Basu judgment, which mandated safeguards during arrest and interrogation, reaffirm constitutional provisions (Articles 20[3] and 21) and provisions within the penal code or related laws. However, unlike the post-1990s, the apex court judgments of 1970–1980 were not forthcoming in their denunciation of torture, as they failed to protect the rights of the victims while expressing concern over custodial torture. For a discussion on this, see Lokaneeta (2011, 144–148).

10. In her study of torture, 'India's Silent Acceptance of Torture Has Made it a "Public Secret"' (2019), Baljeet Kaur notes the torturous routes of the 2008 and 2017 Prevention of Torture Bills and the predictable position of the government in March 2018 in its statement that it has sought changes in the Indian Penal Code (Sections 330 and 331) in lieu of a proper act against torture. See https://www.epw.in/engage/article/indias-silent-acceptance-torture-has (accessed October 2021).

11. For instance, see Nanci Adler and Selma Leydesdorff's Introduction in their edited anthology, *Tapestry of Memory: Evidence and Testimony in Life-Story Narratives* (2013). Adler and Leydesdorff contribute to the debate between testimony and memory by arguing that memory is 'selective', whilst the aim of testimony is 'factual' and evidential. They, however, reject the juridical turn of testimony and study testimony as a crucial tool within oral history. See also the section on 'Trauma and/of Witnessing' in the Introduction to Piya Chatterjee, et al., *States of Trauma* (2009), which also

underlines the perils surrounding testimony insofar as it leads to the danger of 'fetishization' of trauma (p. 16).

12. While this is not a chapter on trauma and its retelling, it is important to remember that Cathy Caruth has been influential in proffering a cultural theory of trauma with regard to the Holocaust. The Yale deconstructionists such as Shoshana Felman also widened the scope of cultural trauma theories. For a critique of cultural theories on trauma, see Kansteiner (2004). Also see Chapter 1 of Roger Luckhurst's *The Trauma Question* (2008).

13. See section on 'Trauma and/of Witnessing' in the Introduction to Chatterjee, et al. (2009, 16). The editors argue for the need to move beyond the fetishising of pain and the 'politics of *ressentiment*' (pp. 16-17).

References

Adler, N., and S. Leydesdorff. 2013. 'Introduction'. In Nanci Adler and Selma Leydesdorff (eds), *Tapestry of Memory: Evidence and Testimony in Life-Story Narratives*. New Brunswick: Transaction Publishers.

Association for Protection of Democratic Rights (APDR). 1999. *Bharatiya Ganatranter Swaroop?* Kolkata: Barnamala.

Amnesty International. 1974. 'Detention Condition in West Bengal'. *Economic and Political Weekly* 9 (38), 1611–1618.

———. 1984. *Torture in the Eighties*. London: Amnesty International Publications.

Bandyopadhyay, K. 2008. 'Naxalbari Politics: A Feminist Narrative'. *Economic and Political Weekly* 43 (14), 52–59.

Bandyopadhyay, T. 2005. *Lal Shalu*. Kolkata: Mitra & Ghosh Publishers.

Banerjee, S. 2008. *In the Wake of Naxalbari*. Kolkata: Sahitya Samsad.

Caruth, C. (ed.). 1995. *Trauma: Explorations in Memory*. Baltimore: John Hopkins University Press.

Dasgupta, R. 1990. 'Deaths Under Police Protection'. *Economic and Political Weekly* 25 (5), 245.

Dutta, N. 1987. 'Torture Victim Fights Back'. *Economic and Political Weekly* 22 (34), 1438–1439.

———. 1991. 'Democratic Rights in West Bengal: Issues and Approaches'. In A. R. Desai (ed.), *Expanding Governmental Lawlessness and Organized Struggles: Violation of Democratic Rights of the Minorities, Women, Slum Dwellers, Press and Some Other Violations*, 246–247. Bombay: Popular Prakashan Pvt. Ltd.

Díaz, G. 1998. 'Gladys Díaz'. In T. C. Wright and Rody Oňate (eds), *Flight From Chile: Voices of Exile*, 79–84. Albuquerque: University of New Mexico Press.

Díaz, N. 1992. *I Was Never Alone: A Prison Diary from El Salvador.* Melbourne: Ocean Press.

Editorial. 1974. 'The Maimed and the Dead'. *Economic and Political Weekly* 9 (30), 1171–1173.

Franco, J. 1992. 'Gender, Death and Resistance: Facing the Ethical Vacuum'. In Juan E. Corradi, Patricia Weiss Fagen, and Manuel Antonio Garretón (eds), *Fear at the Edge: State Terror and Resistance in Latin America*, 104–118. Berkeley: University of California Press.

______. 2013. *Cruel Modernity.* Durham: Duke University Press.

Ghosh, D. 2013. 'Revolutionary Women and Nationalist Heroes in Bengal, 1930 to the 1980s'. *Gender and History* 25 (2), 355–375.

Ghosh, M. 2011. *Lalbajare 64 Din*. Kolkata: Setu Prakashani.

Guha, L. 2001. 'Narak Prakashya Hok: Lalbajar Torture Cell-e Sataash Din'. *Parichay* February–July, 18–55.

Guha, R. 2009. 'Calcutta Diary (1978)'. In Partha Chatterjee (ed.), *Ranajit Guha: The Small Voice of History: Collected Essays*, 609–611. Ranikhet: Permanent Black.

Kansteiner, W. 2004. 'Genealogy of a Category Mistake: A Critical Intellectual History of the Cultural Trauma Metaphor'. *Rethinking History* 8 (2).

Kaur, B. 2019. 'India's Silent Acceptance of Torture Has Made it a "Public Secret"'. *Economic and Political Weekly Engage* 53 (36), 6 September.

Lokaneeta, J. 2011, *Transnational Torture: Law Violence and State Power in the United States and India*. New York: NYU Press.

Luckhurst, R. 2008. *The Trauma Question*. London: Routledge.

Mitra, J. 2004. *Hannaman*, translated from Bangla by Shampa Banerjee. New Delhi: Women Unlimited.

Mukhopadhyay, A. K. (ed.). 2006. *The Naxalites Through the Eyes of the Police: Select Notifications from the Calcutta Police Gazette, 1967–1975*. Kolkata: Dey's Publishing.

Panjabi, Kavita. 2017. *Unclaimed Harvest: An Oral History of the Tebhaga Women's Movement*. New Delhi: Zubaan Books.

Partnoy, A. 1998 [1986]. *The Little School: Tales of Disappearance and Survival in Argentina*. New Jersey: Cleis Press, 2e.

Rehman, I. A. 2017. 'Non-Fiction: An Extraordinary Diary'. *Dawn*, 8 October. Available at https://www.dawn.com/news/1362294 (accessed October 2021).

Roy, S. 2006. 'Revolutionary Marriage: On the Politics of Sexual Stories of Naxalbari'. *Feminist Review* 83 (1), 99–118.

———. 2009. 'Testimonies of State Terror: Trauma and Healing in Naxalbari'. In Piya Chatterjee, Manali Desai, and Parama Roy (eds), *States of Trauma: Gender and Violence in South Asia*, 141–171. New Delhi: Zubaan Books.

———. 2013. 'On Testimony: The Pain of Speaking and the Speaking of Pain'. In Nanci Adler and Selma Leydesdorff (eds), *Tapestry of Memory: Evidence and Testimony in Life-Story Narratives*. New Brunswick: Transaction Publishers.

Scarry, E. 1985. *The Body in Pain: The Making and Unmaking of the World.* New York: Oxford University Press.

Sen, Atreyee. 2014. 'Slaps, Beatings, Laughter, *Adda*, Puppet Shows: Naxal Women Prisoners in Calcutta and the Art of Happiness in Captivity'. In Raminder Kaur and Parul Dave-Mukherji (eds), *Arts and Aesthetics in a Globalizing World,* 119–134. London: Bloomsbury Academic.

Sen, M. 1993 and 1994. *Jailer Bhitor Jail*. Kolkata: People's Book Society.

Sinha Roy, M. 2011. *Gender and Radical Politics in India: Magic Moments of Naxalbari (1967–1975)*. Oxon: Routledge.

———. 2016. 'Sexual Economies of Caste and Gender: The Case of Naxalbari (1967–1975)'. TISS Working Paper No. 11, 1-15. Mumbai: Tata Institute of Social Sciences.

Sundar, N. 2016. *The Burning Forest: India's War in Bastar*. New Delhi: Juggernaut Books.

Tyler, Mary. 1977. *My Years in an Indian Prison*. London: Gollancz.

Women Against Sexual Violence and State Repression (WSS). 2017. *Bearing Witness: Sexual Violence in South Chhattisgarh*.

Chapter 3

Narratives of Confinement, Harm, and Resistance

Mahuya Bandyopadhyay

Narratives of women prisoners are at the centre of this chapter. Narratives are relegated to the realm of storytelling (Chamberlain and Thompson 1998). Storytelling from within the prison may be seen as creative ways of record-keeping, engaging with the world, and negotiating it to reclaim agency. For the researcher in prison, the narrative method is invaluable for the kind of freedom it offers the researcher and the subject, in gathering data and representing lives. The storytelling tag attached to this method, the creative import of crafting a story and telling it to another make this method questionable, in terms of validity and reliability. In a controversial essay, Seidman (1991) called for the renouncing of scientism in developing theoretical insights, placing value on the social narratives that represent 'stories of origin and development, tales of crisis, decline or progress' (ibid., 131). Sociological theory, according to Seidman, was trapped in the search for a universal language and disengaged from local conflicts and public debates. I present two narratives of women prisoners to think about the possibilities that narratives offer in theorising and understanding the prison as an institution, and the prison experience in India.

Further, through these narratives, I grapple with the challenges posed to the narrative method, which render this valuable data source irrelevant for policy discussions on the prison system and its reforms. Such concerns around narrative as a method within qualitative inquiry correspond to a new focus on how narrative can contribute to the realm of evidence-based policymaking (Boswell

2012; Epstein, et al. 2014; Lowndes 2016). Contrary to assumptions of irrelevance, I argue that prisoners' stories about their lives in prison and their reflections on life outside and beyond the prison enable us to rethink how the prison has been conceptualised, both in academic writing and in popular discourse.

What do these narratives tell us about the prison? First, I reiterate an argument that is germane to many of the chapters in this volume, that sense-making of the narratives cannot be trapped in the structures and boundaries of our convictions, our academic disciplines, or even our understanding of how a narrative of a life is to be ordered. I rely on Stauffer's work (see Stauffer 2015) on ethical loneliness to advance this argument. According to Stauffer (ibid.), ethical loneliness is the isolation that a violated person or a member of a persecuted group feels upon encountering complete desertion by humanity, or by those who have power over the potentialities in one's life. It is a condition whereby persons who have been on the receiving end of dehumanisation by other human beings and by political structures emerge from such injustice and realise that no one will listen or correctly hear their testimony on their terms. They find that there is no space for them to voice their claims about their suffering and about what is now owed to them. So ethical loneliness is the experience of being 'abandoned by humanity compounded by the experience of not being heard' (ibid., 1). Such loneliness is a form of social abandonment, imposed when human beings and institutions are responsible for 'multiple ethical lapses'. In understanding and representing the worlds of women prisoners, the dearth of material, the invisibilisation of their experience, and their grotesque representations show that there have been such lapses on the part of the wider society. The uncovering of narratives, their multiple translations and interpretations, their retellings and representations are then ways of uncovering and addressing these ethical lapses.

The author's central argument is that this form of loneliness is widespread, and is caused not only by dehumanisation, oppression, and abandonment, but also by the failure of just-minded people to hear well. It is a failure to understand what recovery or reconciliation after massive violence or longstanding injustice would require. Such failure to hear is vital to those who do not listen and those who are not heard, not only because stories without an audience do not survive but also because being heard or ignored affects human processes of revision. The two narratives presented here resonate with the sense of abandonment that Stauffer articulates. Women prisoners indicate a sense of continuing loss as they move from the intimate and private institutions such as family, marriage, and kinship to the public spaces of the street, the prison, the brothel, and the hospital. The narratives also fulfil the crucial functions of revealing multiple truths and unsettling power (Ewick and Silbey 1995).

Second, it is important to foreground the polyvocality that a narrative encapsulates. Although located in a particular time and space and told mainly through the speech of one person, narratives have many interlocutors, who then disrupt the here and now and tell tales of other times and spaces. In the prison, these stories of other times and spaces have the power to disrupt the binaries with which we see and understand the prison as an institution, as well as the binaries that we often impose on the voices that we, as researchers, generate through our research. This too is a kind of entrapment, one that does not allow us to fully represent what we hear in the 'field', thus perpetuating ethical loneliness.

Narratives of women prisoners are about the exercise of total power and of the complete dehumanisation of identity, personhood, and the individual body. They reveal and speak of the individual body, burdened with humiliation, fear, and the weight of uncertainty. These narratives also enable an unmasking of individual and collective resistances to prison regimes and everyday prison practice. Resisting everyday prison practice also means that prisoners display tremendous agency in reconstituting this everyday practice, thereby moving beyond being submissive recipients of structures of authority and everyday routines as laid out in the jail codes and implemented by the hierarchical structure of prison administration. The two empirical and textual registers that I draw on are separated by two decades, but they tell deeply connected stories of ordinary women prisoners' lives. These narratives articulate the contours of everyday life in prison for ordinary women prisoners. They also narrate the synergies that political prisoners made with ordinary prisoners and the unusual friendships among prisoners, despite the strict surveillance and rule prohibiting socialisation between the two groups. Through the shared sense of pain as women traversed the sites of the home, family, the public space, and the prison emerged a sense of camaraderie, one that challenged the fault-lines stemming from the normative hierarchies of a society divided along caste, class, religion, and regional lines.

Champarani's Death-life

This narrative is drawn from Minakshi Sen's (1993) book, and I have translated it from Bengali.[1] Narratives involve polyvocality as they make it possible to record many voices within a given social context, while at the same time allowing for a single person to speak in multiple voices, without necessarily marking one voice as valid and the others as invalid. Sen wrote this narrative based on her conversations with Champarani. The presentation of this narrative here involves many layers of translation. The first and obvious one is the translation of the written narrative from Bengali to English. The process of linguistic sense-making is complex. What meanings was the author trying to convey? Is there a purity that must be attributed to authorial intentions, and can these intentions be known? Take, for instance, the title of the piece—which uses the words *moron-bancha*, which I have translated as death-life. The term implies living like death or death-like living. As a political prisoner, Sen interacted closely with the ordinary prisoners, to understand their worlds and articulate the chasm between the political prisoners and ordinary prisoners. What sorts of violations of structures of authority and resistance to normative worlds did the ordinary prisoner represent? How was this different from the clearly articulated resistance of the women political prisoners during the Naxal movement? These questions mark out an insightful register with which to translate and re-present the narratives that Sen heard, methodically collected, and then wrote up. Champarani was a convicted prisoner with a punishment of six months imprisonment; she had been convicted for attempted suicide. For the first time, a prisoner convicted for attempted suicide had come to stay in the convict ward (*meyadi number*). Champa's presence was also unusual as the convict ward was generally overflowing with undertrials and innocent prisoners. The prisoners were curious about Champa—why had she done that? What had made her take such an extreme step? Even though she was a convict in the eyes of the law, the prisoners did not perceive her as a criminal. Not only was her case unusual and curiosity surrounded her, but she was also unusual in her silence and her avoidance of most prisoners, including the political prisoners, writes Sen. She was sentenced to simple imprisonment and was not expected to provide her labour while in prison, yet she toiled on silently. She followed the matron's orders and distributed food, cleaned the ward, did the head count, and took care of the matrons. All this kept her busy through the day. She never spoke to anyone and nor did she try to contact anyone within the meyadi number (which means the ward for convict prisoners) or in the rest of the female ward. She worked on through the day with quiet determination, her face hardened and lips pursed tightly together as if signalling her resolve to refrain from any conversations. She was like a machine working away, following the orders of the matrons.

At first, Sen thought that Champarani was petrified, that she had been threatened and warned against talking to anyone, especially the political prisoners—there would be harsh punishments if anyone spoke to the political prisoners—but then she realised that Champa spoke to no one, not even the ordinary prisoners. Despite efforts to befriend her, by looking at her and trying to catch her eye and smiling at her, it took a long time for Champa to relent. Sen writes:

> Initially, when our eyes met, she would look away. Then gradually, she began looking at me fleetingly. After that, I could see her eyes smiling just a little bit and even before the smile could reach her lips, it disappeared. This is how we

> began talking. She would sometimes have long conversations, though this was rare. The first day when she came and sat next to me, I was a little surprised. From afar, she seemed much older, but up close she looked much younger; maybe just about eighteen, not even an adult yet. A soft face and pleasant expression framed her dark-skinned, slim body. Her eyes were beautiful in their calm. They were filled with fear. Disinterest and anxiety were writ large in her gaze.
>
> Then one day she removed the sari from her back and showed me. I was shocked. A burn mark was embedded deep in her back, diagonally. She told me, '*I poured kerosene on myself and set my body on fire, as soon as it caught fire, I wanted to be saved. So, I lay on my stomach on the floor. There was some water, so the front did not burn.*' Her voice was heavy with regret. Although I was inquisitive, I could never bring myself to ask her why she had tried to set herself on fire. She would reveal herself through her words, fragmented words that I would then piece together and understood that she was being forced into sex work, and to resist that she had set herself on fire. 'Then you were punished, but what about those who were forcing you into prostitution? What happened to them?' She did not answer these questions.
>
> Then she would say strange things. For this young girl, the *dalals* (middlemen or go-betweens) of the prostitute house were all-powerful, very strong. They have the power to punish as they have punished her by pushing her in jail. However, they can never be punished. Who will punish the powerful? Who has the power to punish the all-powerful? What conditions forced her towards prostitution—this is a question she does not answer, and it remains masked. Then suddenly, the mask is removed. So much grief and the weight of her narrative, silenced and unheard to all but her, was too much to bear in isolation. So, one day, she spoke openly. (Sen 2014, 277–278)

Sen admits that if she had heard this narrative outside the confines of the prison walls and under the free skies, she would have thought it was fictional, the kind of things one reads in a novel. But this was real.

Champa was from East Bengal—from a lower middle-class Hindu family. She was brought to Kolkata by a man and then sold for prostitution. East Bengal was then in the process of becoming

Bangladesh. At that time, Champa's father wanted to send her to her aunt's home in West Bengal. In those tumultuous times, he thought that was the only way to ensure her safety. Champa's family, though residents of East Bengal, would marry their daughters in India. Champa's aunts were all married in India and so too would Champa be. Travel between India and Bangladesh was not strictly monitored then. Her family decided that her aunt would fix the marriage and let the family know. Her father sent her to India along with a big group, but the primary responsibility was entrusted to a middle-aged man, a distant relative of their neighbour. He had stayed in the neighbour's house for six months and earned the trust of the families. So Champa's father did not hesitate to hand over the responsibility of his daughter to this man.

Even while being in the larger group, he was to take care of Champa and accompany her safely to her aunt's home. There was no doubt in Champa's father's mind that this is what would happen. With the specific identity of a trusted guardian, this man walked out of Champa's home, holding her hand. Later, they were separated from the larger group, and he took her to a sex worker colony in the big city of Kolkata. Sen realised that her words lacked the depth and the strength to articulate what Champa would have gone through. She had grown up in a protected environment and had not stepped out of her home on her own. Other than her little neighbourhood, Champa did not know the world outside. She had not even seen her whole village. A simple young village girl ended up in a sex worker colony of a big city. Initially, she could not even fathom what the place was. Why did the women dress the way they did? Why did they speak in a language of abuse? Why the strange, distorted life? Even as she was trying to find answers to all these questions, a man was sent to her. Maintaining bodily purity and respect were almost naturalised for her. Resolved to maintain this purity and respect, Champa reacted violently, hitting, biting, scratching the client, and forcing him out of the room. For her denial, Champa was beaten up violently by the brothel owner. She was then sent to other women, to be trained, to open her up to submission. After a few days, a young boy was sent to her room. She told her story to this young boy. The young boy changed. He had come to the brothel to satisfy his curiosity about women and sexual life. But on hearing Champa's story and her plea for help, he wanted to save her. The boy promised to find Champa's aunt's home and take her there, after freeing her from the brothel. He promised to make some arrangement, or, if nothing worked, he would ask his mother for help.

Sen writes that they were both novices. They did not know the nature of surveillance in the brothel. There is a sense in Sen's telling as well as from Champa's life itself that while you could be released from prison, once you enter a brothel, you cannot get away. When Champa attempted to escape from the back door as the young boy had planned, it comes as no surprise that she saw the brothel owner waiting outside. She had tried to use bodily force, expressing her refusal to be captured. This was not possible. Champa did not know the strength of the brothel. Her bodily resistance was nothing compared to that strength. Champa's friend, Pushpa, had been there long enough to know that the walls have ears. As the story is revealed, we learn through Sen's words that the night Champa was supposed to escape, a young man died. Champa hoped that the young man would return to help her escape. He never returned. Champa got the news that the morning after they were to escape, a young man was found with his throat slit. In the city, such murder is not unusual. Unsolved, unexplained deaths are also common. It sent tremors of a dangerous message to the community—the consequences of trying to interfere in the brothel.

As Champa looked back on this incident, she thought about whether his mother had received news of what happened. Sen reminds us that Champa did not always verbalise these thoughts as she spoke of her life; they were pieced together from the fragments, from the words she uttered (Sen 2014, 282). After a couple of days, the brothel owner again sent a client to her room. Sen thinks that by then, Champa had no other way of escaping. She used the small stove in the corner of her room and the kerosene to burn herself. However, she could not die. She was severely burnt and had to be hospitalised. This is how she came out of the brothel. The nurses and doctors were very supportive. They asked Champa what had happened. The police were informed. Champa would have been taken back by the brothel owners; however, they could not do so as the doctors and nurses, who wanted to help her, did not allow her release. They asked her to tell the police everything, and she did. However, everything was not all right. Despite the police being informed, people from the brothel came to the hospital in the guise of visitors. They kept her under surveillance. The doctors and nurses did not dare to deal with them (ibid., 283). The brothel owner would come with fruits and sweets and threats for Champa—that she must return to the brothel or face the consequences. The case of attempted suicide emerged as a way of solving the problem. She continued to remain in hospital as she was not fit to be released, and went to court on her case dates. Then, when her case ended with a six-month imprisonment sentence, she moved from the hospital to the jail. The doctors and nurses had all written their addresses in little notes for her, places she could return to when her jail term was over, places of promise.

Sen questioned Champa about why she was afraid: 'Why are you afraid then, Champa? Money? Bus fare? We will manage it. Do not worry. We will give you some money.' However, as Sen realised, Champa was not assured, despite the friendship that had developed between them. The doubt never left her eyes. The anxiety persisted. Sen asks rhetorically: 'Why didn't you tell the judge your whole story? The judge would have legally sent you back to your family.' Champa had no answers. Perhaps she was unable to distinguish between the people and the institutions—the police, the court, the judge. Was this because she was unaware? Because she had no exposure to any reality outside of her life in the home and the village? Or was it because she had witnessed the nexus between these different institutional spaces? She was at the end of her sentence, yet the authorities, with all the knowledge and understanding of her case, had made no arrangements for a safe life for her beyond the prison. Was this not a valid question for the court? Why did she choose to set fire to herself? Her case went to the lower courts. The brothel people gave evidence that she had attempted suicide. How they identified themselves in court, Champa did not know. Champa's implicit understanding of this nexus is made apparent to us through Sen's words:

> One day, Champa came to us, dejected, broken. In this jail, too, their people are here. They threaten Champa; that they will take her straight to the brothel. Who are these people? We tried to ask her, but she did not say anything. We had to be silent. We learnt that the *dalal*s (pimps or middlemen) from sex worker colonies come to prison on petty cases to seek out eligible women. They then stand as guardians in their court cases and on their release. I realised that this is how one of the people from the brothel where Champa was from came to threaten her. There were days when she felt hopeful. She came to us to discuss her release, how she would ensure her safety. We would plan to stay quiet and then, just before release, we would write letters to the doctors and nurses. If any of them show their courage and come to jail, then she would be saved. If no one comes, then she can go to them. We would coach her; she must ask people and reach the bus stop and take a bus to the hospital. If this did not work, then she should go to Sealdah station and from there, take a train to Bongaon. (ibid., 286–287)
>
> Then one day, some women complained about Champa being violent, hitting them unnecessarily. Such behaviour was uncharacteristic of Champa, but not unbelievable. Then another day she started screaming, came into the *meyadi* number screaming, stepped on someone's hand, and pushed someone else. I stood stunned. What happened? Then she came towards us and screamed—release, my release. I felt relieved. Isn't it only three months since your sentence? I asked. 'Yes, but because of my good behaviour, I am being let go,' Champa said. (ibid., 287)

Sen tried to reassure her, saying that she should not be afraid, that she would be able to go to the hospital and if she spent all day there, she would certainly find someone she knew from her previous stay. She would find one of the kind nurses or doctors who had promised to help her. However, before Sen could finish explaining all this to her, she heard a sharp sound come from Champa's voice. In Sen's words:

> She distorted her face; her beautiful eyes were full of desperation and sadness. She did not cry. In her strange, distorted voice, she said, *'warder, the warder, their people... it is them'*. Then she told us that the warder was behind all this. The warder was complicit with the brothel. The warder had told the matron and organised her early release. She would be on duty when Champa was released. Outside the jail, the brothel people would be waiting. If Champa tried to escape or create any commotion, she would not be spared. If she wanted to live, she would have to return to the brothel. As we were asking who the gate warder on duty was, the warder came. She is a figure of danger. There are stories of torture that circulate about her. The warder was angry that Champa was speaking with us. She glared down at us, her eyes red with anger. What happened, we screamed. Whom are you threatening? As soon as we screamed, Champa screamed too. Then she began saying things, incoherent, utterly disjointed. She called out to her father. All night, Champa was restless. (Sen 2014, 91)

The next morning, Champa was to be released. As Champa was leaving, the author, Minakshi Sen, gave her a five-rupee note, in support of the plan they had made together. She threw it away. 'What will happen? What will I do with the money?' Saying this, she ran towards the gate. The note lay in the middle of the meyadi number. The author then saw her stop and pause for a second. She turned around and returned to where the note was, picked it up, and walked on (ibid., 291).

The family, the border, the brothel, the hospital, and the jail are, in Champa's experience, spaces of control, encapsulating constraints of varying degrees and violence. There are extreme and radical events that force her move from one institution to another, but there is also a seamlessness to her mobility and journey through these disparate sites. The continuities are marked through the similarities of her experience in these spaces and the complicity between them, which she is deeply aware of and voices time and again. It is resolutely discovered and presented to us towards the end of her narrative when she tells Sen that it is the warder who ensured her early release and who, she fears, will ensure she returns to the brothel. Sen concludes the narrative with Champa's act of hope, after an extended telling of despair, something that Champa comes to accept as a part of her life. She picked up the money which was offered to her. Was she able to go to the hospital, as advised? Was she able to resist the brothel owner and make a new life for herself with the contacts she had made during her hospital visit? We will never know what happened to Champarani. Her narrative reveals many crucial aspects of women prisoners' lives. The inextricable link between incarceration in a state institution and perceived betrayals (intended or otherwise) of intimate relations and spaces such as family, marriage, and kinship are a recurring theme in the narratives of women prisoners. One way of articulating these linkages has been to show how everyday prison life and in-prison relations are shot through with the influences of pre-carceral ties of prisoners (Da Cunha 2008). An articulation of pre-carceral ties nuances the analysis of everyday prison life as deeply cultural, encompassing the organisational dynamics of prison governance and the attempts to replicate 'normal' lives within prison (Clemmer 1958; Goffman 1961; Sykes 1958).

Prison sociality has been portrayed through the categories of inmate subculture (Irwin and Cressey 1962), convict code, and prisonisation (Clemmer 1958). 'Gang' life and the culture of gangs has also been one of the threads in the discussion around issues of prison governance, culture, and coping with prison life. Discussions revolve around the relative impact of external influences and factors indigenous to the prison environment. Locating the embeddedness of the inside and the outside of the prison through any one of these categories tends to impede an understanding of the women prisoners' experience and articulation of the fragility and precarity in their lives, irrespective of their involvement in gangs, their ability to subvert the oppressive practices of prison life, and their various attempts to beat the system. This chapter side-steps the argument of the influence of one or the other aspect on prison lives and shows how the women prisoners' narratives presented here mark a sense of continuity between the inside and the outside. Prison sociality may seemingly be marked by the instrumentality of benefits and material gains, the fragility of bonds based on immediate needs and impermanence, defined by external constraints. From the narratives of women prisoners, it is observed that such fragile relationships abound, not emerging simply from such utilitarian urges, but rather arising from prisoners' complex experience of the continuation and embeddedness of distrust, control, and violence in spaces within and outside the prison.

However, in policies concerning the treatment of women prisoners, women's personal histories have no bearing on the process of incarceration. Policies focus on the well-being of women prisoners and employ strategies such as filling time, giving work, making them responsible for other prisoners, and in some cases, providing skill-based training. Such skill-based training is aligned to the gendered division of labour and revolve around the domestic tasks of sewing, cooking, and caregiving. Champarani's narrative, as well as the one that follows, shows that personal histories enfold multiple, contingent, and case-specific measures to ensure the well-being of women prisoners. The crimes they are charged and/or convicted with are entwined with the patriarchal conditions of their lives and relationships in the institutions they encounter. To view the prison and the experience of imprisonment as marked aberrations from their lives perpetuates stereotypical notions of female criminality, perceiving women in crime as either weak accomplices (in crimes committed by men) or as demonic women transgressing all societal norms. The female prisoner then oscillates between these stereotypes, and this precludes the possibility of perceiving and treating them as humans, with their strengths and their frailties. The resolution of questions about what the period of incarceration is likely to achieve and how women prisoners can be prepared to reintegrate upon their release is firmly rooted in these common perceptions regarding women prisoners. Reduced to the extreme categorisations of superwomen or complete failures, their treatment within the prison with full human rights becomes an impossibility.

Champarani transgresses such stereotypical notions time and again in her journey through physically and spatially distinct institutional spaces, which paradoxically reveal deep continuities of experience. Her life personifies the experience of confinement in spaces outside the prison. The conception of physical and mental harm begins before imprisonment and is amplified in the prison, not necessarily through the violence that is experienced, but through an understanding of the nexus between the prison and the brothel. Champarani feels these institutional spaces tightening their hold on her life and her impending freedom. But the seemingly insignificant acts of resistance that she essays with the help of other prisoners mark her subjectivity with a sense of power. These acts of resistance have been narrated in terms of her friendship with the author, her uncharacteristic behaviour towards some prisoners, her defiant scream at one of the warders, and finally, her acceptance of the money that the author had given her. Her narrative reveals an overwhelming sense of foreboding tied to her implicit knowledge of the nexus between the prison, the police, the judiciary, and the brothel, and a quiet resolve to not submit to the power of that nexus. Similar continuities across divergent institutional spaces are revealed in the narrative that follows.

No One Like Me Here: Adulteress, Murderer, Widow

'There is possibly no one like me in this jail here. I am cursed in many ways. Accused of being unfaithful, of murder, and of bringing on my widowhood. Supposedly all for love.' With these words, Reshma began slowly unfolding her life to me. Among all the narratives I collected while doing fieldwork in one of the central prisons in West Bengal, India, I was particularly struck by the way she began her story. She squarely placed her identity within the prison right at the beginning of her narrative. It was perhaps a strategy to establish that identity as one that we were both aware of, and suggest to me that her narrative was hinged on that identity. Her opening words were also a telling reminder of one of the significant ways in which women prisoners, charged with or convicted for violent crimes, conceived of the effects of imprisonment. Reshma is imprisoned by this identity. She resists it time and again, even as she narrates her role in the construction of this identity. The narrative that I present here is an excerpt from the notes that I made based on several conversations and two pre-organised and somewhat more formal interviews with Reshma. She had become one of my closest friends in prison. I would look for her as soon as I entered the 'female ward' and she would always ask me why I had not come if I had taken a day off fieldwork. She would talk at length not just about the circumstances of her own life, but that of the others too. She came across as a sensitive, compassionate person, and I had not seen her arguing or engaging in fights with another prisoner. If there was any disagreement, she would sulk and mutter to herself or talk to her confidantes, but she refused to be confrontational. '*Inke mooh lagne ka koi fayda nahin hai*' (no point arguing with these people), was her general refrain.

Reshma is around thirty-five years old. She was convicted as a conspirator in the murder of her husband, along with a brother-in-law. She was allegedly having an affair with her brother-in-law, who was now her 'case partner' and was lodged in the male wards of the same prison. Her husband was an influential person in the neighbourhood. The first time I asked Reshma for an interview, she politely declined and said that she had no time.[2] 'I do not even have any time for myself,' she had said. She worked as a 'writer' in the female ward. She had to ensure that the 'gunti' or the regular head count of prisoners, was done at the specified time, that prisoners were sent off for their court dates, for the interviews within the prison and medical check-ups outside the prison, that the necessary medicines were available for the prisoners, and she reported all the goings-on in the female ward to the 'matron'. Her hands were always full. She rarely had time for herself. She said:

> I can sit down and think about my day only after lock-up in the evening. In a way, it is good. If I begin to think about my life, I

> know that my head will become hot. It is a relief that all day I have no time to think of anything other than the female ward and all the prisoners here.

Reshma comes from a wealthy Muslim family. She had a pampered and happy life. Her family was not as strict as many other Muslim families, even the one she was married into. This was because of her father, who was very open-minded and did not impose *purdah* (veiling) or other restrictions on the girls as they were growing up.

> We had money, so we generally got whatever we wanted. We did not go to a school, but were taught at home. My father wanted us to be educated, wanted us to be able to read and write. Today I am grateful for that. The little education and intelligence that I have is a boon for me in jail here. I can do so much with it. More than anything else, I feel that my father taught me to think. He gave me the strength to think. That is what counts the most. What more can I tell you about my childhood? I got married at the age of fifteen or sixteen. I did not know anything about love and marriage. I just knew that I had to get married someday. It happened like this. Sahab saw me at a fair near his area, and he liked me. At that age, I was good looking. Not like now. I was fairer, healthier. He approached my father with a proposal to marry me. My father was a liberal man and did not want to send his daughter off at such an early age. My mother wanted me married off. She said now is the right age. Proposals are coming for her; people are asking for her. It is better to marry her off now. Later, we will have to go looking for men. I did not know what would happen or what was right. But I knew my father would do what was right. Now I think that my father tried to resist the marriage. You can say that the marriage took place because of Sahab and his adamancy. He just wanted to marry me. At that time, I was young, and I think I liked it that someone wanted to be with me so much. I did not understand much. There was no question of love and all that. I did not know what it meant. I knew I had to get married and that my father knew best, so I never raised any questions about the person I was to marry or about the time. My father was a liberal and 'free' person, and he called me and asked me whether I wanted to marry Sahab. In those days and in our kind of families that was unheard of.

I told him that I knew he would decide what was best for me. I now think that my father must have had a difficult time taking such a big decision, and I am glad that he is not here to be a silent witness to my misery. Who knows, maybe if he were here, he would have been able to protect me from this. It is not that my life changed very much after marriage. I could not stay with my husband's family. They were conservative Muslims, with purdah and all that. So my father made this house for us, and we lived there. I had children, took care of my family, and had a contented life like most other married women of my age.

Sahab was extremely caring and loving, and honestly, despite what has happened to me, I can say that he took care of my every need. In that way, it was like I had not left my father's house. My father too was very careful about providing for us well. My father was very cautious and would often visit us to find out how I was. I think marrying me off at such an early age made him uncomfortable, and he wanted to make sure that I was happy. The minute he realised that I would not be able to stay with my in-laws, he built us this house. Sahab was very supportive when I told him that I would not be able to stay with his family as I had led such a different life at my father's house. He had no problem moving into the house that my father built for us. When we were married, he was not well-known. Through the years, his influence in the area increased. You can say that I stayed with him through thick and thin and never did I once doubt what he did. Now that he is gone, I can say that he was not completely honest with me. He was not as devoted to me as he made it out to be. Only later, I came to know that he would be with other women. I suppose after I gave him children, I was no longer the same person he was once so adamant about marrying. I never faltered in my duty towards him as a wife. I did whatever he asked me to. I even helped him with his work, meeting people, talking to people. Like when he was injured, just before his death. I would go to the people he wanted me to go to and deliver messages. Everyone knew me, and they all liked me.

When his rivals beat him up, we came to Calcutta for treatment, and we were staying at a hotel. I took care of his every need and was slowly nursing him back to health. He would do all his work from the hotel room. People came to visit him all day. Despite having done all that I did for my husband, today I am in this state. I sometimes think—why this had to happen to me? I know I have been a good wife. I think, 'Where did I go wrong?' Today I am not only charged with and convicted for the murder of my husband, but am also accused of being unfaithful. That I could have ordered his life to be taken away so I could be with my 'lover'—it is unthinkable. What hurts me most is this charge that I am having an affair with my brother-in-law. I have never had any place for another man in my life, and he is my brother-in-law. I have not looked at him in that way. He cares about me.

I know that people here and in the society outside consider me *badchalan* (of bad character). Not only did I take away my husband's life, but I also did it for the love of another man. It is like numerous curses are on me—I have lost my husband, I am responsible for his death, and the reason for this is my interest in another man. Whenever I hear all this, my blood starts to boil. I must put up with two kinds of *badnaami* (bad name)—first of being a murderer, and then of being an unfaithful woman. I cannot cope with the fact of a bad name as a woman and a wife. I know how I have served my husband and so do all those who know me. I have never looked at another man. I was married at a time when I did not have any idea about the meanings of love and man-woman relationships. It was only in my marriage and with Sahab that I came to know and understand these things.

I know nobody believes me here. They might talk to me nicely and be friends, but deep down they think of me as a murderer, as someone who has brought ill upon herself, and as an unfaithful woman. When I sit with the other women, like the other afternoon when you were also there, they are always talking about the three or four men they have in their lives. I sit and listen to their stories and wonder how is it possible for one woman to love so many men? I think it cannot be. You could see how they reacted when I said the same thing that afternoon. They all looked at me strangely. I am intelligent enough to know what that look means. They can't say anything on my face because I do things for everybody. That way, being a writer helps me. I know that they are thinking that having

> killed my husband just to have another man, I should not talk like that.

Gita, a younger prisoner charged with kidnapping, was a close friend of Reshma's. She was a relatively new prisoner. Considered slightly 'off' or '*halka*' (literally, 'light', implying foolish and mad), Gita looked out for Reshma. She coaxed her to eat on time, spent time with her, did her work for her willingly, and stood up for her whenever needed. If anyone said a word against Reshma, Gita was there to defend her. Their personalities were very different. Reshma was well turned-out, calm and collected, polite, and always had a respectful demeanour. Gita was loud, scruffy, and argumentative. Most of the other prisoners disliked Gita. Reshma, however, felt protective towards her. 'She has a good heart,' Reshma would say, 'if only she knew how to behave.' The guards and other prisoners were watching with interest the closeness between the two prisoners. I heard the guards say that if they continued in this way, one of them would be sent to a district jail far away.

Navigating intimate relationships and maintaining a sense of dignity are the focus of Reshma's narrative. She presents incarceration and prison time in stark opposition to her life as a young girl and bride. There are slippages in her narrative, which unmask the sense of confinement in her intimate relationships and in the institutions of marriage and family. For instance, while she acknowledges the continuity of care she received in her natal home and her marital home, she also expresses a sense of loss in her marital home. Multiple meanings of confinement emerge. A loss of freedom experienced in her natal home, controls on mobility and free will through purdah and other practices of bodily control, the constraints of submitting to traditional norms and a traditional life as a wife—Reshma navigated these controls with the help of her father who gifted her a separate home, so she did not have to live with her in-laws. After her children were born, she lost her special place in her husband's life. Through the articulation of her stoic acceptance of other women in her husband's life and her unfailing work attending to his every need, her narrative brings out another sense of being trapped. In reflecting on her life, she expresses a continuum, marked through specific definitive points, such as her early marriage, her husband's neglect and her submission to his life, her husband's death, and finally, being charged with and found guilty of conspiring to kill him and being sentenced to prison for life. The joys she experienced in the institutions outside the prison are now coloured by the prison experience. They were short-lived, not eventful or impactful in the face of her encounter with death, betrayals, abandonment, and imprisonment. This encounter frames her identity for her, and everything else is in the past, of which she speaks as if it were in another life, another time. She is trapped in this identity of a murderer, a widow, and adulteress. No action of hers will ever free her from this entrapment. The pains of incarceration are not merely physical for her; they are mired in this identity that she fears she will never be able to erase.

Conclusion

Three crucial aspects of everyday life emerge from the narratives. Everyday life is not just about the material grounding of the experience of imprisonment, about how prisoners cope with the regular challenges of prison life, such as the food filled with insects or the work that must be done. It is also about the painstaking task of negotiating relationships, institutions, and one's sense of time within the prison and outside. Therefore, everyday prison life also narrates the register of the world outside.

The narratives reveal moments in which the binary of the prison as a space of confinement and violence and the institutional spaces outside, such as the neighbourhood, the family, marriage, brothel, is called into question. In Champarani's narrative, this binary is disrupted for the carceral subject. Moreover, the carceral subject is the one whose story is being told and the one who is engaged in the retelling. There is a sense of continuity in the experience of confinement, dehumanisation, and threats to mental and physical well-being in the institutions that Champarani traverses—the family, the neighbourhood, the brothel, and the prison. Narratives of women prisoners respond, in varying ways, to the connections between the home, the prison, and the brothel. While the brothel is in many senses the other, the opposite of the home, it is never too far away in the lives and imaginations of the women prisoners. In Champarani's narrative, the connections become apparent as she tries to resist the brothel, even while being in it, and the prison becomes for her a preferred space, a space of relative freedom, in comparison to the brothel. When she learns of her early release, she is upset as she fears that she would have to return to the brothel. Although the brothel does not figure explicitly in Reshma's narrative, we find that her narrative hinges on her eagerness to restore a sense of dignity to her identity, marred by the accusation and consequent validation through her conviction of conspiring to murder her husband along with her lover. The pains of the identity she is trapped in revolves around a moral code that is universally applied to judge women who have multiple relationships, who live and work in brothels, and those who challenge the institutional codes of the family and marriage. If Champarani's narrative reveals a woman trapped within the brothel, Reshma's shows us the meanings of an identity based on a moral code. Deviations from this moral code are then similarly viewed. Many women prisoners who shared their stories perceived the brothel as the place of last resort. If nothing else worked out on their release, there was always the brothel. The lived experiences leading to the prison and the phase of incarceration had thus diminished the distance between the prison and the brothel.

For Reshma, the murder of her husband had erased all his failings and her experience of isolation, distrust, and neglect in the institution of marriage and her marital home. This experience has no place in the identity ascribed to her as an adulteress, murderer, and widow based on the crime that she is convicted for. Stauffer's (2015) profoundly philosophical work on the idea of ethical loneliness resonates with the silencing of the various narratives of women prisoners in two ways: *first*, as women prisoners are generally not heard, and *second*, they have experienced moments of collapse of their taken-for-granted everyday as they journeyed through different institutional spaces. Their experience of dehumanisation erases the boundaries of the different institutions that they pass through and talk about in their narratives. The presentation of narratives in this chapter, as well as in others in this volume, mark an attempt to 'hear' how women prisoners present their subject formations, their conceptions of selves in different institutional spaces. The narratives of women prisoners not only reveal how they see themselves against the backdrop of the reasons for their being in prison, but they also speak of freedom and unfreedom in different institutional spaces such as the family, neighbourhood, kin group, brothel, and prison. Unfreedom and constraint appear as the cornerstones of their lived experiences, shaping their perceptions of varied institutional locations. In both narratives in this chapter, an attempt is made to hear and represent their stories of being in and passing through these institutions on their own terms. Their sense of being in the family and marriage is framed by patriarchal betrayals and the failure of these institutions to protect, thereby beginning a cycle of harm. However, the prison experience for Reshma and the prison and brothel experiences for Champarani reveal these patriarchal betrayals and failure, not as aberrations (which is how they were probably first conceived) but as defining characteristics of these institutions. Such betrayals and erasures of trust in everyday relationships then become central to their existence and their experience in other institutional spaces, weaving a common thread.

Stauffer argues that violence persists not only because of enabling structures, but also because of the incomprehensible capacity of human beings to destroy the selves of others. According to Stauffer (2015), not being heard aggravates the experience of dehumanisation. Spaces designed for hearing, such as truth commissions and courts, and people entrusted with the task of listening, such as lawyers and researchers, can fail in the task of hearing. Stauffer (ibid.) argues that the reason for this could be that people only hear within the frameworks of their disciplines, training, or requirement, or because some stories are too frightening, as they lay bare the capacity of humans to harm others. Rather than engaging with the formidable stories of human capacity for harm, it is perhaps easier to hear familiar stories of struggles, resilience, and recovery of the self. Stauffer points out that it is perhaps difficult for us to accept that in some instances of suffering and dehumanisation, there is a part of the self that is not repaired. Instead, it is obliterated or relegated to the point of no return. Listening with sensitivity implies engaging with the resilience of the survivors of extreme dehumanisation, and in some cases, even the destruction of the capacity for resilience.

The narratives represent a raw articulation of the carceral logic in the process of subject formation for these women prisoners, through the connections that they draw between the intimate spaces of marriage and family and the institutions of prison and the brothel.

The act of representing subjectivities through the narratives is deeply political. So my third point about the narratives is that they reveal the political nature of the everyday. Everyday life and prison sociality are contingent upon and mediated by desire, need, coping, and responses to deprivation of different kinds. This contingent and mediated nature of everyday life could suggest its slipping into a mundane realm, that of merely going through a series of repetitive acts. In this 'imponderabilia of daily life', the prisoners do not recognise the dynamics of power or have the understanding that they can be changed. This is purportedly a sharp difference between the ordinary prisoner and the political prisoner. For the ordinary prisoner, everyday life is simple, and not mired in the complexities of the political life of the political prisoner. The narrations that I present debunk, at least partially, this idea and bring out the entangled power relations between different groups of prisoners and show how these entanglements suggest a prisoner's awareness of and resistance to these relations and to the institutions, within which they become visible. Therefore, the narratives from prison have the potential to disrupt the dominant ideas of resistance and the question of 'what is political' to include many mundane, simple acts of women's existence and social action in different institutional spaces, revealing alternate understandings of the machinations involved in the exercise of power and the processes of dehumanisation.

Endnotes

1. I have retained some sections in the way that Sen narrates them in her book, and these sections are included here as indented text. To retain the nuances of the narrative, I have chosen to reproduce Sen's voice and her narration of Champarani's life. For some other sections and the background to the narrative, I have used my own words to summarise Champarani's life story and Sen's understanding of it. In translating, I have tried to retain the colloquial and informal way in which Sen narrates her version of Champarani's life. The connections that I draw out from the story are only implicit in Sen's narration and Champarani's performance of everyday life, to which Sen is a witness.
2. A part of Reshma's narrative is presented here to build on the idea of institutional continuities as experienced by women prisoners. Some details of the case have been masked to protect the identity of the prisoner.

References

Boswell, J. 2012. 'Why and How Narrative Matters in Deliberative Systems'. *Political Studies* 61 (3), 620–636.

Chamberlain, M., and P. Thompson. 1998. *Narrative and Genre*. London: Routledge.

Clemmer, D. 1958. *The Prison Community*. New York: Holt, Rinehart, and Winston.

Da Cunha, M. I. P. 2008. 'Closed circuits: Kinship, neighborhood, and incarceration in urban Portugal'. *Ethnography* 9 (3), 325–350.

Epstein, D., J. Heidt, and C. R. Farina. 2014. 'The Value of Words: Narrative as Evidence in Policymaking'. Paper 1243, *Cornell Law Faculty Publications*. Available at http://scholarship.law.cornell.edu/facpub/1243 (accessed November 2021).

Ewick, P., and S. S. Silbey. 1995. 'Subversive Stories and Hegemonic Tales: Toward a Sociology of Narrative'. *Law and Society Review* 29 (2), 197–226.

Goffman, E. 1961. *Asylums: Essays on the Social Situation of the Mental Patient and Other Inmates.* New York: Anchor Books.

Irwin, J., and D. R. Cressey. 1962. 'Thieves, convicts, and the inmate culture'. *Social Problems* 10, 142–155.

Kopijn, Y. J. 1998. 'The Oral History Interview in a Cross-Cultural Setting: An Analysis of its Linguistic, Social and Ideological Structure'. In M. Chamberlain and P. Thompson (eds), *Narrative and Genre.* London: Routledge.

Lowndes, V. 2016. 'Storytelling and Narrative in Policymaking'. In G. Stoker and M. Evans (eds), *Evidence-Based Policymaking in the Social Sciences: Methods that Matter*. Bristol: Policy Press.

Seidman, S. 1991. 'The End of Sociological Theory: The Postmodern Hope'. *Sociological Theory* 9 (2), 131–146.

Sen, M. 2014. *Jailer Bhetor Jail* (*Prison Within Prison*). Kolkata: Karigar Prakashan.

Stauffer, J. 2015. *Ethical Loneliness: The Injustice of Not Being Heard*. New York: Columbia University Press.

Sykes, G. M. 1958. *The Society of Captives.* Princeton, NJ: Princeton University Press.

Part II

Confronting Institutional Spaces

Chapter 4

Women, Crime, and Punishment

Indian Rhetoric and Realities

Shereen Sadiq

Academic and general interest in the female offender has seen a recurrent pattern of decline and growth. For much of the time in history, the female offender has remained invisible, neglected, and misrepresented. She has been portrayed as peculiarly evil, unstable, and irrational. In contemporary times, however, the female offender is back in the limelight. In an increasingly punitive climate, and at a time when discussions have shifted to the emergence of an 'incarceration binge', the female offender has come under its fold (Selman and Leighton 2010).

With a dramatic and alarming increase in the number of women in prisons in the past decade, the female offender now occupies an essential place in the government and criminological agenda. The increase in female offending (NCRB 2019) and the emergence of the figure of the female criminal, not just as an ally in the crimes of men but as an independent criminal actor, has made the female offender a category to reckon with. In the treatment of crime and criminal behaviour, this category can no longer be sidelined.

In this chapter, I draw on the shifts in the perception of the female offender in the Indian context and show that to understand the actions of women that are marked as crimes and that take women to prisons, it is necessary to delineate the structures, the dynamics, and constructs that form their everyday lives. It is crucial to identify the cultural constructs represented by the practice of dowry, the patriarchal family structure, economic marginality, spousal abuse, and non-consensual and unhappy marriages as significant elements of female violent offending. This chapter relates to the women lodged in the women's jail of Aligarh District, Uttar Pradesh, India. It aims to understand the prisoners' lives through their experiences presented by them in my interactions with them.

In the early writings on female criminality, the idea that women engage with a crime in the same way as men is dominant in the works of scholars such as Pollak (1950) and Adler (1975). In *The Criminality of Women,* Pollak argued that women's crime was vastly underestimated and that women were more prominent than men in the figure of crime. Adler (1975) also tried to make sense of the rise and changing nature of female crime throughout the 1960s and 1970s in her controversial book, *Sisters in Crime.* Adler identified a 'new breed of female criminal', who was changing her pattern of offending to a more 'masculine' style, becoming more aggressive, violent, and unfeminine. Inherent in her argument was the idea that liberation caused crime, and that female criminality could be treated as an indication of the degree of freedom achieved by women. The role of the women's movement in changing perceptions around women's crime became the subject of extensive media and scholarly attention. Research, however, gave little support to the hypothesis that there was a 'new female criminal', suggesting that she was more a myth than an empirical reality. In the recent past, there has been a shift in how female criminals are viewed, insofar as they are equal partners in the field of crime. This idea is gaining ground within media and policy circles, and it seems that works by Pollak and Adler are enjoying somewhat of a renaissance (Dowey and Silvestri 2008).

Theories on female offenders focus on women's increased involvement in crime, with scant attention paid to violent crimes. Theories have generally sought to explain why women are less likely to commit violent crimes than men. Early on, the biological theories concentrated on the physical differences between men and women, and invariably included references linked to impulsivity and the greater muscular strength of men (Rafter 2008). More commonly, however, cultural and socialisation theories have dominated the literature on gender differences in violence. Pivotal to these theories is the idea of the differential socialisation of men and women, where men's violent behaviour is condoned, while women are punished and taught to suppress any aggressive impulse (Kruttschnitt 2013; Macoby 2000; Steffensmeier and Allan 1996). In response to this, liberation theory suggests that with changing socialisation patterns, women have adopted masculine behaviours and are likely to engage in violent behaviour (Bottos 2007). None of these theories addresses the issue of gender disparity in violent crime rates, and the normative and cultural contexts of female offending.

At a theoretical level, mainstream criminological research in India often hits a wall. No theory can provide an exhaustive account of all aspects of a social phenomenon. According to Shankardass (2000, 403):

> The separate dilemmas of feminism and criminology both overlap and conflict with empirical detail in the context of India. Criminology's collusive search for 'properties, essences, and unities' continues to plague the Indian female offender who, as a target of stereotyping, fits either too many or none of the slots of her European counterpart who is pigeonholed into prevalent categories of the 'menopausal shoplifter', the 'sophisticated criminal', or the endogenously depressed killer.

The classificatory parameters and the theoretical dimensions of criminology need to be questioned for the generalisation they seek, in order to have convenient categories, universal codes, and punishments. To study women's crime through newer approaches, we need to go beyond modernist paradigms and categories. There are macro-level structures, like the economy, which contextualise women, their crimes, and their lives in the prison, but there are also hidden dynamics situated in culture and the family structure. This chapter elaborates on some of these macro-level structures and hidden dynamics in marriage and family to understand female criminality and women's imprisonment. Crimes and violations move women (especially poor and lower-caste women) from their imprisoned lives within the domain of the patriarchal family to the State-controlled institutionalised space of the prison (Cherukuri 2008).

Methodology

The subject matter and area of interest for the present work is feminist in its approach. Feminist approaches typically generate research that is for women, rather than about women. It employs a variety of strategies for creating knowledge about women and their social worlds, which are often hidden from mainstream society (Biber and Yaiser 2004). I met women inmates of the Aligarh District Jail in 2017–2018. My curiosity to know why they were in prison led to conversations with them, whereby the inmates narrated their path to prison, experiences of being away from family, and their interactions with the criminal justice system. Their narratives have been presented in the form of quotes along with the respective cases. Narratives reveal how people define reality and how they make sense of their past, present, and future. Narratives are social products, not measurable truths. They are a translation of lived life into told life (Girshick 1999).

At the time of the field visits, there were 125 women inmates in Aligarh District Jail, of whom eighty-five (68 per cent) were undertrials and forty (32 per cent) were convicts. The women had been convicted by the lower court, but their cases were pending for trial in the higher court. Out of a total of 125 women inmates, sixty-one (48.8 per cent) were accused of or convicted for murder (including attempt to murder), forty-eight (38.4 per cent) for dowry deaths, and the remaining sixteen (12.8 per cent) for other crimes, such as drug trafficking, kidnapping, and cheating. Of the sixty-one women accused or convicted of murder, fifty-eight were accused of spousal murder. The other three were undertrials and had been alleged with having murdered a minor, a parent-in-law, and a sister-in-law along with her three minor daughters. Out of the 125 inmates, 101 (80.8 per cent) were unlettered. The remaining twenty-four inmates (19.2 per cent) were educated either till middle school, high school, intermediate, or graduation levels. More than 60 per cent of the population belonged to the lower castes, comprising of the Scheduled Caste (SC) and Other Backward Classes (OBC). About 96 per cent of the inmates were not engaged in paid work outside the home. The remaining few were engaged in work considered menial. More than 96 per cent (121 out of 125) were married before coming to prison. An overwhelming majority (96 per cent) of women belonged to a joint family. In this chapter, I use my interactions with these women prisoners and the understanding of the structure of family and marriage in Indian society to reflect on the perceptions and treatment of women and crime.

Hierarchy, Patriarchy, and Women

Discussions on the relationship between women, violence, and culture in India must be situated within the notion of hierarchy along with the principle of purity and pollution. Norms of purity and pollution are thus significant in women's experiences of patriarchal structures in the familial domain and the criminal justice system. Here, I draw on Dumont's (1970) understanding of the nature of hierarchy in Indian society, premised on the principle of opposition and separation between the pure and the impure. This opposition is ingrained in Indian society through the idea of purity and pollution, which pervades all aspects of social life. Women play a central role in the operationalising of the principle of purity and pollution in everyday life within the patriarchal structures of family, kinship, and marriage (Dube 1996).

These norms of purity and pollution were upheld ultimately through the threat or the actual use of violence. Violence against women is a prominent risk factor for violence among women (Livne 2015). The issue of female criminality cannot be understood in isolation from the context of violence against women. The collusion and contestation between patriarchies and Brahmanism (upper-caste practices and ideologies) reveal the exercise of power through the differential definitions and management of gender by caste. Gender is crucial to the maintenance of the reproduction of caste inequalities. As Rege pointed out, Dalit women's labour is essential for the survival of the Dalit family. So the controls on labour, mobility, and sexuality that apply to upper-caste women do not frame the reality of the everyday lives of Dalit women, rendering them 'impure' to begin with. Consequently, in several instances of the rape of Dalit women, these are not considered rape at all because of the customary access that upper-caste men have to Dalit women's sexuality and the perceived lack of virtue of Dalit women, owing to the above-mentioned lack of controls. In almost all regional languages in India, the expression for rape is equivalent to the phrase 'stealing the honour of', and since lower castes, by their double oppression, have no honour to speak of, the right to redressal is denied (Rege 1996, 10).

Rege goes on to argue that the legal courts were unable to distance themselves from this patriarchal and casteist ideology. The cases that I draw on in this chapter further this argument with reference not only to the survivors of violent acts of crime, but also with regard to women offenders. Rege (1996) mentions the two cases of rape that received a lot of media coverage and occupied centre-stage in the women's movement—that of a lower-caste beggar woman (Lakshmi) and a landless tribal labourer (Mathura). In both cases, the courts acquitted the rapists, who were policemen, on the basis of the questionable character of the women. The women's movement made these two cases the pivotal points while raising concerns of violence against women, and the Supreme Court was compelled to reopen the cases and finally amend the law against rape. Two critical changes were introduced: *first*, the law recognised custodial rape, and *second*, it placed the onus of proof on the rapist and not on the woman (Rege 1996, 10–11; see also Jogdand 2013).

In rural India, defiance of caste restrictions by the Dalits has most often resulted in arson and gang-rapes of women from the lower castes (Tharu and Niranjana 1994). A caste-wise analysis of the violent practices against women would reveal that the incidents of dowry murders, controls on mobility and sexuality by the family, and widow burning are more frequent among the upper castes, while Dalit women are more likely to face the collective threat of rape, sexual harassment, and physical violence. This has implications for the sociological analysis of caste, volumes of which have overlooked the essential links between caste and gender (Jogdand 2013).

Violence against women takes varied forms, such as female infanticide, the abortion of a female foetus, the neglect and undernourishment of the girl child, denial of education to girls, pre-pubertal marriage, and the harassment of a bride, leading to her suicide or murder. On one pretext or another, female children are unwanted or treated as a burden by their parents. The yearning for male children is a cultural preference that cuts across the class divide. It clearly expresses every parent's intense desire for male progeny in an intensely patriarchal setting. Within the patriarchal system, society perceives a son as the legitimate heir to the family name. Besides, sons are perceived as assets for parents in their old age. Sons also hold an important ritual space around key events in social life, such as birth and death. For instance, it is only the son who bears the religious obligation to perform the funeral rites. These specific ritual aspects dominate an individual's life choices and determine familial goals (Bhattacharya 2004).

Motherhood and the Idea of Purity

Rani, an inmate of Aligarh District Jail, was booked under Indian Penal Code (IPC) Section 364. She is a 21-year-old unlettered woman. Her mother died very early, and she lived with her father and stepmother. The nagging about being a burden forced her to leave the family. She worked as a domestic help and eventually married a man almost twice her age. Initially, her in-laws did not object to the match, but things did not stay the same when, after two years of marriage, she did not have a child. She was advised to *cure* herself by sacrificing a child to the Devi (Goddess). Rani admitted to killing a child and said:

> I was afraid that my husband would remarry and I would be thrown out for not having a child. I was in distress. There was no one to whom I could turn for help. I visited a *tantric* who

> advised that sacrificing a child would rid me of my problem. I did not know that the sacrifice would bring me to prison.

Rani, her husband, and in-laws have been in prison for the past three years. They are without a lawyer, and there is no one left in the family outside to arrange for the same.

Mothering is considered fundamental to women's lives and to the organisation of the family. The concept of motherhood determines the values and norms that dictate what women ought to do, and offer ideal patterns of maternal behaviour and nature. Cultural symbols and society in general glorify women's role as mothers, to the extent that it is considered obligatory (Chandrababu and Thilagavathi 2009). Despite the cultural and symbolic significance of the figure of the mother, in reality, she recedes to the background immediately after she attains motherhood, at least until the next delivery. She can offer worship and oblations, and observe vows for the health, longevity, and well-being of her children. Not only is motherhood often imposed on women, but they are also conditioned to regard it as the *summum bonum* of life; barrenness is deplored, and those who cannot fulfil their roles as mothers suffer untold torture from rituals directed towards the fertilisation of the womb. Women condemn and ridicule the childless woman because they have internalised the male social values regarding the merits of having a son (Bhattacharji 1990). In Indian society, married women who remain childless are invisible in social research. However, they are far from invisible in the social and cultural life of families and communities. While they are forced to remain on the margins of social life, they are also clearly marked out as inadequate and incomplete.

Whether it is for the attainment of motherhood, the cure of prolonged illness, or avenging of loss, recourse to spiritual healers, tantric priests, *babas* (spiritual leaders), and *ojhas* (exorcists) is not uncommon in rural and semi-urban areas in India. They range from curing through such practices as smoking out spirits with the aid of *jhaar-phook* (burning concoctions in dried vegetation and waving the smoking jar over the possessed), driving out curses through sacrifices, vanquishing *bhoot-pret* (ghosts) through nocturnal rituals, and human sacrifice. The prevalence and power of ojhas, spiritual healers, witch doctors, and exorcists cannot be ignored just because the urban educated are relatively free from it. The ignorant and uninformed are continually exploited in villages, remote tribal abodes, and small towns, where charlatans advocate the need to appease or combat the power of evil spirits to avoid further disasters. It is a situation that calls for urgent action. Some states like Maharashtra and Karnataka have sought to pass a bill against black magic and superstitious practices to address this issue, which has implications for women's criminality and incarceration.

Complete ignorance of the legal machinery and the propagation of so-called divine and supernatural or magical powers commonly known as black magic often guide women to legally punitive acts. Empirical studies relating to female criminality in India often support such happenings. Bajpai and Bajpai (2000), in their study of female prisoners, mention the case of Chando and her neighbour, who were guided by a tantric (a healer guided by occult practices) to eat a piece of an infant's liver to fulfil their wish of having a child. Both of them were charged with the murder of an infant. Shankardass (2012) mentions the case of Bina, who took an ojha's advice and allegedly threw her neighbours' children into two separate wells to repel the curse which had led to her illness and the death of her 5-year-old son. She was charged with kidnapping and intent to kill and was given life imprisonment.

The ideology of hierarchy and purity and pollution shapes the everyday life and experiences of women in the Indian family (Dube 1988). Although the family is projected as a sanctuary for women, it also has the potential to serve as a prison with a restrictive code of conduct. The hierarchy of relationships that typically characterises a patriarchal home develops along age and gender lines, so that young women entering a patriarchal household are vulnerable to acts of violence from their marital family in the event that they refuse to conform to traditional gender roles. These acts of violence also tend to be socially accepted. Violence against women may be generally disapproved of, yet there is a cultural acceptance of men disciplining women (Chowdhry 1997). One of the more common forms of the patriarchal family in India is the joint family, in which the wife comes under the patriarchal control of the head of the household, typically a senior male member of the family. A woman is more susceptible to abuse from joint family members.

Institution of Marriage

Shabnam, an inmate of Aligarh District Jail, was booked under IPC Section 302 for the murder of her husband. She was in a relationship with Shahid, but Shahid's parents did not want him to marry Shabnam. She was married to another man against her will. Her husband often accused her of continuing the affair even after marriage, which led to frequent conflict and abuse. She said:

> I had given up everything and surrendered to the will of my family. For the sake of my husband, I forgot the past and adjusted to the new life. All this was not easy. But despite all my sacrifices, I was blamed and abused for being unfaithful. I could not take it anymore. What did I get by sacrificing my happiness? Whenever there was a quarrel between me and my husband, my parents never stood by me. They doubted me. I was fed up and wanted to end the ordeal once and for all.

Despite frequent mental and physical torture, women often persist in their marriages. Lack of familial and societal support can leave a woman with a feeling of helplessness, and as a consequence the need to remain in an abusive relationship is reinforced. The lack of financial security and independence also plays a key role in women's decision-making capacities in the context of intimate partner violence. Social stigma and taboos around divorce, failed marriages, childlessness, and the status of being single further heighten psychological harm. In the long term, survivors experience the risk of tremendous anxiety, depression, post-traumatic stress disorder (PTSD), and problems of low self-esteem. A woman facing violence needs support from her family and friends, who can help her express herself without being judgemental or forcing the victim to take action

(Dutt 2018). It is in the search for this support that married women become the new 'infidels'. She feels the lack of either affection or the novelty element of the relationship, and when she comes across a situation where she finds this value in another person, she gives in to instant gratification. Such links are forged for emotional reasons and for some focused attention, caring, respect, self-esteem, self-worth, and companionship. Women's act of considering the risky terrain of adultery and their eventual murder of their violent partners with the newfound 'support' is a response to cumulative abuse rather than to a single provocative act. Shabnam's case provides evidence of this as she negotiates the pressures of family honour and choice in marriage.

Honour is central to the sustenance of the patriarchal family and the institution of marriage. Women are considered the repository of family honour as daughters, wives, and mothers. The fear of losing honour is used as a justification for masculine aggression, control over women's decision-making, and violence against women. Caste, class, and community identities are accomplices in such reasoning and normalise practices within the family that marginalise women. For instance, a family may want to settle the matter of an inter-caste marriage amicably, but there are more considerable community pressures that compel that family to treat it as a matter of honour. Honour, in the last resort, is protected through the sacrifice of their sons and daughters in the collective interests of the caste group (Vishwanath and Palakonda 2011). Such honour killings have been reported from areas where *khap* or caste panchayats are more active. The existence of khap panchayats has been justified in the name of preserving honour, and upholding the values of the community and the sanctity of customs and practices (Chowdhry 1997).

Akbari, a 70-year-old inmate of Aligarh District Jail, booked under IPC Section 498A and convicted for bride burning, was in prison for eight years. She was arrested along with her husband and son. The family sold their belongings to arrange money to get her husband and son released on bail. No such effort was made for Akbari's release. Akbari continued to remain in prison. During the eight years of her imprisonment, her husband had visited her only once, and her son had never come to meet her since being bailed out three years earlier. She said:

> I am illiterate and thus ignorant. Things are decided by men in the family. They are knowledgeable. My marriage was decided by my father and other close male relatives. Women in the family endorsed it. I was never consulted. It was the same after marriage. I was to prove my worth for household work. That was my only domain. My husband and son shared nothing with me. I simply had to go by their decisions. Now, I am old. Not of much use for the family. They have to spend on my medicines and doctors. If I am not at home, it hardly makes a difference. Why would they spend on bringing me back? I don't want to die in prison. That is my greatest fear. I just pray to God that by any means I don't die in prison. I want to be in my home for this.

Traditionally, marriage in India is characterised by payments of dowry and, among certain groups and in some areas of the country, bride price. In popular opinion, and in the perception of some anthropologists (Goody 1973), dowry should be seen as an inheritance that daughters receive on marriage, or pre-mortem inheritance, while sons receive their inheritance following the death of the parental generation (Dalmia and Lawrence 2005). However, there are several arguments against this idea of dowry as pre-mortem inheritance, which revolve around the principles of distribution of a family's assets and the kind of control that a daughter has over the items received as dowry (Sharma 1993). Only a fraction of the dowry gifts are intended for the bride for her consumption and control. A significant portion becomes a fund of goods and cash, managed by the husband's family and often put to the service of the marriages of his sisters (Pocock 1993).

Far from declining, the 'dowry system' has gained ground. Within two years of Independence, the legislature had sought to curb the giving and receiving of dowry, deeming it a 'social evil', and this was followed up by guest control regulations introduced during the Indian Emergency (1975–1977) to restrict conspicuous spending on feasting and hospitality. Discreetly flouted even during the Emergency years, these regulations have increasingly been disregarded. In the 1970s, the gruesome phenomenon of 'dowry deaths' and some well-publicised cases of suicide by young women became the focus of attention in the second phase of the women's movement in India. Notwithstanding successive State interventions, the 'problem' of dowry has not gone away. If anything, it has been exacerbated and taken on new forms. There is a cultural ethos which supports dowry and the concomitant view of brides as objects to be passed from one social group to another for the procreation of children and as vehicles for aspirations to social prestige (Uberoi 1993). Therefore, the harassment of women in their marital homes is related to their financial dependence on and location in the Indian family structure, which concentrates economic and decision-making power in the hands of men. There is a high degree of tolerance among women and denial of domestic violence. The myth that wife battering is a private matter has silenced victims for centuries. Even today, thousands of women remain trapped in life-threatening relationships. During the course of their marriage, women defend abusive husbands. As a result, wives rarely report domestic violence; in fact, they choose to deny its existence (Bhattacharya 2004).

Such forms of harassment and violence are borne by women and their natal families. For instance, if the woman is killed or forced to leave the house by her husband, the parents have an economic reason to project dowry demands as the primary or only cause of harassment, as they hope to get the dowry back (Kishwar 2005). In the experience of violence and ironically, even in death, the focus continues to be on the amount of dowry paid, rather than on the woman herself, her pain, and her ultimate destruction. Dowry is a patriarchal enterprise where the benefits of land, money, and gifts are used and controlled by the male members of the household. Women (mothers-in-law, sisters-in-law) derive fringe benefits which include household appliances, jewellery, etc. Such practices of limited control over the material goods that come as dowry reinforce the perversity of this patriarchal enterprise as these fringe beneficiaries are made to defend and participate in the practice of dowry actively. It is also not surprising, therefore, that popular opinion highlights the participation of these women beneficiaries in the dowry crimes to dilute its patriarchal essence (Cherukuri 2008).

Most of the older women in Aligarh prison are mothers-in-law booked for dowry death/harassment. These women are overlooked, even in the limited number of studies on women offenders. Older women in society feel vulnerable even at the best of times; as prisoners, they receive the kind of attention that borders on pity and contempt. The Committee on Women Prisoners (Krishna Iyer Committee) and judicial pronouncements have provided guidelines for prison administrations to release older prisoners when they reach sixty years of age. Prisoners with disabilities related to old age are specifically targeted for early release under these provisions. However, even a cursory look around the prison reveals both the presence of the elderly and the general apathy towards their needs. Most of them are scared and confused about their future and fearful of dying in custody. The prison administration is not sensitised to the age-specific disabilities of older women prisoners. That they are in prison is a slur on our society, and that this is accompanied by general apathy towards them in the system and in society itself reveals the complexities of the problem (Shankardass 2012).

The dowry question is critical, not only because it brings women into prison, but also because it places unmarried sisters-in-law and elderly mothers-in-law behind bars. The stigma of a prison experience reduces all chances of a decent marriage proposal for any of the women in the family. The mother-in-law is generally illiterate, elderly, and economically dependent, and marked with physical disabilities and diseases peculiar to her age. This standout contradiction in how a crime against women re-victimises women and how a reform institution is oblivious to the difficulty of rehabilitating a woman in the last phase of her life exposes a whole range of ideological as well as institutional lapses in the criminal justice system (Cherukuri 2008). It is also unfortunate that rarely has a dowry death-related judgment taken note of the lack of support from the natal home in the perpetration of such violence. Every time a girl informs her parents that she is being physically or mentally ill-treated, she is asked to adjust and return to an abusive marital home. Such adjustments and compromises are called for as any additional financial burden is a threat to the survival of the family, or it could be because the family is unable to withstand societal pressures. Challenging societal and community norms also threaten the family's ability to access livelihood options. The harassment and torture continue for a long time, and finally culminate in tragic death. Parents who choose to ignore marital abuse and are silent witnesses to their child's growing despair share the criminal liability, and are as much an accessory to the crime as those who are guilty of physical and mental torture (Singh 2010).

Shabnam and Akbari's cases draw attention to the patriarchal tenets of marriage and how women's decisions beyond the prescriptions of the institution are identified as criminally deviant. This conservative attitude towards marriage and parenthood can survive the change from the extended to the nuclear type of family (Uberoi 1993). When a woman decides to terminate her marriage—for reasons that may vary vastly—she encounters powerful resistance from within her family. In a domestic violence case, the victim may want to leave her violent partner, despite mounting opposition. Even in a life-threatening situation, a woman's motives for leaving the husband are questioned in the severest manner.

Experiences with the Judiciary

Maya, a 50-year-old widow and inmate of Aligarh District Jail, was booked under 8/20 NDPS (Narcotic Drugs and Psychotropic Substances) Act. After her husband's demise, she could not think of any means to support herself and her only son. Maya agreed to carry charas (cannabis concentrate, classified as a narcotic substance) from Bihar (where she hails from) for a sum of Rs 500. She said:

> I did it for money, not even knowing it to be an offence. I kept the *charas* in polythene and tied it to my stomach. It began to bloat because of heat and people in the train suspected it to be an explosive and reported it to the police.

She had been in prison for eight years when I met her. Her son and daughter-in-law had visited her only twice during this time as they could not afford the fare from Bihar to Aligarh. She was entirely unaware of the progress of her case, and her family was too poor to fight the legal battle. According to jail authorities, a lawyer from the district legal aid cell was appointed in her case, but there was no communication between the lawyer and the accused. Maya knew nothing about her lawyer or the case in court.

Naima, a 27-year-old prisoner, was booked under IPC Section 302 for the murder of her spouse and had been in prison for eighteen months. Her only child, a 4-year-old son, lived with her in-laws. Her elderly mother looked after her case as there was no one else in her natal family. Her in-laws did not visit her, nor did they allow her son to meet her. She was not aware that as a mother, she could keep her son with her in prison till he was six years old. When she reached the prison, she found children living along with their mothers. She was also unaware of the fact that women prisoners could not be deprived of meetings with their children, which is one of the many rights of women who are in prison. She said,

> After my husband's death, I was taken to the police station by my in-laws. There I was interrogated and then arrested. It was all very sudden and surprising. I wanted to meet my son, but could not even say goodbye to him. I miss him a lot. I fear he will forget me or people will make him see me as the one who killed his father. I want to explain to him that all this happened in order to eliminate my husband's share in the family property. When will you come next? Can you bring my son to meet me?

Her lawyer was requested to submit an application in the court, whereby the court would summon her in-laws to bring her son to meet her. To this, the lawyer replied, 'This is out of the question. Her in-laws are angry and they will never allow this to happen. In any case, this is not my job. She was unfaithful to her husband. Why should she meet her son?'

The majority of women in prison are unlettered and economically marginalised. Due to their lack of legal awareness and inadequate financial and physical resources, they fail to get justice. In the administration of justice, there are two major systems for the dispensing of justice, the adversarial system and the inquisitorial system. India follows the adversarial system. Under such a system, two advocates represent their party's position before an impartial jury or judge, who attempts to determine the truth of the case. Justice is believed to be served only when a capable adversary can argue their perspective on the case as the legitimate one; thus, the prosecution and the defence stand opposed to each other.

As such, in this system, lawyers play a vital role in deciding the fate and destiny of prisoners. Due to a variety of factors for which the bar alone is not responsible, public perception about the profession has not been appreciative. In the field of criminal justice, this public perception has done a lot of damage, not only to the profession but also to the quality and efficiency of criminal justice administration. The general opinion is that lawyers treat their profession as a business. They choose at their pleasure to not appear for clients in the courts. The accurate measure of a competent advocate is whether he can delay cases even longer than his colleagues. Lawyers do not seem to help very much in arriving at a just settlement of disputes. On the contrary, they sometimes endeavour to prolong conflicts and make them bitter. They use the courts to further, rather than solve disputes (Deva 2005). The laws are complicated and have many loopholes; the legal process is costly, lengthy, and tiring. Cases are dragged on for years and even decades, while the victims of justice continue to suffer. Going to a court of law costs so much money because of the high fees charged by the lawyers and the court fees, and it is so time-consuming that most people cannot afford to take advantage of the legal system. While the rich and privileged have the resources to bend laws and the legal processes to their advantage, the ordinary people barely have even workable access to the legal system. There are many loopholes in the law through which those in positions of privilege and power can escape without much difficulty. They can hire the best and the most expensive lawyers. Those at the margins of social hierarchies cannot engage competent lawyers, and often do not have even elementary knowledge about the laws that govern them. The judge attempts to demonstrate neutrality by remaining passive, leading to compromises on the truth and the consequent failure of the system to assert the truth. Thus, the search for truth eludes the criminal justice system because of errors in investigation and prosecution, loopholes in the law, etc. I argue here that this idea of 'truth' is hinged on observable facts as evidence, while there are many hidden aspects to women's crime that are an integral aspect of the truth in crimes committed by women.

The administration of the criminal justice system in India has deficiencies that are both substantive and procedural. The most severe manifestation of these deficiencies is reflected in a distorted proportion of the number of convicted prisoners versus the undertrial prisoners. At the end of 2015, 1,401 jails in India were already overcrowded, housing around 419,623 people against a sanctioned capacity of 366,781. Besides, of the total jail population of 419,623 prisoners, around 282,076 (67.2 per cent) were undertrial prisoners. Their increasing numbers have largely been responsible for overcrowding in prisons (NCRB 2019). Congestion severely limits the ability of the prison system to provide a life of dignity, following the fundamental human rights of prisoners. Their basic needs, such as healthcare, food, hygiene, and accommodation, are far below minimum acceptable standards, thereby endangering the physical and mental health of prisoners.

These conditions tend to affect women more adversely than men. The proportionately low numbers of women prisoners, their differential circumstances as mothers and primary caregivers, their role as repositories of family honour, and their patterns of offending, which are often linked to male criminality and perceived as deviance from institutional norms, are crucial to understanding the impact of incarceration on women (Marsh 2004). It is evident from criminological literature that women's pattern of offending is different from that of men. Women's status within the family and society is used as a context to understand and ascertain their delinquency (Steffensmeier and Allan 1996). In all likelihood, they are first-time offenders, and many serve as accomplices in crimes committed by the male members of their families, or by other men with whom they share an intimate relationship.

There is also a strong assumption that women offenders are unlikely to be recidivists and hardened or professional criminals, and the crimes they commit are less dangerous. For these reasons, women offenders are viewed as not posing any grave threat to society and public order (Dowey and Silvestri 2008). However, the paradox arises when women offenders are treated far worse than their male counterparts as they traverse the criminal justice system. If their crimes can be viewed leniently, why are they treated differently in the criminal justice institutions? It is crucial for criminal justice institutions to take into account the specificities of women's crimes, and this consideration should be reflected in the treatment extended to them by the criminal justice system, aligning the system to the broader goals of social justice and the compassionate treatment of women.

In developing countries like India, economic dependency sometimes leads women to commit crimes to fulfil their basic needs. The cases I have presented here reveal the lives of women who have been exposed to painful events, which they perceive as beyond their control. Finding no way of escape, women tend to develop feelings of passivity and helplessness, and are unable to seek out stimuli or options that can allow them to escape the conditions of their pain. Instead, they are resigned to the conditions of suffering. If they do seek escape routes, these are located in drastic and radical measures. The experiences of being mistreated further reinforce their low self-esteem and the belief that they are powerless to alter their situation or take effective action. The vulnerability of women, in terms of their backgrounds or lack of family and social support, leads to them being accused, and can play a role in increasing the likelihood of their being victimised while also making it more likely that they will be disadvantaged in terms of escape routes. The dynamics of abuse creates a vicious cycle in which the victim becomes increasingly more passive and frightened, and the abuser becomes more able to control and terrorise. The more the victim gives up her external sources of support, the easier it becomes for the abuser to dominate her.

For many women, being sent to prison is just one of the social and economic injustices they face in their lives. They are often there because they have finally returned the violence that was imposed on them by their partners, or had become involved in drug smuggling to alleviate the extreme poverty that they and their families face. The women experience internal conflicts and a sense of self that is contradictory, inconsistent, and incoherent. This conflict is not simply the product of social relations of inequalities of class, race, gender, religion, caste, and community; rather, it assumes pathological tendencies as there is an acceptance of these perverse inequalities and discriminatory and violent practices. This gives 'coherence' to the contradictions in societies. Such coherence needs to be analysed to expose its false assumptions.

As far as dowry death is concerned, the likelihood of the participation of female members in the murder cannot necessarily be ruled out. However, given the power dynamics within the family and the fact that dowry benefits men more than it does women, it can well be mentioned that their participation in the act is not on equal terms, and that the returns of such involvement are questionable.

In several contexts, women confront a 'devil and the deep blue sea' predicament when faced with two contesting justice systems—traditional (social and cultural) and modern (legal)—leaving them without conclusive justice. Each specific social and cultural fact of the accused becomes a failing, and she stands indicted well before the investigative machinery begins its work. If we seek to study women offenders through fresh approaches because of the faulty theorising and faulty frameworks that prevent a proper understanding, then women's punishments need an even more radical reappraisal because they address none of the problems that relate to women and crime. Penological theorising needs as much reanalysis as criminological theorising. Are women offenders to be treated by the punitive machinery as 'women', or as 'humans' entitled to the same respect and dignity as other humans? These questions have received few, if any, answers, given the vast differences in the social, economic, and cultural circumstances that surround the lives of women in India. The images of women in prison might be tainted and require a rigorous probe, while their treatment at the hands of the machinery of justice, which boasts of neutrality, needs another type of investigation. These separate, distinctive, and complete enquiries about women in prison are required for a fair interpretation and assessment. Such an analysis has not gained ground in India. There has been a tendency to ignore it because women in prison are fewer; they are also socially marginal, and the criminal justice machinery claims neutrality and is blind to social realities. It is thus vital for legal and judicial practitioners, scholars, and activists to learn to work together (Shankardass 2000).

Conclusion

Incarcerated women share histories of violence and marginalisation. Their criminal acts cannot be seen in isolation from their experiences within the intimate, but hierarchical institutions of family and marriage. These narratives from the Aligarh prison demonstrate how the idea of purity-pollution and honour provide a link between female deviance and criminality. The stories also trace the pathways from violent homes to the prison. These aspects of women's incarceration must be taken into account for any significant analysis of the impact of imprisonment, and to conceive of the reformative potential of imprisonment. Keeping in mind the subservient position that women occupy in their families of orientation and procreation, the criminal justice system must take into account the totality of thesewomen's lives. Women offenders need to be presented first and foremost as persons before they begin their life behind bars, defined by their status as offenders or criminals.

References

Adler, F. 1975. *Sisters in Crime: The Rise of the New Female Criminal*. New York: McGraw Hill.

Bajpai, A., and P. K. Bajpai. 2000. *Female Criminality in India*. Jaipur: Rawat Publications.

Bhattacharji, S. 1990. 'Motherhood in Ancient India'. *Economic and Political Weekly* 25 (42), 50–57.

Bhattacharya, R. (ed.). 2004. *Behind Closed Doors: Domestic Violence in India*. New Delhi: Sage Publications.

Biber, S. N. H., and M. L. Yaiser (eds). 2004. *Feminist Perspectives on Social Research*. New York: Oxford University Press.

Bottos, S. 2007. 'Women and Violence: Theory, Risk, and Treatment Implications', Research Branch Correctional Service Canada. Available at http://www.csc-scc.gc.ca/research/092/r198-eng.pdf (accessed November 2021).

Chandrababu, B. S., and L. Thilagavathi. 2009. *Woman: Her History and Her Struggle for Emancipation*. Chennai: Bharathi Puthakalayam.

Cherukuri, S. 2008. *Women in Prison: An Insight into Captivity and Crime*. New Delhi: Cambridge University Press.

Chowdhry, P. 1997. 'Enforcing Cultural Codes—Gender and Violence in Northern India'. *Economic and Political Weekly* 32 (19), 1019–1028.

Dalmia, S., and P. G. Lawrence. 2005. 'The institution of dowry in India: Why it continues to prevail'. *The Journal of Developing Areas* 38 (2), 71–93.

Deva, I. (ed.). 2005. *Sociology of Law*, New Delhi: Oxford University Press.

Dowey, C. C., and M. Silvestri. 2008. *Gender and Crime*. New Delhi: Sage Publications.

Dutt, A. 2018. 'The Code of Silence'. *Hindustan Times*, 4 February.

Dube, L. 1988. 'On the Construction of Gender: Hindu Girls in Patrilineal India'. *Economic and Political Weekly* 23 (18), WS 11–WS 19.

———. 1996. 'Caste and Women'. In M. N. Srinivas (ed.), *Caste: Its Twentieth Century Avatar*. New Delhi: Viking Penguin.

Dumont, L. 1970. *Homo Hierarchicus: The Caste System and its Implications*. London: Weidenfeld & Nicolson.

Girshick, L. B. 1999. *No Safe Haven: Stories of Women in Prison*. Boston, MA: Northeastern University Press.

Goody, J. 1973. 'Bridewealth and Dowry in Africa and Eurasia'. In J. Goody and S. J. Tambiah (eds), *Bridewealth and Dowry*. New York: Cambridge University Press.

Jogdand, P. G. (ed.). 2013. *Dalit Women in India: Issues and Perspectives*. New Delhi: Gyan Publishing House.

Kishwar, M. 2005. *Strategies for Combating the Culture of Dowry and Domestic Violence in India*. Vienna: UN Division for the Advancement of Women. Available at https://www.un.org/womenwatch/daw/egm/vaw-gp-2005/docs/experts/kishwar.dowry.pdf (accessed December 2021).

Kruttschnitt, Candace. 2013. 'Gender and Crime'. *Annual Review of Sociology* 39, 291–308.

Livne, E. 2015. *Violence Against Women in India: Origins, Perpetuation and Reform*. Pittsburgh: Carnegie Mellon University.

Macoby, E. 2000. 'Perspectives on Gender Development'. *International Journal of Behavioural Development* 24 (4), 398–406.

Marsh, I. 2004. *Criminal Justice: An Introduction to Philosophies, Theories and Practice*. London: Routledge

Mishra, K. K. and J. H. Lowry (eds). 2007. *Recent Studies on Indian Women: Empirical Work of Social Scientists*. New Delhi: Rawat Publications.

Nariman, F. S. 2006. *India's Legal System: Can It Be Saved?* New Delhi: Penguin Books.

National Crime Records Bureau (NCRB). 2019. *Prison Statistics India—2019: Executive Summary*. Available at https://ncrb.gov.in/sites/default/files/Executive-Summary-2019.pdf (accessed December 2021).

Pandey, S. P. and A. K. Singh. 2006. *Women Prisoners and their Dependent Children*. Lucknow: Serials Publications.

Pathiyan, P. 2016. 'Adultery Among Women: The State of Affairs'. *Outlook*, 2 January. Available at https://www.outlookindia.com/magazine/story/adultery-among-women-the-state-of-affairs/298294 (accessed November 2021).

Pocock, D. F. 1993. 'The Hypergamy of the Patidars'. In Patricia Uberoi (ed.), *Family, Kinship and Marriage in India*, 330–340. New Delhi: Oxford University Press.

Pollak, O. 1950. *The Criminality of Women*. Philadelphia: University of Pennsylvania Press.

Rafter, Nicole. 2008. *The Criminal Brain: Understanding Biological Theories of Crime*. New York: New York University Press.

Rege, S. 1996. 'Caste and Gender: The Violence Against Women in India'. EUI Working Paper RSC No. 96/17. San Domenico: European University Institute.

Riessman, C. K. 2000. 'Stigma and Everyday Resistance Practices: Childless Women in South India'. *Gender and Society* 14 (1), 111–135.

Sadiq, S. 2013. *Women and Bail*. New Delhi: APH Publishing Corporation.

Selman, D., and P. Leighton. 2010. *Punishment for Sale: Private Prisons, Big Business, and the Incarceration Binge*. Lanham, MD: Rowman & Littlefield Publishers.

Shankardass, R. D. (ed.). 2000. *Punishment and the Prison: Indian and International Perspectives*. New Delhi: Sage Publications.

———. 2012. *Of Women 'Inside': Prison Voices from India*. New Delhi: Routledge.

Sharma, U. 1993. 'Dowry in North India: Its Consequences for Women'. In Patricia Uberoi (ed.), *Family, Kinship, and Marriage in India*, 341–356. Oxford: Oxford University Press.

Siddiqi, F. E., and S. Ranganathan. 2001. *Handbook on Women and Human Rights: A Guide for Social Activists*, Part II. India: Kanishka Publishers.

Singh, A. K., S. P. Singh, and S. P. Pandey. 2009. *Domestic Violence Against Women in India*. Gurgaon: Madhav Books.

Singh, P. 2010. 'The Deepest Cut of All'. *Hindustan Times*, 8 January.

———. 2014. *Dalit Women: Fear and Discrimination*. New Delhi: Centrum Press.

Steffensmeier, D., and E. Allan. 1996. 'Gender and Crime: Toward a Gendered Theory of Female Offending'. *Annual Review of Sociology* 22, 459–487.

Tharu, S., and T. Niranjana. 1994. 'Problems for a Contemporary Theory of Gender'. *Social Scientist* 22 (3/4), 93–117.

Uberoi, P. (ed.). 1993. *Family, Kinship and Marriage in India*. New Delhi: Oxford University Press.

———. 2006. *Freedom and Destiny: Gender, Family and Popular Culture in India*. New Delhi: Oxford University Press.

Verma, J. S. 2004. *The New Universe of Human Rights*. New Delhi: Universal Law Publishing.

World Health Organization. 2009. *The Evidence: Changing Cultural and Social Norms that Support Violence*, Series of Briefings on Violence Prevention. Available at http://www.who.int/violence_injury_prevention/violence/norms.pdf (accessed November 2021).

Vishwanath, J., and S. C. Palakonda. 2011. 'Patriarchal Ideology of Honour Crimes in India'. *International Journal of Criminal Justice Sciences* 6 (1&2), 386–395.

Chapter 5

THE MANY TALES OF 'LOVE'

Prison, Survival, and Resistance

KANUPRIYA SHARMA

> *To be in love in prison is like daring to be human...like catching that last breath when you are drowning, knowing that this may be your only way to survive.*
>
> Aisha, undergoing life-term in Punjab women's prison

The importance of relationships in the lives of women offenders during and post incarceration has been well-established in existing prison literature (see Covington 2001; Girshick 1999; Greer 2000; Leverentz 2006; Mehta 2014, 2018; Owen 1998; Pollock 1998; Stephen, et al. 2005). Studies on the subject have pointed towards the role of supportive networks in helping women cope with imprisonment and ensuring a smooth transition back into the community (see Giallombardo 1966; Leverentz 2006; Owen 1998; Stephen, et al. 2005). However, much of this literature continues to be focused on familial relationships, with little or no attention to the intimate partner relationships of women.[1] The few studies which have touched upon the themes of 'love and intimacy' within the walls of the penitentiary have mostly been based on female partners of male prisoners or have focused on same-sex relationships (see Comfort 2008; Comfort, et al. 2005). Importantly, much of our knowledge about what matters in women's prisons stems from a Western context. These factors limit our understanding of the alternate forms of heterosexual relationships that women possibly engage in after coming to prison, such as relationships with male prisoners, prison staff, or men outside, and how these relationships take shape in non-Western prison settings.

This chapter, while addressing the void in existing literature, aims to explore the ways in which women resist, manipulate, and negotiate penal and societal norms to form new intimate relationships with men during incarceration. Through field observations in one of the largest and only all-women's prison in Punjab and court lock-up (*bakshi khana*), and in-depth interviews with fourteen female offenders, the chapter seeks to provide a culturally nuanced understanding of women's motivations in engaging in these intimate relationships within confinement. Unique to this chapter is an exploration of the ways in which women select and approach these men during incarceration—providing new, alternate meanings to the idea of prison as a 'total institution' (Goffman 1962). Ultimately, it points towards the porous nature of the prison and its important role in helping women constitute a sense of self and agency within prison.

Immersing in the Field: Exploring 'Love' through an Ethnographic Lens

> 'Eh *Didi*, are you the one writing love stories?' shouts a young woman, probably in her mid-twenties, as I walk through the long, circular prison corridor towards the main office compound. The group of women prisoners standing beside her burst into a loud laughter. 'Which one of them do you want to know about? The one behind the wall or the one who landed me here?' she asks, as I stop, nervously smiling back at her. The women continue to giggle. 'Didi, finding a man in prison is not such a big deal...it's like those matrimonial websites...only there are much less choices here!'
>
> Fieldnotes (8 May 2018)

'Love' was certainly not one of the themes I was exploring when I first conducted fieldwork in one of the largest and only women's prison in Punjab. Being a novice researcher in my mid-twenties, I had initially set out to explore the everyday life of women in imprisonment and their contemplations of life post-prison within the framework of State reformatory policy. Among the many themes that emerged from my data—fear of stigma, anxiety about separation from family, and anger towards institutional control—love was one of the least anticipated but most discussed themes in the narratives of women prisoners. Unlike the mainstream heterosexual imagination of love, rooted in marriage or procreation, these women spoke of 'love' in a multitude of forms. For them, love served not only as a painful reminder of their past, but was also an important means to survive their everyday 'pains of imprisonment' (Sykes 1958). Having been brought up in traditional Punjabi families, most of my research participants were married off at an early age or were coerced to leave their love alliances in favour of an arranged marriage. Mody (2002, 226) points out that conventionally in India, 'the construction of the relationship between love and marriage is that love should never precede marriage'. Exercising autonomy to choose one's spouse is considered unacceptable—a challenge to natural caste hierarchies and community norms (ibid.). This is partly the reason why most of my participants chose to take recourse to violent, unlawful means to pursue their love interest or escape abusive marriages. Ten of the fourteen women I interviewed were in prison for murdering their husbands or one of their family members so as to marry their romantic partner or escape domestic violence and physical abuse. Two others had been imprisoned along with their partners for murder. The remaining two were unmarried, and shared their experiences of not being allowed to enter into romantic relationships with men before they get married.

Despite experiencing violent love relationships in the past, these women considered 'love' an important source of their survival, both inside and outside prison. Whether married, single, widowed, or separated from their husbands, all the interviewed women spoke of an involvement in romantic relationships with male prisoners, prison guards, or 'new'[2] men outside. These relationships, mostly developed through a tactical negotiation of time, space, and movement, shaped the way women organised their life inside prison. This chapter, while focusing on some of these relationships, investigates the different routes that women resort to in prison to develop and maintain new heterosexual ties with men, and the meanings they assign to these relationships. The prison encounters I describe in this chapter resonate with the literature on 'love' of Bangladeshi women prisoners (Mehta 2014, 2018), where the author examines the connections between intimate relationships, the total institution, the border, and the question of nationality. The intersections of border, nationality, patriarchy, family, marriage, and love reveal narratives of agency, control, and survival. While I draw on similar ideas of survival, resistance, and challenge to patriarchal and institutional norms, this chapter differs from Mehta's insofar as its focus is resolutely on women prisoners accused or convicted of crimes around familial and intimate partner relations. The intersections of family honour, expression of agency, and social acceptance through heterosexual relationships of choice, accompanied by the violent contexts of the crime and the continuities and disruptions of women's pre-prison and incarceration experiences help to glean an understanding of the complex nature of these relationships. When located within the larger cultural matrix of Indian and South Asian society, we can therefore see the discordant elements that the lives of women prisoners represent, and the strategies that they continue to adopt from within the frames of honour, protection, and conceptions of traditional roles.

The ensuing data analysis is based on two months of ethnographic fieldwork in a women's prison in Punjab. Built in 1988, the facility was separated from the men's prison only a decade later, and was named *Janana Sudhaar Ghar* (Women's Correctional Home). Today, the building stands as a separate structure, just a few yards away from the Central Prison for men. My first round of fieldwork, conducted in 2014, had broadly identified the theme of 'love' in the lives of incarcerated women. This was further explored in depth during my second round of field visits in the same prison, four years later. While returning to the field put me through heightened surveillance, it helped me gain easy access to the site. Although there were new staff recruitments in the prison, most of my interactions took place with the deputy superintendent who acted as my 'gatekeeper' (Minichiello, et al. 1997), giving me unrestricted access to all areas of the prison.

Most of my interviews were conducted in the legal aid clinic or the storage room, both of which were empty during my visits. These interviews were supplemented by informal conversations in the barracks, corridors, or near the phone booth where women often hung out. Unlike traditional one-to-one interviews, some of my participants preferred being interviewed in pairs or in groups of three. Contrary to my expectations, these interviews turned out to be more candid and natural. They were mostly conducted in colloquial Punjabi or Hindi and transcribed in English. As I was not allowed an audio recorder in the prison, I would take detailed notes during and after the interview.[3] These were later 'tidied up' (Gibbs 2007, 14) into formal interview transcripts.

Apart from women prisoners, I conducted casual conversations with the prison staff to understand their perceptions of the intimate engagements of women. These conversations mostly happened during *bandi* (lock-up) hours or while waiting outside the superintendent's office. As most of the exchanges between male and female prisoners were carried out in the bakshi khana (court lock-up) located in one of the nearby district courts, special permission was taken to access the site for a few hours. I spent nearly two days in the court lock-up every week, observing women's interactions with men, sometimes even facilitating their exchange of love letters or barrack numbers through the bars. These subversive practices in the field, while placing me in an ethical fix, gave me unique access to the intimate lives of prisoners and helped me establish greater trust with them. It was also through these 'favours'[4] that I gained a deeper ethnographic insight into new forms of intimacies that women sought to engage in and the meaning these relationships held in the lives of incarcerated women. This chapter is an offshoot of my field research conducted as a part of my Masters dissertation at the University of Cambridge, UK.

The Hunt for 'Love': Strategies, Negotiations, and Resistance

> There is a strange smell in here…like a dingy basement that has been locked up for years. I cross the dark corridor that leads to a small room, dimly lit with no sunlight. There are thick, long bars on either side of the room separating male prisoners from female. The room is unbearably noisy with men shouting swear words at each other from across the bars and women giggling at them. 'Hey, look at this new bee!' shouts a male prisoner, as I make my way towards the far end of the room. All eyes turn towards me as I try to find a familiar face. Just then, Reena, who I had previously interviewed in the prison, comes running towards me… 'Didi, isn't this place just like I described you?' she asks, 'Men all around you… like lions in a cage,' she adds, laughing hysterically. 'Wait…. Do you wish to see a trailer?' she asks. Before I can respond, Reena looks towards some of the male prisoners and gives them a sly wink. Within no time, around five-six men come flocking towards the bars smiling at her, signalling her to come and talk to them. I start to feel uncomfortable as she makes her way down to these men and notes down one of their barrack numbers on her hand. She comes back, looking proud. 'This is our love abode Didi…the place where all the action is!'
>
> First visit to the court lock-up (8 May 2018)

Court visits were one of the most anticipated events for most women prisoners on remand. On the one hand, it evoked hopes for their release; on the other, it also opened up possibilities for meeting men. In fact, eight of the fourteen women I interviewed found their romantic partners during their court visits in the bakshi khana. These visits were treated like celebratory affairs in the prison and involved a range of preparations beforehand. For instance, many women would stitch new clothes in the prison factory days before their scheduled court date, or would borrow clothes from the female guards by paying them money. Others would spend the previous night applying henna to their hands, plucking their eyebrows, or getting facials done from their fellow prisoners. These beautification activities, mostly carried out in secrecy from the prison staff, formed an important means of expression for women's desire to exercise their autonomy to be with men. As Rani explained:

> It is important for us to look our best on the court date .... I know women spend hours on this shit...and the staff thinks we are doing it to attract men there...*well, yeah*! How else will you get a man's attention in the first place! I remember being approached by multiple men on days when I have done my hair in a fancy bun or wore that red lipstick of mine.

Female prisoners often travelled in the same police van as male prisoners while going to the court, giving them a chance to interact with each other. In the bakshi khana, a common waiting room separated by bars in the middle, these interactions were highly dramatised. Here, men approached women directly by calling out their names, singing songs or whistling. Prison guards were often accomplices in these relationships, allowing men and women to interact freely. Women were often selective about the men they chose. One of the important criteria for this selection was the way men approached them during the court visit. For instance, many women suggested that they only agreed to be in relationships with men who were 'decent' in their approach.

Other women also agreed to form relationships with men who went 'out of their way' to pursue them. Seema was one such woman who became romantically involved with a male prisoner after he paid off the guards to enter the female section of the court lock-up and knelt down in front of everyone to confess his love. For her, his public confession of love was proof of his seriousness towards this relationship. Some women, however, did not want loud admissions of love, and preferred being approached through letters or other non-verbal means of communication. These women were extremely conscious of their 'reputation' in the prison or feared losing their existing ties with their partners outside. Interestingly, these women would not reveal their real names when forming romantic ties with male prisoners, and replied to letters anonymously.

Apart from male prisoners, court visits also offered women an opportunity to form intimate relationships with male guards. As opposed to the prison, which only had female security guards, the bakshi khana mostly had male guards on duty, which gave women ample time for interaction with them. These relationships, women claimed, were mostly initiated through an exchange of 'special favours'. For instance, Mandeep entered into a romantic relationship with a guard after he started doing small favours for her. He arranged private visits with her family in the bakshi khana, allowed her to make phone calls through his personal phone, and brought her food from the canteen. These favours, she explained, served as a testimony of his 'love' for her. Parminder, another female prisoner, also shared her experience of developing a relationship with a prison guard after he offered to pay for her lawyer:

> I was really tense that day…the judge had adjourned my hearing and my lawyer was asking for more money…God…it was a tough day and this guard, who kind of knew about my case, offered me help. I was so overwhelmed, you know…my own parents have not done that for me. The next few court visits, we just exchanged glances and nothing really happened. Then one day, when I was in the bakshi khana, he brought me some Chinese food. That was it…I just couldn't help but feel attracted towards him. The next time, he just held my hand and asked me to be his girl (blushes) and I agreed…. I mean, he had done so much for me already.

Relationships with prison guards were the most coveted among women prisoners as they opened doors for certain 'privileges'. Women who were married or had children inside prison particularly expressed their preference towards forming these relationships, due to their transient nature and possibility of economic benefits. These women would often ask their lawyers to adjust their court hearings to match the duty hours of the prison guards in the court lock-up in order to spend more time with them. The ease with which these negotiations were made points to the porous nature of prisons, thus marking a shift from it being 'total'.

Women who were convicted often resorted to other institutional means to find men. Popular among them were the hospital visits. Many women who were convicted or had delayed court hearings would often pretend to be sick in front of the prison doctor in order to be referred to the government hospital. These visits would give them a chance to interact with the male prisoners and guards travelling in the same prison van as them. As prisoners would be taken in groups of six inside the hospital, women would often be required to stay in the van with men for long periods of time. This gave them ample opportunities to exchange flirtatious words and gestures with each other, or pass 'love letters' from their fellow prisoners. Soniya was one such prisoner who met her long-time partner, a prison guard, through one of these hospital visits:

> I waited for some time for my husband to return…but I soon realised that I had to look for other options. I was suffering from a heart ailment at that time…it wasn't that bad, but was enough to get me a hospital visit every week…. I met many men there, but no one really came to my fancy. Until I met this security guard…he was married and all…but he would often hold my hand in the van. It all started from there…then one day he took me to the hospital bathroom and we had a little snuggle. To be honest, that was my best day in prison till date…. It's been a year now, and I still sometimes go to the hospital to meet him. The other day I acted as if I was suffering from diarrhoea to get a hospital visit (*laughs*). I know it's crazy…I have started faking sickness for him.

For women who were imprisoned along with their husbands or family members, hospital visit was a 'safer' way to meet new men and allowed for more private interactions. Raima, for instance, preferred to interact with male prisoners or guards during her hospital visits. As she shared most of the court dates with her parents, who were also imprisoned for the same offence, she felt reluctant to initiate any intimate conversations with men in the bakshi khana: 'I mean, I cannot flirt around with men on my court date…my parents would feel embarrassed…so I often act sick to go to the hospital instead…. it seems less of a public spectacle of your intimate life.' Interestingly, the prison staff, including the doctor, seemed to be aware of these tactics, yet readily sanctioned these visits. According to the medical officer, these visits were 'harmless' as long as they did not disrupt the disciplinary routine of the prison:

> These women think that we do not know what they are up to… they dress up like anything when they go to the hospital and some even come back without seeing a doctor…. I mean, I really understand what they go through and if that means they need to meet someone in the hospital…it's okay…no problems for me. I just expect them to tell me honestly, you know. Like the other day, a woman told me that she wants to go to the hospital to meet this male prisoner. I allowed her to go on condition that she should at least get the prescription signed from the doctor…as long as it doesn't put me in any trouble and the women aren't going all crazy, I am fine with everything.

The medical staff, especially the chief doctor, were usually placed on duty for only six months before being replaced by new staff members. Owing to their short working tenure, they were quite phlegmatic in their approach towards women's relationships. Narratives of women prisoners revealed instances where members of staff took bribes to arrange their visits to the hospital on specific dates. Many women claimed to often strike 'deals' with the nurse to meet with their partners or families during hospital visit. 'It's definitely easier with money…but sometimes she (nurse) would agree to arrange my visit in return for head massages or facials…if her mood was right, she would sanction two hospital visits!' (Aisha). The visits in the hospital were considered more convenient than those carried out in the prison visitation room or bakshi khana as they allowed women to spend more time with their new partners with no security restrictions. It was also one of the ways in which women sustained their relationships post-conviction. For these women in particular, hospital visits served as an alternate institutional arrangement to perform intimacy within the penitentiary.

Social Networks: '... It's Like Match-making in Prison'

A few of the women I interviewed during my fieldwork found their partners through their strong social connections with fellow prisoners. These women were usually those who had lost all familial connections and had a preference for more stable, long-term relationships with men. They tactically forged strong bonds with women prisoners who had strong familial support or had more links to the 'outside' world. Sweety was one such woman who got married in prison after one of her fellow prisoners arranged a match for her through her connections outside. Having been abandoned by her family and husband for fifteen years since her coming to prison, Sweety had lost all hopes of rebuilding her life until she met Parmeet, a fellow prisoner who introduced her to a man from her community:

> I used to work for Parmeet...cook meals for her, wash her utensils and clothes, and sometimes even clean her *khadda* (bedding area). In return, she would give me some money to buy groceries. I knew she had strong connections outside... she had told me she was the *sarpanch* (head) of her village before coming here. So, I just casually asked her one day if she had someone she knew who could support me, you know... like a man. After a few days, she told me about someone in her village whose wife had left him. I did not react much... but I was thrilled. I pursued Parmeet for a few days...did some extra work for her. Then, one day she just took me to a corner and told me that she has spoken to this man and he is keen on visiting me in prison. I just couldn't stop smiling... I immediately got ready...wore my favourite *salwar kameez*. And there he was...this handsome young chap in the visitation room...even the staff knew that it was a big day for me. It felt like one of those arranged marriage situations outside.... Only now, it was like match-making in the prison!

After a couple of visitations, Sweety filed for parole[5] on her partner's surety and got married in an informal ceremony outside prison.

During her interview with me, she was pregnant with her first child and was preparing to apply for her second parole visit. Like Sweety, other women strategically networked inside prison to find long-term partners for marriage. For instance, women who were single or had separated from their husbands often chose to form bonds with elderly women who were imprisoned for dowry death[6] offences. This gave them a clear chance at marriage, as the older women would have sons who were now single or were in prison for the same offence. Owing to the stigma surrounding the dowry death offence, the elderly women knew their sons would have low chances of getting remarried outside. Therefore, they would actively respond to the subtle advances of young women within the prison and show an interest in getting their sons married off to them. Nalima got married after an elderly woman prisoner, whom she shared a close rapport with, asked for her hand in marriage for her son. In this case, the fact that the man's family was also in the same prison worked in Nalima's favour, helping her to gain both emotional and financial support from them:

> I used to do all the chores for aunty in the prison and sometimes even cook food for her…she was old and I knew she was looking for a match for her son. I am not saying I did that to get married to him, but it worked in my favour, you know…she did my full background check as well. But luckily, I had no prior convictions and I was unmarried… I know it's a big thing… which is why maybe my in-laws value me because they know they wouldn't have gotten a girl like me on the outside for sure…especially with their son being booked for dowry death…. In prison, too, I feel women see me differently now. After all, not everybody is lucky to find a man in here.

Some elderly women serving life terms would specifically look out for women prisoners who were unmarried, divorced, or had lost familial connections during incarceration, and were about to be released on bail. These prospective brides, elderly women believed, were 'ideal' to be married off to their sons as they would be available to take care of their families on the outside. This match-making within the institution proved to be a useful means by which women could rebuild and secure their familial lives outside. It also gave them an opportunity to regain their feminine identity and fulfil their learned domestic roles. As Gilligan (1982) points out, 'a woman's role in a man's life cycle has always been that of a nurturer, a weaver of relationships on which she in turn relies'. These relationships give women a sense of meaning and self-worth, in turn reassuring them of their identity as a woman (Mehta 2014).

While women like Nalima focused on forming interpersonal bonds with fellow prisoners to meet prospective men for marriage, there were others who leveraged their connections with the prison staff members. These women were usually those who worked for the administrative staff as *munshis* (assistants). Owing to their closeness to the prison staff, they would approach them, albeit subtly, to find prospective marriage alliances for themselves or their fellow convicts. Sarika was one such woman who found a marriage alliance through her close association with the supervisor of the prison stitching unit, who belonged to the same caste as her:

> I used to work closely with this supervisor...and we were both from the same caste and village community. So, I just casually asked her if she knew anyone in the village looking for a bride ...she said she would ask the local matchmakers. I offered to pay for the service, but the supervisor was nice enough to not take money...after a few days, she contacted me with a man's profile. Initially, I was reluctant and his family too had problems with me being in prison. But I said I am going to be released soon and the man himself had severe health ailments...he had children to take care of as his wife had left him for another man. Certainly, I was his best option.

Unlike Sarika, there were women who would wait for their parole or furlough[7] visits to meet men. These women would go outside and rekindle earlier romances, or would rely on their kin to arrange inter-caste marriages. Interestingly, in the women's narratives, caste was observed as one of the major criteria for the selection of men. Many women, particularly those belonging to higher Hindu sub-castes, would brag about the fact that their partners were from the same caste as them. They would sometimes even look down on each other's relationships on the basis of their partner's caste, in a way reinforcing the politics of caste hierarchy that exist in Indian societies outside (see Uberoi 1994 for an analysis of caste and marriage in India). While in some ways women conformed to these social expectations, they also defied them in other ways. Many women chose to convert to other religions to be with their partners outside. For instance, Mohana, who was a Hindu by birth, decided to embrace Islam after her partner, who was a Muslim, asked for her hand in marriage. Having lost all ties with her family during the course of her imprisonment, she claimed she had no social obligations towards her family to retain her religion. A few months later, she and her partner applied for a parole visit and got married in an informal ceremony in a mosque. Currently, they are both serving life sentences in prison and meet each other frequently during hospital visits or celebratory festivities inside prison.

In India, where choosing a partner for marriage is conventionally proscribed, women in prison were observed to take an active lead in the process of selecting men for marriage, in a way exercising a freedom of choice that they had been deprived of in the past. Even in cases where these relationships were not formed with the aim of getting married, women seemed to experience a greater measure of control in their dealings with men, thereby acquiring agency over their life choices and actions in prison. The means through which these relationships were developed served as an important tool of resistance for women, *first*, against the institutional norms of the prison, and *second*, against the moral strictures of society. As Fili (2013, 5) explains, 'The elevation of female inmates as resistors is attributed to how the very notion of feminity is negotiated in prison and the ways women resist penal imperatives and shape them towards their self-interest.' Through subtle negotiations of institutional space and norms, women in my research inadvertently acted as passive resistors to both corrective and societal demands that bind women's desires, inside and outside the prison.

Performing Intimacy Behind Bars

> We are far away, but I shall meet you in my dreams today. As I lay in bed thinking about you, I wonder if I could cross these bars and fly to you. The walls that separate us haunt me, but then I think about you and I thank the heavens that I met you.
>
> Excerpt from one of the prisoner's letters (Translated)

Unlike 'typical' marital alliances, where home appears to be a powerful ingredient in maintaining relationships, relationships established during incarceration were marked by separation, heightened surveillance, and punitive management. Despite such institutional impediments, women strove to maintain these ties through their unique ways of communication. Among them, the exchange of letters was perceived as one of the primary ways through which women maintained contact with their 'new' partners in prison—particularly male prisoners. Ten of the fourteen women I interviewed wrote letters to their partners every day, and identified this as one of the most gratifying experiences of their courtship.

In contrast to fixing meetings in the bakshi khana or the hospital, this form of correspondence was considered less risky, with no immediate engagement of the correctional staff. Owing to strict communication regulations in prison, these letters were mostly exchanged between female and male prisoners in secrecy, during court dates or hospital visits. Many women would carry letters for their fellow inmates and pass them on to the male prisoners in the police van or the bakshi khana. Women folded and rolled up the letters into tiny cigarettes and carried them in their undergarments before leaving for their court dates. Interestingly, while the staff was aware of these exchanges, they mostly preferred to ignore these 'small breaches'. In fact, there were times when the female security guards themselves facilitated these exchanges by taking money from the prisoners.

> The other day, the superintendent ordered a full checking before we went for the court date and the guard found five letters stuffed in my bra. I had to give whatever money I had

> to that guard to let me through, or else they would have taken my letters and I would have to work extra shifts in the office. (Sarika)

Letters were sometimes used as a tool of negotiation by the prison administrative staff to make prisoners work long hours in the prison office or sewing factory. Many women claimed that the superintendent would conduct surprise checks of their barracks on days when there were huge orders in the factory, or when monthly reports needed to be sent out from the office. If letters were found, women were forgiven on the condition that they would work extra hours that day. During my fieldwork, there was an instance when a 'full search' of barracks was ordered by the administrative office. The next day, women revealed how they had dug holes in the prison ground to hide their letters, along with other *maal* (drugs and cigarettes). Despite such institutional constraints, women openly engaged in reading and writing letters in their barracks. Every night they would assemble in groups of two or three and share their partner's written love verses with each other. As many women in the prison were illiterate or spoke different languages from their partners, they would often ask their fellow prisoners to read and write letters for them, and sometimes even pay them for these services. Reena explained that this was one of the most lucrative 'trades' for women inside prison:

> There are hardly any women here who have gone to school. Obviously, they are in demand when it comes to writing love letters.... They usually charge per page and sometimes a little extra for poems or songs. I remember last time on *Karva Chauth*,[8] there was absolute ruckus and women actually had to book appointments with these women.... They also doubled their charges during those days...so I decided to send Rakesh a small card with drawings of hearts on it.... It was definitely not what he was expecting, but it was still better than nothing.

Despite the barrier of literacy, women persisted in sending long letters to their partners frequently, indicating the symbolic importance of these missives in their relationships (see Ahearn 2001). For them, these letters served as a means of communication and an instrument to combat their 'pains of imprisonment' (Sykes 1958). Many women explained how they would save all the letters received from their partners in soap cases and often re-read them at night to overcome their fears of loneliness. Some would paste these letters in their personal dairies, along with their partners' passport-sized photographs or photocopies of their prison identity cards. The amount of energy, time, and thought devoted to the safekeeping of these letters readily suggests the sacramental importance of prison correspondence in women's lives. In fact, two of my research participants who were married cited letter exchanges as one of their primary motivations for forming new intimate relationships inside prison.

> It's the letters, you know… nothing else. If you have someone outside, he can come and meet you for twenty minutes in the visitation room. That's it and then he is gone! He cannot send you letters everyday…. But men in the prison…it's different with them…. Though you do have that fear about what will happen if they get released. So, it's just good to keep your options open. Like, I have these three men I write to regularly… and there is never a day I don't receive a letter from any one of them…it's just so much better than meeting in person.

For many women, the letters received from male prisoners were more emotionally comforting than visitations from their partners or husbands outside. These letters, women claimed, were more intimate in nature, and provided them with a unique sense of security that they had never experienced in their relationships.

> It's just the way he writes these things…like the other day, he wrote long proses of love and how he dreams of getting released with me. I mean, men usually don't say these things in person…. Right? In five years of my marriage, my husband [who is outside] never even told me he loved me, forget all of this!' (Aisha)

Although immersed in a hyper-masculine environment (Sabo, et al. 2001), women observed that some men in prison were more expressive and communicative in their letters than men on the outside.

Apart from emotional sustenance, letters were also one of the ways of enacting intimacy within confinement. With no opportunity for physical contact with their partners, women often relied on prison correspondence for sexual interaction. These letters acted as 'body substitutes' (Comfort 2008, 73), in a way compensating for the lack of bodily presence in their relationships. As Rajni, while showing me one of her letters, said,

> I sometimes just put my lipstick mark over here…just right before signing my name off. He says he kisses it before sleeping every night…the other day, I drew a picture of breasts towards the end of the page…just to get him excited (*giggles*). I mean, he does that too…like write sexy stuff and all on the margins for me.

While the women were aware that these letters might be read and condemned by the correctional staff during barrack searches, they persisted in including sexually simulating images in their correspondence. Thereby, they exercised their sexual freedom through a resistance of both institutional and societal norms that control women's desires and sexual behaviour, both in the prison and outside.

Phone Calls: 'I Live for those Five Minutes Every Day…'

Apart from exchanging letters, phone calls were another means by which women communicated with their partners. Many women who had formed relationships with male security guards or men outside relied on phone calls to maintain contact. Every day at 6 AM, women would start queuing up near the phone booth placed in one of the empty prison barracks near the corridor. The prisoner in charge would then note down the number placement of each woman in the queue on their wrists and in a small diary to avoid queue jumping. The phone booth would usually be opened from 9 AM to 12 PM, and then from 3 PM to 6 PM. During these hours, every woman was allowed to make one phone call from their account for a duration of five minutes, after which the call would disconnect. All women prisoners had to pre-register two phone numbers along with the names in the phone machine prior to making the call. As the calls were chargeable, women had to deposit a minimum amount of Rs 100 in their accounts every day. These accounts were solely handled by the prisoner in charge of the phone booth, who exercised full authority during the phone duty hours. In this scenario, the frequency of the phone calls made by women was mostly dependent on three factors: a willingness to wait in long queues, the availability of monetary resources, and their ability to effectively negotiate with the prisoner in charge.

Women would work overtime in the sewing factory or the prison office to earn money to call their partners. Others would offer to do personal chores for the prisoner in charge for a couple of days in return for quick access to phones. As the phone machine would only allow women to make one phone call a day from their accounts, many women would strike 'deals' with fellow prisoners in order to use their accounts. Hardeep offered to share her food and clothes with another woman prisoner for a month in return for using her phone account.

Phone calls were also used as a tool of disciplinary control. For instance, if a prisoner flouted any rules, she would not be allowed to make phone calls for a week, or even a month, depending on the nature of the infraction. Interestingly, in order to encourage women to work as munshis (assistants) in the prison office, the staff used to offer free phone calls for at least a month, along with extra phone hours. This encouraged many women to take up work in the administrative offices. As Kanika revealed,

> I took up this clerical work...just to get those extra few minutes. It's a lot, I mean.... You don't have to queue up and you save money. Also, it's not like you have to go around asking favours from other prisoners. It feels like you earned this.

Kanika was convicted for life after spending six years in prison on remand. Her husband left her for another woman, and it was then that she got romantically involved with a prison guard whom she met during one of her court dates. As the prison does not allow women to have visitations with or letters from prison guards, phone calls were her only means of communication with him:

> It's like I live for those five minutes ... I get up and then I eat... and then wait in queues just to hear his voice...and when I am calling, the clock is ticking in my head...the screen says five minutes left, and then four minutes, and at one minute, my head is panicking. I just fade out and then pain engulfs me... and then I feel the need to talk to him again.

Apart from the short time allotted for phone calls, women cited lack of privacy as one of the biggest hindrances in their communications. The phone booth was located in a loud and busy area, making it difficult for women to engage in intimate conversations. Therefore, they would sometimes pay the prisoner in charge to give them 'alone time' during their phone calls. This was done discreetly by booking a date and time in advance, usually early mornings or late evenings, when there would be relatively fewer staff members in the prison. As Hardeep elucidated:

> It's like preparing for a date...but in a different way...me and my partner decide on a time...I inform the woman in charge beforehand and pay her Rs 10. But it's weird because she would tell all the women in the queue to disperse for a while and then everybody knows that I am having sexy chats...and when you come out, they give you those looks like, 'I know what dirty things you have been doing in there'. But then you know in your head that they would also do the same.

Unlike letters, phone calls were a more authorised forum for performing intimacy for women during incarceration. Although all phone calls were recorded, it did not involve the direct censorship of the correctional staff. This method, which provided relative freedom of correspondence in the prison, had a huge impact on the ways women resisted or negotiated penal norms to interact with men. Instances were cited where women would pay female guards to make duplicate keys of the phone booth, and take turns to use the phone at night. Others brought in mobile phones illegally inside the prison and lent them to women on an hourly basis for money. These means of communicating with men reflected the many ways in which women prisoners exercised agency, resisted norms, and exerted power in a relatively powerless institution such as the prison (Bosworth and Carrabine 2001).

Food Sharing: '…More Intimate than Usual'

One of the unique ways in which women maintained contact with their partners behind bars was through the sharing of food. Many women explained in detail how they would get up early in the morning on their court dates to prepare meals for male prisoners or security guards with whom they were romantically engaged. On reaching the bakshi khana, these women would give their prepared meals across the bars to their partners, or sometimes pay the guards to have meals with them in person. Women who were in relationships with security guards[9] would discreetly pass their food during lunch hour in the court lock-up, and would maintain eye contact with them from across the room while eating. According to Parminder, these lunch hours counted as among the most intimate moments of her relationship during incarceration:

> It's not that we would ever eat together…he would walk up to me in the bakshi khana…and I would give him half of my food when no one else was watching. He would then sit across me in the room and we eat at the same time. It's a different feeling…like we both are looking at each other and eating, but are not really doing anything. You know what I mean…it's a different kind of connection…more intimate.

Many women who were convicted but had partners on remand would prepare and send meals through their fellow prisoners. During festivals, when special meals would be cooked in prison, many men and women would, in fact, save their meals to send to their partners the next day. This exchange of food was common and was one of the ways in which couples created a symbolic presence of each other in their lives inside prison. As Comfort (2008, 106) remarks, 'In tightly controlled relationship with scarce opportunities for shared activities… provision and partaking of food becomes central acts for the creation of connectedness and closeness.'

For women who got married during parole visits, the sharing of food during visitation was also a way to recreate family life and fulfil their traditional feminine roles. As Lupton notes (1976, 62), 'In the general atmosphere of family disintegration…producing a "proper" meal … is seen as a symbol of family reinforcement.' Many women, during interviews, revealed that they would cook traditional Punjabi meals for their partners who would come on visitation, and would sometimes take special permission to eat together in the office rooms. Here, food was used as a tool to domesticate the carceral environment, thus blurring the boundaries between the home and the penitentiary. 'By relocating intimate activities inside the confined walls, women attempted to "civilize" the prison existence through mimicry of external life' (Comfort 2008, 123). In their illustrations of exchange, the correctional apparatus—despite its enormous degradations, controls, and curtailments on communication—served as an indispensable element in maintaining intimacy and domesticity in their relationships.

Unmasking 'Love': Gender, Prison, and Survival

Cohen (2001), in his study of the 'states of denial', emphasised the importance of understanding not the structural causes of behaviour (the reasons), but the accounts given by the deviants themselves (their reasons). While the author presented this as an explanation of the various forms of denial, this analytical approach could be extended to understand women's motivations for engaging in 'love' relationships. In my research, women's accounts of their reasons for entering into new heterosexual relationships were often multilayered and largely influenced by sociocultural factors. Three-fourths of the women prisoners I interviewed, whether married, single, or separated from their partners, cited emotional sustenance as a primary motivation for engaging in relationships inside prison.

Among them, 50 per cent of the women held that relationships with male prisoners in particular were more emotionally fulfilling than their prior associations with men outside (see Comfort 2008). For them, their shared experiences of pain and struggles with incarcerated men provided them with a unique sense of closeness and comfort that they had not felt before. As Parveen remarked:

> With men in prison, it is different…they know what you are going through because they have been through the same, if not worse, you know. Like, my guy would exactly say the things I want to hear…and it gives a sense of relief that you would not get talking to someone else.

Having separated from her second husband after coming to prison, Parveen met her partner during one of her court dates in the bakshi khana. Her partner, she revealed, was already married and had two children prior to incarceration. However, that did not deter her from entering into a relationship with him: 'I don't want his marriage to break off or something. It's a temporary thing where we both give each other emotional support and we know that it's important and needed here…. It's an unsaid thing.' Interestingly, Parveen's relationship was not limited to just her partner as she often spoke of being in close contact with his immediate family members. According to her, this relationship fulfilled her need for companionship and compensated for her loss of familial ties:

> I often speak to his family on phone, especially his mother…. That day, his mother addressed me as her *putt* (daughter) while talking, and I could not control my tears. After so many years, I had heard someone call me like that and all memories of my own family came flashing by…it's just not about him. It's everything that comes with him.

Like Parveen, many women who did not wish to form long-term, 'serious' relationships, or who already had partners outside prison, often became involved with men who were married. This, women claimed, posed less risk to their existing relationships and helped them to alleviate their emotional distress. 'It's safe with married men…they wouldn't get serious. You know in your head that it's just an emotional exchange and it will end after you go from here' (Jashan). Unlike her, some other women entered into relationships with men inside prison to escape their current abusive marriages. For them, their relationships with male prisoners offered idealised forms of domestic tranquillity and emotional closeness that they had not experienced earlier. In fact, many of my research participants spoke of experiencing a new sense of 'self' through the development of intimate relationships during incarceration. This idea of preserving and reconstituting the self via close affiliations has been richly and abundantly documented in existing prison subculture literature (Faith 1993; Forsyth, et al. 2002; Giallombardo 1966; Owen 1998; Ward and Kassembaum 1965). In this scenario, however, this positive selfhood did not seem to generate from family dyads or same-sex relationships in prison, but through an active engagement in heterosexual intimacy (also see Mehta 2014).

Apart from emotional sustenance, many women cited monetary and material support as among the major incentives to form heterosexual relationships inside prison. Women in relationships with prison security guards openly regarded their relationships as 'transactional' and deemed them an important source of economic survival in prison. These relationships were not based on romantic love or attraction, but on a dire need to compensate for their lack of financial resources. For instance, Raga entered into a relationship with a security guard after her family cut all ties with her. According to her, she and her partner entered into an unspoken agreement whereby he would send her weekly groceries, clothes, and cosmetics in prison, in return for sexual favours. While the prison staff offered prisoners opportunities to earn money through administrative jobs or work in the sewing factory, many women considered this amount insufficient to meet their expenditures. They relied on alternate means to survive in prison, which often involved asking their family members for money or doing menial jobs for fellow prisoners, the latter being considered 'degrading' by many. 'I would rather date a man than clean someone's dirty undergarments.... Many people do it for money, but nah...I can't stoop that low' (Sarika).

Interestingly, some women who were imprisoned along with their husbands formed sexual relationships with security guards to economically sustain both themselves and their husbands in prison. These relationships, the women claimed, were known to their husbands, and helped them attain certain privileges in the bakshi khana. With no resources available to pay for a lawyer for herself and her husband, Puja decided to enter a romantic liaison with one of the security guards, hoping to receive some economic support:

> My husband does get offended by my relationship with Surjeet [prison guard] sometimes. But it's not like we have any other option as well.... Surjeet pays for our lawyer ...and sometimes even lets me and my husband sit together in the bakshi khana. He hands me money and groceries during those rough times.... Now you tell me Didi, how else would we survive here? The prison money is not enough to pay for our court fee and we have children outside...and it's not like I am sleeping around with Surjeet. It's just some flirting around and touching...not such a big deal, I feel.

There were also women who did not enter relationships with the sole objective of seeking financial support, but acknowledged it as one of the most significant gains from their alliance. According to them, women who had greater economic resources in prison were considered more influential than others, and could 'pay their way out' of any situation. These women, in order to sustain their prominent position inside the prison, would seek to develop and maintain ties with men in prison and outside. Hardeep got married to her family friend's son during one of her parole visits for reasons of economic security. Although her husband was physically and verbally abusive towards her, she continued to maintain her relationship with him because she feared losing her influential position in prison:

> I have always had my say in prison...the other day, I got a special chicken meal delivered to my barrack and it's all because of the shit loads of money I have paid these guards. Not everybody can afford this...so even if my husband beats the shit out of me outside, I have no option but to stay with

> him…he pays for this status…you know what I mean, I cannot part with that.

This idea of engaging in prison intimacies for purposes of 'economic manipulation' has been well-documented in the context of homosexual relationships in prison (Forsyth, et al. 2002; Greer 2000) and prisoner-staff intimacy (Allen and Bosta 1981; Worley, et al. 2003). However, against the sociocultural backdrop of India, where marriage has always been considered the most important determinant of women's economic sustenance (Banerjee, et al. 2013), the development of these fleeting, transactional relationships within prison becomes all the more fascinating and offers alternatives to our understanding of heteronormative love.

Another recurrent theme among women prisoners when asked about their reasons for engaging in new intimate relationships with men were visions of domestic stability. Many women who had lost all connections with their families post-incarceration viewed these relationships as an opportunity to rebuild their lives after their release, and reaffirm their identities as 'good' women. As Das (1976) observes, ties generated through sexuality and procreation are the most valuable relationships in Punjabi societies. In other words, a woman's identity is centred on her capacity to fulfil her roles as a mother or a wife (Uberoi 1994). Therefore, many women in prison attempted to regain their lost domesticity through an engagement in new heterosexual relationships. Reena entered into a relationship with a male prisoner with the objective of getting married. Having been in prison with her 4-year-old daughter, she felt that it was an opportunity for her to 'turn her life around':

> I am doing this for my daughter's sake…. He told me that if he gets released first, he would take care of Aaina [daughter] and if I get released first, I could stay with his family…I know he might be lying to me, but for now I am at ease. I have seen him treating Aaina like his own daughter…he buys her snacks. On her birthday, he had even sent her this huge box of chocolates through the prison guards…. That day, she went around the prison saying that her dad had sent her a gift…honestly, I would do anything to keep her happy.

Four days after our conversation, Reena got engaged to her partner in the bakshi khana itself. Like her, other women in prison formed long-term relationships with men during imprisonment for the well-being of their children outside. For instance, Babli deliberately formed an alliance with a male prisoner who was about to be released on bail. Although they never got legally married, he took responsibility for her children and even stood surety for her while applying for her parole visit:

> He gave me a stability that my own man couldn't give me in years.... Today, I am relaxed because I know my children are in safe hands.... It's strange that I say that, you know, because he is in for murder.... But he is the only one who can give them a real home.

Both Reena and Babli had suffered years of domestic abuse and were imprisoned for the murder of their husbands. Despite such violent experiences, they expressed a desire to return to the same institution of marriage that was responsible for their imprisonment in the first place. This highlights the sociocultural importance of marital alliances in the lives of women, inside and outside prison. Interestingly, this longing for domesticity was also seen among women who had short-term, fleeting relationships with men in prison. For instance, many of my participants who were not married were also observed to wear *sindoor* (vermillion red powder) on their foreheads or a *mangalsutra* (black beaded necklace), both of which are traditional motifs of marriage. There were also women who addressed their love partners as husbands in front of the staff and kept fasts for them on Karva Chauth, attempting to enact the heterosexual family life in prison. Interestingly, these expressions of domesticity were further reinforced by the prison administration, which allowed informal marriage ceremonies in the *mulaqat* (visitation) room or even arranged prospective matches for them.

In anthropological literature, this innate desire for domestic life among women has been observed by Ghosh (2011) in her essay on sex workers. She explains how women who are stigmatised attempt to invoke the missing elements of affection and respectability in their lives by engaging in transient relationships with men. This personal space of domesticity that they share with their partners, Ghosh observes, is a replication of the heterosexual, reproductive family from which they have been excluded (ibid., 362). In the case of women prisoners, this pursuance of domestic stability through intimate engagements can be interpreted in terms of their desire to gain acceptance and recognition in the society that stigmatises them. But at the same time, it can also be viewed as an act of resistance against the penal norms that essentially deprive them of the benefits of domesticity and conjugality.

For many women, these heterosexual ties were also seen as a means to acquire social status. As Owen (1998) states, 'social capital' in prison is embodied in the social networks that women possess or develop during imprisonment. In my research, this social capital was mostly determined by the nature of the intimate heterosexual relationships of women. For instance, women with long-term, permanent relationships with men outside were seen to have greater social capital in prison, and were thus accorded higher respect and social status. Women who were involved in relationships with male prisoners were on the medium rung of this status hierarchy due to the temporary, often fleeting nature of their relationships. On the lowest rung were the relationships with security guards, as these were mostly transactional in nature and were considered 'iniquitous' by many women prisoners. Fascinatingly, however, women who were involved with security guards occupied the most 'influential' position in prison in terms of power, thereby making prison hierarchies more indistinct in character. As Jashan remarked:

> These women do things that no moral woman would do.... So, nobody really respects them. But you don't want to be in their bad books either...because if they tell their guard lovers about you, your life is going to be hell. Like, I remember having an argument with one of these women who had a relationship with a guard ...the next court hearing, her chap did not let me talk to any men in the court waiting room...he constantly called out on me and even abused me in front of all other women...it was such a drama.

Pressure to conform to this social status also existed in prison. Many women who were new to prison expressed a desire to form new intimate relationships in order to 'fit in' with the prison culture. Tanu was one such prisoner who expressed her urge to find a man in the bakshi khana the day before her first court hearing. Having been in prison for two weeks, she explained how women in her barrack had already started advising her on the different techniques of approaching men:

> It's like you come here and women tell you all kinds of stories about the bakshi khana…nobody asks you to do anything but you feel kinda pressurised to find a man to have something to talk about…and it's strange as all they discuss about before a court date is what to wear and how to give those sexual gestures to men…and then somewhere in your mind, you start feeling the need to do this or you know you will be left alone.

Through women's narratives, it can be established that while there is no singular explanation for women's involvement in these intimate relationships, their selections of prospective men are largely influenced by their present socioeconomic circumstances, cultural expectations of their gender roles, and their need to acquire a certain social status in prison. While in the sociocultural context of India these non-monogamous engagements of women might be viewed as unscrupulous, almost sinful in nature, their occurrence in the context of prisons seems almost indispensable.

Conclusion

Gender-segregated prison spaces, penal imperatives, and sociocultural norms operate in multiple ways to regulate women's desires (Mehta 2014). Despite these restrictions and institutional impediments, women learn to negotiate their intimate lives within confinement in a manner that can fulfil both their conformed and desired gender roles in prison. This holds true in the narratives of the fourteen women prisoners I interviewed during my fieldwork in the largest women's prison in Punjab, India. Having been raised in sexually repressive cultures and backgrounds, these women viewed relationships in prison as an opportunity to practice a new sense of freedom, whilst reaffirming their identity as a 'cultured' woman. Their decision to actively engage in new romantic ties with men during incarceration reflected much more than a coping strategy or a means to alleviate their 'pains of imprisonment' (Sykes 1958). These were seen as ways to acquire and exert greater agency over their life choices and decisions. As Bosworth (1999) remarks, in even tightly controlled situations like the prison, people possess the power to resist control and shape their environment towards their self-interest.

Therefore, although most of the women interviewed in my research cited marriage as one of the most important determinants of their lives, they moved beyond the socially sanctioned monogamous practices of marriage to experience love and intimacy in a multitude of forms. This plurality of expressions among my research participants throws light on the complex, often multifaceted nature of these relationships. While on the one hand women attempted to conform to their prescribed gender roles through an enactment of domesticity within the prison, on the other hand they challenged the intrinsically patriarchal power structures by exercising greater choice and autonomy in their relationships with men. In a way, therefore, they put forth alternatives and parallels to the hegemonic heterosexist norm governing intimate relationships in India, based on procreation and copulation. As Biswas (2011) points out, it is important to explore sexual intimacy beyond the 'penetrative eros', such that it helps us to explore not only the sphere of non-normative sexuality, but also the exceptions within the heterosexual normative itself.

In this context, much of my findings resonate with those of Mehta (2014, 2018), who explored the homosexual and heterosexual relationships of Bangladeshi women prisoners in correctional homes in Kolkata. Through narratives of 'love', Mehta points out the different ways in which women prisoners use love as a tool of resistance to constitute a new sense of self and agency within prison. My work, while extending this analysis to include relationships with prison guards and men outside, further provides meaning to the myriad ways in which 'love' is perceived, enacted, and negotiated in prison through the paradigm of shame and honour, social acceptance, and gender confirmation. It is interesting to note how women, despite experiencing violent intimate relationships in the past, continue to yearn for domesticity in order to mask the shame that comes with imprisonment, whilst rediscovering their agentic self. These 'patriarchal bargains'[10] (Kandiyoti 1988) that women engage in shape their unconscious gender subjectivity and enable them to achieve social sanction and rewards.

Thus, many women, when asked about their motivations for entering into new heterosexual ties, mostly oscillated between short-term economic fulfilment and long-term domestic stability. Decisions were usually dependent on women's prior life experiences, their current socioeconomic standing in prison, and their desire to indulge in specific social and emotional trajectories during imprisonment. While findings on economic support, emotional sustenance, and the need to reconcile with their lost domesticity do bear similarities to existing prison subculture literature (see Giallombardo 1966; Greer 2000; Owen 1998; Pollack 1998), what is unique in this analysis is the implication that these relationships have for women's social status and power hierarchies in prison. The observation that women who had long-term, stable heterosexual relationships were accorded higher social status while women in relationships with security guards were considered more influential in terms of power underlines the complex nature of prison governance, and the changing interpersonal environment within Indian prisons.

It also propels further explorations of the role of prison staff in providing access to or defying these romantic relationships, and the impact that sociocultural factors may have on prison administration. While this aspect has not been covered at length in this chapter, the allowing of informal visitations, phones, or staff members facilitating the exchange of letters within prison offers a good starting point to understand how the import of societal attitudes and cultural expectations from the outside may have a direct implication on prison policy and practice. Therefore, it comes as no surprise that Punjab and Haryana are the first and only states to grant conjugal rights and artificial insemination facilities to prisoners for purposes of procreation, thus reinforcing the very patriarchal conceptions of procreative sex within the institution that binds women's sexual conduct outside.

This discussion on 'love' should not be misconstrued as an attempt to trivialise the everyday struggles and pains of imprisonment faced by women prisoners. Instead, it should be seen as one of the ways in which women conform to and parallelly challenge the power and authority of two intrinsically patriarchal power structures: the prison and society. As Kandiyoti (1988, 285) remarks,

> A systematic analyses of women's strategies and coping mechanisms can help to capture the nature of patriarchal systems in their cultural, class-specific, and temporal concreteness and reveal how women and men can resist, accommodate, adapt and conflict with each other over resources, rights and responsibilities.

Women's narratives of their desire for love and intimacy in prison offer one such revelation. It reflects the many ways in which women interact and negotiate with institutional and societal boundaries and control, rebuff its demands and intrusions, and come to find purpose in their lives inside prison.

Endnotes

1. For exceptions, see Mehta's (2014, 2018) anthropological inquiry into love, borders, and nationality based on Bangladeshi women prisoners.
2. Many women developed relationships with men whom they had never met before incarceration through their social networks inside and outside prison.
3. I mostly jotted down interesting quotes during the interviews so as to enable close transcriptions of what was said or heard. These jottings were mostly done in the language of the participant to retain its linguistic sanctity.

4. Women would often ask me to do favours for them—like bringing them clothes and cosmetics, passing their legal documents to their lawyers, or making phone calls to their partners outside.

5. Parole visits in Punjab are granted to prisoners after completion of four months of their sentence for a period of not more than sixteen weeks per year (which is not included in their sentence) in lieu of good behaviour. The sixteen weeks are divided and granted in four quarters or two quarters a year, meaning that the prisoner can avail a maximum of eight weeks of parole in six months. It is granted to ensure that prisoners can have a respite from penal custody for some time, and maintain their family and societal links.

6. Causing bodily harm or death to a woman (daughter-in-law) within seven years of her marriage for not bringing in dowry.

7. In Punjab, all prisoners who have been sentenced to at least five years of imprisonment and have completed at least three years of their sentence in prison are eligible to be released on furlough for a period of twenty-one days for the first year, and fourteen days during each successive year thereafter.

8. An Indian festival where women keep a fast for the whole day to ensure a long life for their partners or husbands.

9. The security guards deployed inside the prison complex are employed by the prison department and those manning the gate and outside area are usually deployed by the police department or Central Reserve Police Force (CRPF). The security guards or constabulary who accompany prisoners to the court are from the police department, and are usually the ones to engage with female prisoners the most.

10. The term 'patriarchal bargain' coined by Deniz Kandiyoti (1988) refers to women's decisions to conform to patriarchal notions or gender norms in order to reap benefits of any form, or sometimes just to survive.

References

Ahearn, L. M. 2001. *Invitations to Love: Literacy, Love Letters, and Social Change in Nepal*. Ann Arbor: University of Michigan Press.

Allen, B., and D. Bosta. 1981. *Games Criminals Play*. Susanville, CA: Rae John Publishers.

Bandyopadhyay, M. 2010. *Everyday Life in a Prison: Confinement, Surveillance, Resistance*. Hyderabad: Orient BlackSwan.

Banerjee, A., E. Duflo, M. Ghatak, and J. Lafortune. 2013. 'Marry for What? Caste and Mate Selection in Modern India'. *American Economic Journal: Microeconomics, American Economic Association* 5 (2), 33–72.

Biswas, R. 2011. 'Of Love, Marriage and Kinship: Queerying the Family'. In R. Biswas, S. Sen, and N. Dhawan (eds), *Intimate Others: Marriage and Sexualities in India*, 414–435. Kolkata: Stree.

Bosworth, M. 1999. *Engendering Resistance: Agency and Power in Women's Prisons.* Aldershot: Ashgate.

Bosworth, M., and E. Carrabine. 2001. 'Reassessing resistance: Race, gender and sexuality in prison'. *Punishment and Society* 3, 501–515.

Cohen, S. 2001. *States of Denial.* Cambridge: Polity.

Comfort, M. 2008. *Doing Time Together: Love and Family in the shadow of the Prison.* Chicago, IL: The University of Chicago Press.

Comfort, M., O. Grinstead, K. McCartney, P. Bourgois, and K. Knight. 2005. 'You can't do nothing in this damn place'. *The Journal of Sex Research* 42 (1), 3–12.

Covington, S. Stephanie 2001. 'A Woman's Journey Home: Challenges for Female Offenders and their Children'. In Jeremy Travis and Michelle Waul (eds), *Prisoners Once Removed: The Impact of Incarceration and Reentry on Children, Families, and Communities*, 67–104. Washington, DC: Urban Institute Press.

Das, V. 1976. 'Masks and faces: An essay on Punjabi kinship'. *Contributions to Indian Sociology* 10 (1), 1–30.

Faith, K. 1993. *Unruly Women.* Vancouver, Canada: Press Gang Publishers.

Fili, A. 2013. 'Women in prison: Victims or Resistors? Representations of Agency in Women's Prisons in Greece'. *Women, Gender, and Prison: National and Global Perspectives* 39 (1), 1–26.

Forsyth, C. J., R. D. Evans, and D. B. Foster. 2002. 'An Analysis of Inmate Explanations for Lesbian Relationships in Prison'. *International Journal of the Sociology of the Family* 30 (1), 66–77.

Ghosh, S. 2011. 'Of Women Whoring'. In R. Biswas, S. Sen, and N. Dhawan (eds), *Intimate Others: Marriage and Sexualities in India*, 345–369. Kolkata: Stree.

Giallombardo, R. 1966. *Society of Women: A Study of a Women's Prison.* New York: John Wiley.

Gibbs, G. 2007. *Analysing Qualitative Data.* Los Angeles: Sage Publications.

Gilligan, C. 1982. *In a Different Voice: Psychological Theory and Women's Development.* Cambridge: Harvard University Press.

Girshick, L. B. 1999. *No Safe Haven: Stories of Women in Prison.* Boston: Northeastern University Press.

Goffman, E. 1962. *Asylums: Essays on the Social Situation of Mental Patients and other Inmates*. Chicago: Aldine Publishing Company.

Greer, R. Kimberly. 2000. *The Changing Nature of Interpersonal Relationships in a Women's Prison*. Pennsylvania Prison Society: Sage Publications.

Kandiyoti, Deniz. 1988. *Bargaining with Patriarchy*. Gender and Society: Sage Publications.

Leverentz. M. Andrea. 2006. *People, Places, and Things: The Social Process of Reentry for Female Ex-Offenders*. Chicago: University of Chicago Press.

Liebling, A. 2009. 'Women in prison prefer legitimacy to sex'. *British Society of Criminology* 63, 19–23.

Lupton, D. 1976. *Food, the Body, and the Self*. Thousand Oaks: Sage Publications.

Mehta, R. 2014. 'So Many Ways to Love You/Self'. *International Feminist Journal of Politics* 16 (2), 181–198.

———. 2018. *Women, Mobility and Incarceration: Love and Recasting of Self across the Bangladesh-India Border*. London: Routledge.

Minichiello, V., R. Aroni, E. Timewell, and L. Alexander. 1997. *In-depth Interviewing*. Melbourne: Longman Cheshire, 2e.

Mody, P. 2002. 'Love and the Law: Love Marriage in Delhi'. *Modern Asian Studies* 36 (1), 223–256.

Owen, B. 1998. *In the Mix: Struggle and Survival in a Women's Prison*. Albany: State University of New York Press.

Pollock, J. M. 1998. *Counseling Women in Prison*. Thousand Oaks, CA: Sage Publications.

Propper, A. 1982. 'Make-believe families and homosexuality among imprisoned girls'. *Criminology* 20, 127–139

Sabo, D., T. A. Kupers, and W. London. 2001. *Prison Masculinities*. Philadelphia, PA: Temple University Press

Stephen, J., A. Harker, B. Guild, E. Paul, and K. James. 2005. 'The reentry process: How parolees adjust to release from prison'. *Fathering* 3 (3), 243–266.

Sykes, G. M. 1958. *The Society of Captives: A Study of a Maximum Security Prison*. Princeton, NJ: Princeton University Press.

Uberoi, P. 1994. *Family, Kinship and Marriage in India*. New Delhi: Oxford University Press.

Ward, D. A., and G. G. Kassebaum. 1965. *Women's Prison: Sex and Social Structure*. Chicago: Aldine.

Worley, R., J. W. Marquart, and J. L. Mullings. 2003. 'Prison guard predators: An analysis of inmates who established inappropriate relationships with prison staff, 1995–1998'. *Deviant Behaviour* 24 (2), 175–194.

Chapter 6

Gender and Prison Structures

A Study of Two Women's Prisons in Maharashtra

Sadaf Modak

> *I cannot imagine a place where one might stand and have a clearer view of concentrated disadvantage based on racial, class and gender inequality in the country than from inside the walls of a women's prison.*
>
> Richie 2004, 438

The women's prison as an institution has emerged in feminist research as a site of 'concentrated disadvantage' that reflects and reproduces the social position and condition of women in the society 'outside'. This chapter is based on a study I conducted in April–May 2016 in two prisons where women are lodged in the state of Maharashtra—Yerwada Central Women's Prison in Pune and Mumbai District Women's Prison in Byculla—examining the prison structure by situating it within a feminist perspective. I also examined various prison policy documents which have over the years shaped the current prison administration, and compared them with everyday practice as narrated by women inmates of these two prisons. While the prison administration, through the use of generic words like 'prisoners' in its documents, seems to include both men and women, it remains male-centric (Hesse-Biber 2012).

In India, the disproportionate ratio of male to female prison inmate population serves as a justification for the neglect of women prisoners. The consequent high cost of training for a small number of women, who are considered to present little threat to society, is another reason for making male prisons the priority in spending the limited budgets (Singer 1973, 337). This leads to a disregard for the rights of women and further subordinates their social position. In India, the National Crime Records Bureau or NCRB (2013) estimates that women form 4.4 per cent (18,188) of an almost 400,000 prison population across nineteen separate women's prisons, and other sub-jails or enclosures within male prisons.

Against this backdrop, one of the key concepts that I explore is the understanding of 'gendered organisation' in Acker's (1990) essay, 'Hierarchies, Jobs, Bodies: A Theory of Gendered Organisations'. According to her, 'to say that an organisation is gendered means that advantage and disadvantage, exploitation and control, action and emotion, meaning and identity, are patterned through and in terms of a distinction between male and female, masculine and feminine' (ibid., 146). She further states that there can be no proper understanding of the ongoing processes in such organisations, which are considered gender-neutral, without an analysis of gender. It conceptualises gender as a product of social construction that is reflected at both an individual micro level and at the macro level through social institutions, policies, and practice (Britton 2003, 6). This chapter will explore the prison as one such macro-level social institution in which the social construction of gender takes place.

The documents that I have referred to for contextualising the narratives of women are the *Prison Discipline Committee, 1836–38*, one of the first prison reform documents on Indian prisons under colonial rule; *Report of the Indian Jails Committee, 1919–20*, which is considered the foundation of modern prison reforms in India; the *All India Committee on Jail Reforms, 1980–83*; the *National Expert Committee on Women Prisoners, 1986*; the *Maharashtra Prison Manual*, on which the current prison administration relies; and the *Model Prison Manual 2003*, a document prepared by the Ministry of Home Affairs, Union Government of India, to serve as a model manual, based on which the prison departments of all states and union territories are to prepare manuals adapted and suited to their prisons.

Through the woman inmate, I also attempt to understand the State's construction of its citizens. As an institution of coercion, the prison, through its routine of disciplining and other strategies, denotes the construction of the ideal citizen of the State (Britton 2005). Thus, in examining the woman inmate, this study seeks to understand the State's construction of its female citizens. The fixing of certain roles for women in prison through policy and practice helps to construct a specific identity of the female citizen.

Prison System in India

The prison system in India was operationalised during the colonial period. One of the first documents on the condition of prisons in India was the report of a committee under the membership of T. B. Macaulay in 1835. The report of this committee was followed by other, similar committees over the next few years, and led to the Prisons Act 1870, which for the first time made the provision for the separation of prisoners, including a separate prison or enclosure for women.

The successive legislation, Prisons Act 1894, continues to be the primary legislation governing prisons in the country today. This Act does not address women prisoners specifically, instead making provisions for the gender-neutral 'prisoner'. This overlooks the differential requirements of women in relation to issues of health, their daily living conditions, and social needs. It is left to the discretion of the state governments to formulate prison manuals to ensure that specific provisions are laid out in the rules for women prisoners.

Another significant document that followed the Act was the *Report of the Indian Jails Committee, 1919–20*. It is one of the first comprehensive documents on the modern prison system in India and is considered the foundation of modern prison reforms in India. It also refers to the work done in one of the earliest interventions by Elizabeth Fry,[1] the first penal reformer, who concentrated on the condition of women's prisons and women prisoners (Dobash, et al. 1986, 41). The significance of this report lies in its separate section on female prisoners, under the category 'Special Classes of

Prisoners'. The language of the report is important, too, since it admits to making recommendations with the 'adult male convict' in view (East India [Jails Committee] 1921, 153).

After Independence, there have been State-initiated efforts to take stock and discuss the condition of prisons and prisoners in the country. The All-India Committee on Jail Reforms, also known as the Justice Mulla Committee (1980–1983), is a result of these efforts. The report of this committee suggested significant measures in the area of women prisoners, such as a medical examination of women inmates on admission into prison, transfer of pregnant women to a local maternity hospital at the time of childbirth, and special diets for pregnant and lactating women. It also advised that suitable educational programmes be developed for women prisoners. Further, it also sought special provisions to be made for women willing to get married after their release. The report of this committee also focused on the specific needs of women in incarceration.

This was followed by a National Expert Committee on Women Prisoners, headed by the then Justice Krishna Iyer in 1986–1987. The report of the committee provided the first gender-specific review of the criminal justice system in India. The most significant contribution of this report was the way it addressed women: not merely as offenders, but also taking into consideration their social position. The report stated that the status of a woman in custody is 'an extension and reflection of how she is treated and the esteem or the lack of it, in which she is held outside custody'. The report also dealt extensively with various aspects of women's imprisonment, including the need for socio-legal counselling of women, specific medical facilities, use of probation as an alternative to imprisonment, and after-care assistance.

Apart from some of these documents that specifically address issues faced by women prisoners, most literature clearly reveal that provisions for prisoners were made with men in mind. Special considerations were made for women as and when required, while leaving scope for much arbitrariness and oversight. This aspect can be seen in the committee reports (such as the Indian Jails Committee, Mulla Committee), which first began to look at women prisoners' needs as pertaining only to their biological needs. This biological and essentialist basis was then used to adopt a distinctive and unequal approach towards them. Most of these committee reports do not pertain to women with an understanding of their larger social contexts, or with any approach towards changing the inequalities that persist in their positions outside. The prison, with its objective of 'correction', tends to overlook the corrections required in the injustices meted out to women. The provisions for women in prisons are restricted to maintaining them in custody, with little attempt to change their status quo or help them overcome the inequalities that lead them into the criminal justice system in the first place. An analysis of these documents reflects a paternalistic attitude towards women, resulting in their double subordination—as offenders and as women offenders.

Methodology

The objective behind the study was to understand the role of gender in women's prisons with a focus on their everyday lives and organisational practices and policy. Through narratives of the lived realities and experiences of women and references to policy documents that govern prison administration, the study examines how the prison is a gendered institution. I documented the subjective narration of individual experiences of women prisoners through exploratory qualitative research. Since it involved a closed prison setting, descriptions of the individuals and the prison environment were gained through observations made while conducting the research. This was also done with a view to keeping the focus on the processes as much as on the objectives and the end result of the study. Similarly, I adopted the approach of an ethnographic study within the concept of 'quasi-ethnography'. The limitations of and constraints in closed institutional settings such as prisons have led to this form of ethnography, which is distinct from the standard practice, emerging as it does from the 'structural barriers to full immersion in the field site' (Bandopadhyay 2010, 34). The study was also formulated through the theoretical lens of the feminist perspective.

Data for the study was collected from two prisons in Maharashtra through in-depth interviews and non-participant observation. An issue faced during data collection was my inability to take an electronic recorder due to prison rules. This enabled inmates to speak without becoming conscious of sharing their experiences, and without fear that their conversations would be heard by prison authorities. Notes were taken as the women spoke, but at times, this broke the flow of the conversation. I also realised during the interviews that the women were more comfortable conversing without their responses being written down as they spoke. At such times, to ensure that there was no interruption in the conversations, I would summarise their responses in short in my field notes. Immediately after the conversation, I would write down their complete answers, based on the summary. This may have led to their responses not being recorded verbatim, but ensured a better rapport with the women.

Prison Mapping

Yerwada Women's Central Prison

Yerwada is one of the oldest prisons in the country, built during colonial rule. While the male section of the prison forms part of a large facade with a heavy security cover, the women's section, in stark contrast, is situated across the road with a solitary guard outside the gate. It is, however, built with high walls with a barbed-wire fence over it, which are the signs of a custodial institution. The women's section also has large open fields, used for the cultivation of vegetables and grains, where some of the women convicts worked. At the time of fieldwork, the prison, which was built for 126 inmates, had 268 women residing in eight barracks. Each woman had some space assigned to her, where all her belongings were tied against the wall in many small plastic bags. The women remained inside the barrack from 6 PM to 6 AM, and from 12 PM to 3 PM. These were called the *bandi* (lock-up) hours.

Mumbai District Women's Prison

This is the only prison for women for the two districts of Mumbai suburban and Mumbai city. A separate women's section was created in the male prison in 2002. The prison facade is inconspicuous, despite being located on a bustling street in South Mumbai's Byculla region. The female section of the prison has a capacity for 165 women, but had over 230 women at the time of fieldwork. The women's section is divided into two 'circles', entry to which is through the common areas of the male and female prison. Only women staff members are appointed in the two-storey buildings that house the women prisoners. No woman is allowed outside the door of her circle to access the common areas of the prison. The severe restrictions on movement are only a repeated reminder that the female section is a prison within a prison, separated not just by doors but by a more sinister design that seeks to impose extreme control.

Gendering of Space and Practices

The significance of spaces in the interrelation of gender and power has been elaborated upon in feminist research (Foucault 1980; Spain 1992; Phadke, et al. 2011). Foucault emphasises that the 'history written of spaces would be at the same time a history of powers' (Foucault 1980, 149). The position of women within a prison structure is symbolised through organisational practices in the management of spaces within prison. The spaces allotted to women within prison—and more importantly, those that are out of bounds for them—also reflect the gendered nature of the institution.

Confinement is essentially the main feature of the prison structure. For women, this confinement is further aggravated by restrictions placed on them to remain within their enclosures, which work like prisons within prisons.

Segregation

The segregation of male and female prisoners has been in place since the earliest prison reform documents under colonial rule in India. The Indian Jails Committee, 1919–1920, stated the need to imprison women in separate buildings, or separate parts of the same building, in such a manner so as to 'prevent their seeing, conversing, or holding any intercourse with any male prisoner'. It referred to an exception seen in the Common Prison in Bombay, where male inmates occupied the entire building while the female prisoners remained confined in the upper floor of the building. This required the women to stay confined to their wards at all times.

The committee directed that alternative arrangements be made to rectify such a severe restriction on women. However, a similar restriction on women continues till date, where the women inmate population is confined in sub-jails or annexes and enclosures within the male prison. The restrictions on women and their inability to access most spaces within prison are immense. The situation is comparatively better in prisons that are exclusively for women, but India has only nineteen such women's prisons, where only 1.4 per cent of the total inmate population, that is, over 4,000 women, are lodged (NCRB 2013).

The prison in Yerwada is a separate women's prison, distinct in its physical location as well as its daily administration. Yet, it continues to function like a wing of the male prison. For instance, while the women's section has a separate kitchen, the menu for the preparation of meals and the daily supplies are decided by the male prison administration. Every morning, two male convict warders supervised by a prison guard bring a cart of supplies required for the preparation of food for the women's wing. The cart is pulled till the main gate of the women's prison, after which women inmates on duty in the kitchen pull it forward to the kitchen space, empty it, and bring it back to the main gate, where it is again taken back to the male prison. An inmate spoke of the futility of imposing a common menu on both prisons. The women could have been given the choice to cook according to their needs. Further, a full-time doctor is available only at the male prison, should emergencies arise for women during the night. Other administrative decisions are also taken from the male prison, including those concerning visitors who would be allowed access to the women's prison.

The condition of women inmates in Byculla prison is not very different from the committee's description of the common prison, made almost a century ago. Since the prison has separate enclosures for men and women, the circles housing women have strict rules against freely roaming around in the prison environment. On my first day in Byculla, I was asked by the female staff member to carry a *dupatta* (a long piece of cloth worn around the neck or shoulders by women in South Asia) to cover myself while walking through these 'common' areas towards the women's enclosure. Any woman who wants to step outside the gate separating the women's enclosure from the rest of the prison is scrutinised and needs a good reason to pass through the gate, and she has to be similarly covered with a *dupatta* or a stole. The only space accessible to the women outside their enclosure is the office of the Medical Officer, who attends to both male and female prisoners.

Practices of Access

The spaces that are considered 'common' areas of the prison effectively go from being '"no man's land" to "man's land" since whatever is not the female section is the male section' (Sahni 1988, 325). An inmate from Byculla spoke of the gendering of space within prison:

> In places where women's prisons are a jail within a jail, there is a very severe restriction on movement of women inmates.

> The justification that is given is of security of women inmates, yet it is used to confine them further. There are times when if a male official is entering the women's section, all women are sent in a corner. The prison compound is one, but there is very little information that can be accessed by women. For example, even to know whether escort guards are coming on a particular day or any other information about our lawyers, case status, case hearing dates, we have to depend on our male case partners, who have more access.

This is also a reflection of women's lack of access to public spaces in society. There is often an unsaid protocol regarding spaces that women can and cannot access. Men enjoy disproportionate access to most places at most times of the day and night than women in the public arena. Women cannot be seen loitering or assembling at street corners the way men can. Within prison structures, the restricted spatial access to women reproduces this inequality in order to maintain control over women's movements. It emerges not only as a means of control by the prison staff, but is also about power, where those with wider access are privileged to negotiate with those in power. Men, being allowed to work in administrative offices as 'writers', get a certain sense of privilege and an opportunity to experience a defiance of the principle of a 'total institution' (Bandyopadhyay 2010, 83). These limitations on access and opportunity for women are means of focusing on their sexuality, which is perceived as needing constant control.

Controls over Body and Sexuality

Within prison, some practices overtly emphasise women's gender within conventional roles. An inmate in Byculla spoke about a practice:

> There is this obnoxious practice present that on the very first day, when a woman inmate has to present herself before the superintendent of the jail, she is ordered to remove her footwear and forced to cover her head with her *pallu* (the end of the sari that falls over the shoulder) or *dupatta*. When the

> reason for this was asked, there were different answers given. One official said that it was our culture and another said that it was to maintain discipline. A junior officer denied outright that such a practice existed.

Such practices go beyond the law in segregating women, forcing them into submission before the authorities. They do not merely denote a practice of wielding power and control over the inmates, but additionally reinforce gender roles for women. They reflect a certain perception of women as offenders, wherein their deviance—in terms of having broken a law—is also considered a deviation from their gender role. The *pallu* or *dupatta* on the head is claimed to be a mark of respect, but indicates the imposition of a certain feminine subservience.

Similarly, while there are no separate rules regarding the disciplining of women, the prison assumes the control of their sexuality as a form of discipline. This is situated within the ideas of honour and sexuality, to such an extent that it becomes central to many prison practices. The control of women is seen as an imperative task, which includes their control not only as inmates but also as representatives of the value of honour in society, where a woman's body is constructed to symbolically represent a community, nation, or race (Gangoli 2007, 48). Practices surrounding women's sexuality reproduce the framework within which women are constantly judged in society. It is within certain notions of femininity that deviance is viewed. This constant obsession with maintaining propriety through the control of women is demonstrated through an incident narrated by an undertrial in Byculla:

> Once an Honourable judge, one who is assigned to visit and take down complaints of inmates, appeared suddenly in the office of our circle. Women were standing to take their evening *bhatta* (food). The warden yelled, 'cover yourself, cover yourself' to the fully clad women. One inmate was so confused that she sat down. Others ran and hid themselves in the toilets. One inmate, who was dressed from head to toe, didn't know what else to cover, so she covered herself with a *vati* (bowl). She made a terrible mistake. She miscalculated

> that she had two breasts and one *vati*. Another inmate was clever enough to cover her chest with a plate.

Although women laughed at the hilarity and absurdity of this incident, it represented the misplaced focus on their bodies as a form of discipline. Other practices which are validated as cultural beliefs in prison entail allowing women inmates to wear ornaments like the *mangalsutra* (a necklace that the groom ties around the bride's neck), toe rings, and bangles, each of which is a sign of the marital status of a woman. For most married women, incarceration has an adverse effect on their marriage and other familial ties. At Yerwada prison, a staff member spoke of how they were aware of the need to maintain contact with the family members to prevent abandonment. The prison's duality in stripping women inmates of all their belongings except for those denoting their marital status is merely a symbolic consideration. By permitting the use of such symbols while strictly controlling familial contact, the status quo in prison is maintained.

Labour and Employment

The reinforcement of the subordinate position of women can also be seen in other aspects, such as employment and labour options provided to the female prisoners. On the issue of employment of prisoners, the Indian Jail Committee, 1919–1920 had stated that female prisoners can be employed in the 'usual' method of preparation of some articles of food, such as husking, pounding, sifting grain, etc. It also suggested that it would be useful for inmates to be taught needlework or the preparation of food, which is the 'invariable duty of the women'.

For the generic section of 'prisoners', the forms of labour differ. It states that a prisoner can be given the forms of labour that will 'excite his interest, lead him to exert his powers willingly and so enable him to form habits of industry'. This is linked to the prisoner's rehabilitation through livelihood after his release, and denotes a stark difference in the way work is viewed as a means of reformation for men, while it has no such value for women.

In Yerwada prison, women are employed in the factory in activities like *agarbatti* (incense stick) making, tailoring, floor mat-making, weaving, printing, and beauty parlour training. Many women take up these activities and excel at them. Yet, most do not see these as activities that will help them earn a livelihood once they are released. A general feature of many women's prisons is the allocation of dead-end jobs to women, without these serving as useful training for post-release employment. Vocational training programmes, too, are anchored in the stereotypical roles assigned to women. Inmates in Byculla stated that while there were public-speaking and personality development sessions for men, women were not given these options.

Abandonment and Everyday Survival

Abandonment and separation are the common consequences faced by many women in prisons. The prison as a space that is 'emotionally provocative' (Greer 2002) aggravates their fears of abandonment and isolation in the outside world. As an institution, the prison plays almost no role in preventing this from happening, either through interventions by welfare officers or by allowing frequent communication between women and their family members. It can be seen that in the case of women, even prison is 'no place where (women) ... can be considered as family-immune' (Carlen 1998, 86; also cited in Rhodes 2001, 74). The attachment to and dependence on their families is portrayed as a lack of will or ability on the part of women to equip themselves with social and economic agency. The prison emerges as another institution that fails to address gender inequalities; instead, it reinforces them by ascribing the same gendered identities and roles to women. Through its normatively gendered practices, which begin from the time of admission into prison and extend to daily prison practice, it reasserts the inevitability of the unequal position of women in society.

Further, in trying to grasp the centrality of gender in prison structures, it is imperative to explore how women understand their gender. Some women spoke about the discrimination they faced at the police station when they were arrested, and some spoke of their realisation of a permanent change in the way they were perceived after a parole visit, after neighbours and relatives subjected them to curious questions. Women spoke of their lives before prison and the helplessness of their situation because of abandonment or dependence on their male partners.

One of the most poignant responses I received about women's prisons came from an undertrial in Pune named Mohini, who had been imprisoned for over two years: '*Stree hi shoshitach aste. Ti purna aayusha adjustmentach karte. Mag hai adjust menttichyasaathi kaahi katheen nasta*' ('Women are exploited. All their lives, they make adjustments. This adjustment is not difficult for them'). She believed that women continued to make 'adjustments' all through their lives, and prison, as another adjustment, was not difficult for her.

This is not to say that Mohini survived in prison without much difficulty; nor should one assume that imprisonment is similar to the other forms of subordination that women are subjected to. When I spoke to her, she was preparing to leave for her court hearing, happy in the thought that she would probably be released if the court ruled in her favour that day. Yet, her understanding of prisons was shaped by the expectations that society had from women. Her own experiences as a mother and wife and those of other women around her made her feel that they were always expected to adjust without voicing any inconvenience. She felt that prison life was a continuation of the same expectations. Prison also became a space that led to other realisations:

> I spent my whole life for the sake of my husband and my children. I did not choose to be here. It was the first time that I was in a space all by myself. I realised here that I could stand on my own feet. I had done a course in beauty parlour training when I was young, but with all the responsibilities as a wife, as a mother, I never got the chance to pursue that. Here, there was training for an advance course, which I attended. This sense of being able to be self-reliant makes me want to go out and start my own parlour.

One could see meaning being derived from the prison experience. Women spoke of the constant fights that took place in prison over the scarcity of water or space. The fights turned abusive, and sometimes even physically violent. Yet, one could also see women sitting together during non-*bandi* hours, laughing about an incident. The idea of prison as a space of constant despair and pain found moments of escape, where it could have been any other community space, where women were engaged in playful banter. Women spoke of how they had a sense of togetherness, bound by their situations and the realities they saw each other as having lived through.

This also led to women developing a collective sense of awareness regarding the way gender impacted their imprisonment. Inmates spoke of how, despite functioning on the doctrine of 'equality before law', the quantum of punishment in the criminal justice system differed in its impact based on the social aspects of the offender. The social position of women made their experiences in the prison structure different from those of men. The separation from family and the irreparable damage this did to their social lives and the neglect of their health aggravated the sentences that women were imprisoned for.

The narratives of women reflected diverse interpretations of the influence and impact of gender in prison structures. Entry into prison was recalled as a humiliating experience, which they had to relive each time they entered prison from the outside world. The strict routine, which left them with no choice to exercise their will, continued the degradation they felt. The constant focus on their gender was interpreted as another form of control, which could not be escaped even within the women's prison. The women's prison itself was viewed as being a prison within a prison, which limited their access to the prison environment. The pain of separation from their families aggravated fears of abandonment, and caused untold damage to their close social relationships.

One narrative common to almost all the women I spoke to was the apprehension of being left alone, of permanently losing their position within their families. Women had seen other inmates over the years, some of whom had not stepped out of prison on parole even once in over a decade, others who had been sent divorce papers through mail. A woman who had been convicted under the Immoral Traffic Prevention Act 1986 spoke of how she had not contacted her family for over two years since they did not know her occupation, and getting in touch with them would mean telling them why she was arrested. Such situations made women more vulnerable to the perils of imprisonment.

The multiple and varied negotiations and subversions practised by women prisoners contributed to their agency in redefining notions of the prison as a homogenous unit. In the inmate social system, this reflected the sense of community derived through an awareness of disadvantaged social identities and the associations or dissociations they led to. Women's specific needs and the social contexts of their biographies are neglected in everyday prison practice, which attempts to create a uniform and equal approach to governing all prisoners.

Mental health is one aspect that clearly asserts this point. The absence of counsellors or psychiatrists in most prisons compounds the disadvantages and negative repercussions of imprisonment for women. Davis (2003) discusses jails and prisons as being the dominant institutions for the control of men, while mental health institutions serve the same purpose for women. Many women spoke of not wanting to end up in a mental health institution. This can be seen as a revealing reality for women in prison. For most women prisoners, the prison is a space that at least offers legitimacy to their limited autonomy in their everyday lives. Despite controls over body and movement, women are able to independently script some parts of their everyday. However, they perceive a constant threat of losing control over their cognitive abilities for everyday survival, both in prison and thereafter. They fear that such a loss will result in their transfer to another prison or a mental health institution. The defining and continuing presence of State and social institutions in their lives further weakens their abilities to remain hopeful. These apprehensions regarding their lives in prison and their post-release lives, as well as the damage caused to their social ties, are aggravated through their constant struggle with the gendered spaces and practices within prison and outside it.

Conclusion

This research was an attempt to deconstruct the normative policies and practices within women's prisons through a gender perspective. The women's prison was chosen as a site for examining gender for various reasons. First, prison as an institution functions with the goals of correcting and reforming those who have been alleged, or proven, to have deviated from legal norms. These goals are expected to be achieved through State intervention, by means of control of the citizen. The significance of the prison as a State institution, with State actors being imbued with the legitimate power to exercise control and authority over its citizens, gives it the scope to be examined.

Further, despite notions of the prison as a closed institution and of the 'outside' that lies beyond it, prison remains situated within society. It does not function in isolation from existing social structures. The inmates confined in the prison, who are identified as legal subjects, also retain their social identities. These characteristics of the prison offer contradictions as well as intersections, which make prison a meeting point between public and private, and legal and social.

Situating gender at the centre of these intersections can provide an understanding of the structures that lead to power hierarchies. The exercise of rules by the staff also indicated their notions of female criminality. In prison practice, along with the usual asymmetrical hierarchy between the staff and inmates, notions of subservience and submission attached to women could also be seen. The practice of appearing before the Superintendent with the *dupatta* covering the head was one such example. This signified the role of the staff in contributing to the existing, pre-scripted, and conventional roles in society. Such practices are endorsed in policy formulations concerning women inmates, which reflect and reproduce these roles and biases in each aspect of everyday prison life, including work, education, health, children, etc. The role of other institutions, including family, which remained at the centre of the lives of imprisoned women, and societal perceptions of a woman as offender could also be seen as significant structures connected to the creation of a gendered institution.

The role of the State, through its actors in prison policy formulation and prison practice, as well as in the working of the criminal justice system, is also important. Through its prison manuals and rules, the prison claims to function by exercising complete control over its inmates to enable their return to society as 'law-abiding', 'self-reliant', 'useful', and 'better' citizens. The prison thus claims responsibility for a process that will allow a prisoner to claim citizenship through participation and agency (Mukhopadhyay and Singh 2007, 6). This prescribed outcome is not uniform for male and female inmates. Both prison policy and practice place greater significance on the political, economic, and social agency of the male inmate over the female. This is manifested in many aspects of prison life, where the objective of activities like work or education for 'prisoners' is to make them more aware of their rights as citizens. However, the separate section on women still focuses on their 'functional capability' (Government of India 2003). Such an approach towards women extends the bias beyond the prison to the larger concept of citizenship. The inherent inequalities that women face in our society require a greater assertion of their right to active engagement and participation in political, economic, and social spheres. Instead, the State limits them within their conventional roles, restricting their claim to citizenship as well. It is in this larger context that the role of gender in prison structures has to be situated. This also signifies that in prison structures, merely changing the language and administration alone will not be sufficient to bring about gender justice. The fundamental entitlement of women prisoners to citizenship outside of prisons needs to be recognised.

Endnote

1. Elizabeth Fry (1780–1845) was born in 1780 in England. She worked for the improvement of prisoners across Europe, advocating prison reforms that included opportunities for education, employment, and support after release.

References

Acker, J. 1990. 'Hierarchies, Jobs, Bodies: A Theory of Gendered Organizations'. *Gender and Society* 4 (2), 139–158.

Bandyopadhyay, M. 2010. *Everyday Life in a Prison: Confinement, Surveillance, Resistance*. New Delhi: Orient BlackSwan.

Britton, D. M. 2003. *At Work in the Iron Cage: The Prison as Gendered Organization*. New York: New York University Press.

———. (ed.). 2005. *Gender and Prisons*. Aldershot: Ashgate Publishing.

Carlen, P. 1988. *Women, Crime and Poverty*. Philadelphia: Open University Press.

———. 1998. *Sledgehammer: Women's Imprisonment at the Millenium*. London: MacMillan.

Committee on Prison Discipline. 1838. *Report of the Committee on Prison Discipline*. Calcutta: Baptist Mission Press.

Davis, A. Y. 2003. *Are Prisons Obsolete?* New York: Seven Stories Press.

Dobash, R. P., E. R. Dobash, and S. Gutteridge. 1986. *The Imprisonment of Women*. New York: Blackwell.

East India (Jails Committee). 1921. *Report of the Indian Jails Committee, 1919–20*. London: His Majesty's Stationery Office.

Foucault, M. 1980. *Power/Knowledge: Selected Interviews and Other Writings, 1972–1977*. Brighton, Sussex: The Harvester Press.

Gangoli, G. 2007. *Indian Feminisms: Law, Patriarchies and Violence in India*. Bristol: University of Bristol Press.

Gillham, B. 2005. *Research Interviewing: The Range of Techniques*. UK: McGraw-Hill Education.

Goffman, E. 1961. 'On the Characteristics of Total Institutions'. In E. Goffman, *Asylums: Essays on the Social Situation of Mental Patients and Other Inmates*. New York: Anchor Books.

Government of India. 1983. *All India Committee on Jail Reforms*. New Delhi: Ministry of Home Affairs.

———. 1986. *National Expert Committee on Women Prisoners*. New Delhi: National Human Rights Commission.

———. 2003. *Model Prison Manual*. New Delhi: Ministry of Home Affairs.

———. Prisons Act 1894.

Government of Maharashtra. 1979. *Maharashtra Prison Manual*. Yerwada Prison Press.

Greer, K. 2002. 'Walking an Emotional Tightrope: Managing Emotions in a Women's Prison'. *Symbolic Interaction* 25 (1), 117–139.

Hesse-Biber, S. N. 2012. 'Feminist Research: Exploring, Interrogating, and Transforming the Interconnections of Epistemology, Methodology, and Method'. In S. N. Hesse-Biber (ed.), *Handbook of Feminist Research: Theory and Praxis*. Thousand Oaks, California: Sage Publications.

Mukhopadhyay, M., and N. Singh. 2007. *Gender Justice, Citizenship and Development*. New Delhi: Zubaan Books.

National Crime Records Bureau. 2013. *Prison Statistics of India*. New Delhi: Ministry of Home Affairs.

Phadke, S., S. Khan, and S. Ranade. 2011. *Why Loiter? Women and Risk on Mumbai Streets*. New Delhi: Penguin Books.

Rhodes, L. 2001. 'Toward an Anthropology of Prisons'. *Annual Review of Anthropology* 30, 65–83.

Richie, B. E. 2004. 'Review: Feminist Ethnographies of Women in Prison'. *Feminist Studies* 30 (2), 438.

Sahni, S. S. 1988. *Women Prisoners: The Remand and Undertrial Experience*. Bombay: Tata Institute of Social Sciences.

Singer, L. R. 1973. 'Women and the Correctional Process'. *American Criminal Law Review* 1 (2), 295–308.

Spain, D. 1992. *Gendered Spaces*. Chapel Hill, NC: University of North Carolina Press.

Chapter 7

Time is on My Side
Negotiating Space and Time in Prison

Rimple Mehta

Spaces can be real and imagined. Spaces can tell stories and unfold histories. Spaces can be interrupted, appropriated, and transformed through artistic and literary practice.

hooks 1989

I think about it several times. When I was young, my parents would always scold me for not studying. If my father asked me, I would always tell him that I had finished studying for the day. I would get scolded almost every day for skipping school or for not studying at home. If at that time I had devoted myself to studying properly, then I would not be here [prison in India] today. My teacher used to say, 'The one who skips studying, life skips them someday'. And now I am here. (Aalia, thirty years old, married, worked in a hospital in Bangalore for a year).

I am not scared of saying anything. I have not done anything. I came to India just to feed my stomach. This is my only crime, that I came to India. Here, in the prison, everyone says only one thing—these are Bangladeshi women. They always stereotype Bangladeshis. They don't know our names, so they just say Bangladeshi. So I am now here. Eating food of the prison. They refer to us as Bangladeshis all the time. I can't bear it any longer. I feel like dying. But my desire to see my child again keeps me alive. I understand I have committed a crime, but I have also served a sentence for the same. Four months (including one month and three days in the State Protective Home in Bangalore) since I was first rescued and

> then arrested. How much more time am I supposed to serve in the prison? It had been just a month-and-a-half since I had arrived in India and I was arrested. I hoped to work in India and send some money back home. But as soon as I reached India, I was unwell and could not work. I could not send any money home. I have some issues in my stomach. Other women used to work and feed me. (Kakoli, twenty-two years old, married and the mother of a child)

This chapter discusses the ways in which forty young Bangladeshi women in two correctional homes in Kolkata, India, charged under the Foreigners Act 1946 for crossing the Indo-Bangladesh border without valid documents, negotiate with space and time and how this becomes an integral part of their everyday lived experience in prison. I argue that the space-time context needs to be incorporated as an epistemological question in research. It is important to take note of how the space and time in which research is conducted choreographs research relationships as well as individual subjectivities, and how, in turn, space and time are constructed in the narratives of the research participants.

Conceptions of space and time have gone through several changes, from the Aristotelian understanding to its postmodern detonation. According to the Aristotelian tradition, space and time were among those *categories* that facilitated the naming and classing of the evidence of the senses. Descartes attributed a homogeneous absolute value to space—dominating and encompassing all senses and all bodies. Kantian space belonged to an *a priori* realm of consciousness—transcendental and ungraspable. As opposed to a generalised philosophical understanding of space, scientists, led largely by mathematicians, proposed the idea of a particular space. This idea of space continues to predominate in Eucledian geometry. The Cartesian idea of space as an empty receptacle in which social action takes place is further solidified with Eucledian geometrical shapes that continue to dominate our language and everyday life. Hence, according to this understanding, 'real space' is fixed with its specific characteristics. Lefebvre refers to this as mental space: the 'locus of a "theoretical practice" which is separated from social practice and which sets itself up as the axis, pivot or central reference point of Knowledge' (Lefebvre 1991, 6). Shifting away from an idea of what he calls mental space as propounded by Decartes and Kant, he proposes the idea of a social space, shifting the focus from 'space as a product' to the process of 'production of space'. Lefebvre concurs that there is an abstract logical space, a physical space, and a practico-sensory realm of social space.

Feminist scholarship on space brings forth the ways in which the relationship between women and space is constituted by power, and that men and women experience a certain place in different ways (Massey 1994; Niranjana 2001; Raju 2011). Further, feminist scholarship on intersectionality offers rich conceptual frameworks to understand how relations of power are produced in and through sexuality, gender, race, ethnicity, class, caste, and nationality, among other positionalities (see Collins 1986, 1998, 2000; Crenshaw 1991). Although there is some work on space, there is little discussion of the ways that gender, space, and time intersect in creating different relations of power. Amongst feminists, space has been an important point of discussion right from the second wave of feminism, which gave the clarion call, 'personal is political'. It critiques the capitalist separation of the public and private space, which consequently relegated women to the latter and granted a primacy to the public space that men occupied. Massey (1994, 180) argues that the 'construction of "home" as a woman's place has, moreover, carried through into those views of place itself as a source of stability, reliability and authenticity'. She also points out that women's mobility in terms of space and identity had contributed to their subordination in several cultural contexts by designating home as 'A Woman's Place'. This division between the public and private space began to define women's respectability in such a way that in order to demonstrate their respectability, women have to exhibit their allegiance to the private space even when they are in the public space (Phadke, et al. 2011, 24).

The slogan 'personal is political' does refer to the physical space of the home, where the violence and other forms of marginalisation faced by women are silenced based on a mainstream understanding that these are 'private' matters that are not relevant for discussion in the 'public' space, and hence should not be politicised. The second-wave feminists demonstrated for society how patriarchy and gender norms operate in the 'private' realm. This foregrounded discussions of domestic violence and led to a flurry of legal reforms from the State. In addition, in the 1970s and 1980s feminists in India also grappled with the way patriarchal power was reorganised post-Independence and extended to different spatial locations—at the police station, the court, and the prison (Ray 2000). While the exploitation and marginalisation of women in the public realm was not a new phenomenon, exploitation of women in custodial spaces such as the police stations (for instance, the Mathura rape case in 1972) and prisons (sexual torture of political prisoners; see Chapter 2, this volume) created renewed situations of marginalisation. According to Ranade (2007, 1524–1525), 'the normalization of particular gender-space is a key axis around which the society structures itself and the maintenance of this order is critical to its self-preservation.' Therefore, spatial considerations have been a part of feminist scholarship and activism, although they may not have been foregrounded adequately, particularly in relation to time. In this context, it becomes important to understand how space and time in the prison shape the subjectivities of women, especially when they are in a prison in a different country, as in the case of Bangladeshi women prisoners in India, and the ways in which the space of the home, the country, and the prison form a tripartite in shaping their sense of being.

Space-Time Constitution of Research Relationships[1]

Questions of space and time became apparent to me through a reflexive engagement with the constitution of the research relationships between the Bangladeshi women and myself. From passing through a metal detector, depositing the mobile phone with the duty officer, waiting on a chair opposite the men's toilet in a chaotic office to be escorted to the female ward by a male guard, watching the large red iron gate being unlocked with a voluminous bunch of keys, walking through the prison spaces with loitering male prisoners staring at me, to finally reaching the small, unassuming gate of the female ward, the rituals of entry into the prison set the rules for the way I conducted myself in these spaces. The aura of the prison space warned me against any untoward utterance or gesture, and compelled me to reflect on my own safety and the safety of the Bangladeshi women prisoners while navigating the apparently secure spaces within it. This aside, I had to be careful of every move I made lest it impact my access or affect the well-being of the women.

Spatial considerations are central to the articulation of the logic of everyday life, and more often than not, they find expression through a range of practices (Niranjana 2001). It is 'not a neutral void to be filled up but is differently defined by the various people who inhabit it' (Phadke, et al. 2011, 66). People not only produce particular spatio-temporal configurations, but in the process, are also themselves produced as gendered bodies (Ranade 2007). The prison and its spaces therefore played a major role in mediating the interactions between the Bangladeshi women who were the research participants and myself, the researcher. There was both an invisible and a visible barrier which controlled our conversations. The invisible barrier was in the form of a discursive surveillance while the visible barrier was present in the architectural form as well as the stationed warders and guards.

In addition to the architectural organisation, the prison space needs to be seen in terms of its temporality. Prison time, which will be discussed in detail in the next section, comprised not only the everyday life in prison, but also the time that was 'suspended' and the time in which prisoners visualised their return. Time spent with me to contribute to the research process also became a part of prison time. Time for the staff members/warders was organised in terms of their duty hours, shift timings, holidays, etc. Their time was also organised on the basis of the temporal space that they shared with other prisoners. It was within this temporal space that they jostled over moments of power, and certain specific subjectivities were produced.

It is important to see how the relationship between the Bangladeshi women prisoners and I is constitutive of a space-time context. This relationship affects the narratives of both the researcher and the research participants. Hence, in order to understand the conceptual contours of the experiences of the Bangladeshi women prisoners, it is important to situate them in an episteme of space-time. An acknowledgement of space-time as an epistemological question can lead us to a more situated knowledge (Haraway 1988) of their experiences. This situatedness therefore emerges from not just an exercise in self-reflexivity, but from a spatio-temporal location of that reflexivity. In this context, my own experience of working within the borders of the prison becomes relevant. Despite my discomfort at the constant surveillance in the prison, my ability to leave the prison premises at the end of the day marked my experience as different from those of the prisoners. The insider-outsider divide between us remained, and was much detested by the prisoners due to the sheer helplessness of their own situation. My time in the prison could be scheduled, but theirs seemed like it would never end. This difference in the spatio-temporal location within the prison also shaped our relationship and experience of the prison space; this, however, is not to overlook our differences along caste, class, and other social hierarchies.

Of the two prisons in which I carried out fieldwork between December 2010 and December 2011, the first housed both men and women. The female ward comprised approximately 35–40 Bangladeshis and two Indian women at any given time. The second prison, with a capacity of 400 women, was an all-women's prison, with approximately 12 per cent Bangladeshis. The prison space that the Bangladeshi women prisoners inhabited needs to be broken down into multiple spaces such as the various corners of the female ward, registration desk, interview room, hospital/Out Patient Department (OPD), schoolroom, trees, warders' duty room, and toilets in order to understand how prisoners experience different spaces, where they felt comfortable and where they felt threatened by the power that constantly subjected them to surveillance. It is important for a prison researcher to be aware of the various 'sub-spaces' within the 'given' anthropological space of the prison, because they impact the performance of narratives and gestures of the research participants differently. The comfort level of the women prisoners within a certain space was interpreted based on the change in their behaviour (as observed by me), and the changing nature of the narratives as we moved our conversations from one place to another within the prison, across different times during the day.

The mango tree in the female ward of the prison for both men and women became an important component in the relationship between the researcher and the research participants, suggesting that the relationship is intersected by space and has an impact on critical inquiry. During the initial days of my visits to the prison, the warders asked me to sit in a dimly lit, damp room, which was referred to as the 'schoolroom'. The Bangladeshi women prisoners and I would sit on a blanket that doubled up as a mat. Our conversations were restrained because of the presence of a schoolteacher, who would sit in a corner of the room reading the newspaper. There were no students in the school since the Indian women had been shifted to an all-women's prison. The NGOs had also shifted their teaching programmes to the other prison, leaving no options for education for the Bangladeshi women. The Bangladeshi women prisoners spoke so softly that it was sometimes very difficult for me to hear what they were saying, despite sitting very close to them on the mat. They were apprehensive that their narratives would be heard by the schoolteacher. A few months later, the schoolteacher attained superannuation and the schoolroom was locked. In the absence of an alternative space, the warders asked me to sit under the mango tree and speak with the prisoners. Initially, what seemed like a space that would dissuade them from coming to speak with me, due to the excruciating heat, turned out to be an attractive place that each one from the dormitory vied for. They felt a sense of freedom under the shade of the mango tree. Its changing contours and growth gave the prisoners a sense of movement, which was contrary to their monotonous routine in the prison. The unpredictability of a mango falling from the tree gave them a sense of excitement and something to look forward to. The open sky was a break from the roof of their dormitory, to which they were confined for large parts of the day. The narratives shaped up very differently with the change in the space from the schoolroom to the mango tree. In fact, a shift in the research space brought about a conceptual shift in the entire research, which began with looking at the question of violence in their lives but shifted to their experiences of love in prison.

My visits were scheduled between 11.30 AM and 3.30 PM. The superintendent had suggested this as the best time, as the prisoners would be locked up in the dormitory between 12 PM to 3 PM. The woman I would interview would be brought out of the cell as required. He thought it would be 'safe' for me to visit during this time but to me, it seemed like an unfavourable time given the heat during those hours, which could prevent women from venturing out of their cells. As the months went by, I managed to stay in the prison beyond the suggested time and negotiate my visiting hours. But it is important to note that the space of the mango tree transformed the relationship between me, the researcher, and the research participants, despite the unfavourable time of day and year in which to carry out a conversation in the open, with temperatures ranging from 39–41 degrees Celsius and the humidity above 90 per cent. The mango tree became symbolic of the ways in which Bangladeshi women prisoners used and understood the space-time complex, and how it influenced their narratives and experience of what Goffman (1961) calls a 'total institution'.

Relationships are negotiated in and across space, whether it is within a courtroom, a hospital, a public street, a home, or the prison. According to Dorsch (2013), spatiality and temporality are inseparable in lived and everyday worlds. Therefore, space and time play a crucial role in shaping the direction that research takes, but is often left out of discussions on the relationship between a researcher and research participants in the field, and the way the subjectivities of individuals are shaped by it. Gupta and Ferguson (1997, 34–36) point out that in the social sciences, 'space itself becomes a kind of neutral grid on which cultural difference, historical memory, and societal organisation is inscribed'. Space does feature as a central organising principle in the social sciences, but at the same time it disappears from analytical purview. There are discussions of techniques, representation, and power relations in the context of ethnographic work (see Bandyopadhyay 2010; Bosworth 1999; Stanley and Wise 1983; Visweswaran 1994), but there is little discussion about the role space and time play in formulating these. For instance, the prison space, in terms of its architecture and spatial organisation and in terms of its fixed time schedule, has an overbearing presence and accomplishes the objective of surveillance even in the absence of guards or warders. In a space already under surveillance, the female ward is often referred to as a 'prison within a prison' due to the multiple levels of security that one needs to cross to reach there. Criminology and sociological studies need to engage more forthrightly with custodial space and time, and how they shape the everyday lives of those who inhabit them (for instance, see Bhatia and Canning 2021).

Bangladeshi Women Prisoners Speak Space and Time

Space and time take on specific significance in a circumscribed institution where there is a scarcity of space and an abundance of time. In the case of the Bangladeshi women prisoners in the two correctional homes in Kolkata, they were constantly jostling for space, whether in the cell or under the mango tree or the bathroom or for some additional comfort in the prison hospital. Based on the number of prisoners, the prison administration would keep a dormitory or two operational in the female ward. Therefore, although there were more dormitories and cells in the female ward, there was always a space crunch because some of them were locked and not in use. There was no concept of privacy in the dormitory as they lived next to each other with a thick blanket which doubled up as a mattress, a few utensils, and clothes as their only belongings.

The physical space becomes a site of everyday struggles in a closed institution such as a prison, hospital, or a government-run shelter home. This is because the subjects involved in negotiating their everyday lives in a closed institution have only their bodies and the physical space of the prison in which to place their demands in the larger State rhetoric of reform. In a prison, where an individual is stripped of all their belongings, the only 'possessions' they have are handed out by the State for their survival in the prison. For the State, the prisoner is merely reduced to a number—a number ascribed in the prison and a number that adds up to the statistics of prisoners in the State. The 'docile' body (Foucault 1977) of the prisoner epitomises the ideal citizen, governed by the State-allotted space and time. This 'docile' body is perceived as devoid of any ability to express emotions due to the crime it has committed. The lines between a human being worthy of dignity and a prisoner are further blurred where the prisoner is perceived to be just another body in the prison, stripped of all its possessions. Psychoanalytic feminists such as Grosz (1995, 84) argue that bodies must be reconceived not only in terms of their 'matter' and 'form', but also in terms of their environment and spatio-temporal location. According to her, conceptions of space and time are important correlates of the exploration of corporeality. She argues, 'Corporeality can be seen as the material condition of subjectivity, and the subordinated term in the opposition, can move to its rightful place in the very heart of the dominant term, mind' (ibid., 103). In addition to this, psychoanalytic feminists have also focused on how sexual drives and erotic zones constitute an individual's subjectivity, and how a body is lived and positioned as a spatio-temporal being.

The Bangladeshi women prisoners lived their everyday lives beyond the perceptions of the State and the behaviour expected of them in the prison space. They are the other 'other' in prison because they bear the triple burden of being a woman, a prisoner, and a foreigner. Their status as a 'foreigner' brings upon them additional insults and suspicions from the prison staff, who often believe that each one of them has worked in a brothel and had come to India only for sex work. Their sexuality is often weighed against the sexuality of Indian women who may be accused or convicted of kidnapping, homicide, or theft, but are considered much more 'cultured'. The behaviour of economically disadvantaged migrant women from Bangladesh was viewed through the lens of 'honour', with Indian women prisoners seen as more 'honourable' in comparison to the Bangladeshi women prisoners, who were perceived as 'sexually aggressive'. Ironically, while the prison staff judged the Bangladeshi women based on their understanding of chastity, a number of the male guards also flirted with the women prisoners. An exchange of jokes and statements with sexual innuendos between the women prisoners and the male prison staff was not unknown.

This apart, they were viewed with disdain because they added to the population in India and competed with the domestic labour market. They seemed to have threatened not only the sanctity of the political borders, but also the labour market and the moral order of society. Given their position in the prison hierarchy, there are multiple ways in which the Bangladeshi women prisoners used the space and time in the prison as a site of resistance. It is important to note that their mobility across the borders of one country to another positions them in a doubly vulnerable space within the prison, as it casts aspersions on their 'sexual integrity'. Moreover, since women are considered to represent their family honour as well as the honour of the State, they become the fulcrum in the battle of citizens versus foreigners; their presence is seen as a disruption in the space of the nation-state.

Another difficult aspect of a prisoner's life, apart from the overbearing architectural structure and hierarchical power relations, is dealing with 'time'. The prison, therefore, also needs to be seen in terms of temporality. Activities in the prison, like various other institutions, are organised around time. The cooking and distribution of food, labour, *gunti*, court dates, time at which NGOs or members of the State Legal Services Authority (SLSA) visit are predetermined, and when a prisoner enters the prison, she is expected to adapt herself to the time frame that she has been put into. Prison time is different from the time 'outside' in terms of its meaning for the female prisoners. Prison time is also separate from other parallel times; for instance, the time she looks forward to after her release, the time that she has left behind in Bangladesh, the moment when she crossed the Indo-Bangladesh border. These different time zones lay competing claims on her 'real' time in prison. In this way, their subjectivity is constituted by multiple 'time' claims, of which the future is the one they look forward to. Although the future holds an uncertainty with regard to acceptance or rejection by family members and society at large, it is also indicative of a moment of freedom from the prison. The 'real' time of the prisoners is also intertwined with the time that the staff members/warders spend in the prison. For the latter, time is organised in terms of their duty hours, shift timings, holidays, etc. Their time is also organised on the basis of the temporal space that they share with the prisoners.

Their desire to be in the world outside makes the Bangladeshi women prisoners want to collapse the prison time with the time of the 'outside' world. By talking to me, their expectation was that they can keep themselves updated and find out what is happening in the world outside, that I would bring some *khobor* (news) from the outside world. Their interactions with the warders and attempts to become friendly with them are related to their desire to understand what is happening in the world outside, and collapses the chasm between the time 'inside' and time 'outside' the prison.

When they met me, they mentioned that the most exciting part for them was not realising how quickly time went by. Some of them would walk up to me and say, 'let me come and talk to you, that way you can also kill time and I can also kill time' (this was in the initial stages, when they assumed that if I did not spend enough time in the prison and returned without talking to them, I would not be paid for it). Another common phrase that they would use when they had to leave during our conversations was: '*Didi*, I have no *samay* (time), I need to go'. Some of the women had various duties in the prison, especially in the all-women's prison, where most of the prison work was shared by the prisoners. When a woman said that she could not speak to me any further, it meant that she had to be present for the duty that had been allotted to her. There were ways in which women were kept busy in the prison, but there was a sense of alienation with regard to the way they spent their time. Their time was not their own and they could not choose to do a certain task at a certain time. Tasks were allotted to them based on their physique and visible strength to carry out a particular job. It is important to note that their time in prison was not always determined by a watch. There were wall clocks in the dormitories and in the common room, but a prisoner was not allowed to possess a watch inside the prison. When they spoke to me, they would often ask me the time and were attracted to my watch. This may be related to their sense of alienation from their time in prison.

Some other instances indicate their understanding of time beyond the 'watch' and the 'calendar'. When faced with my specific questions concerning age, when they decided to come to India, when they came to India, when they were arrested, when their trial started, how long their trial went on for, they often paused. Most of them did not know their year of birth, and gave an approximate age at which they were arrested. Often, they said that they were above eighteen years of age, because they had learnt from the police and other rumours that mentioning they were below eighteen would lead to their relocation to a protective home for minor girls, from which they would never be able to return home. Hence, their approximation of their ages was mostly above eighteen years. They would sheepishly tell me their age and initially always stated it to be above eighteen, but gradually, as they came to know me better and were more inclined to trust me, they told me that at the time of their arrest, they had been less than eighteen. They would calculate their approximate age based on when they started menstruating. Their sense of time was based on seasons and their bodily experiences and not on the Roman calendar or the watch, directing us towards an embodied understanding of time. It is the difference between their embodied time and the prison time that brought about a sense of alienation with time that was imposed on them.

Their everyday bodily prison experience reminds them of the various moments that led them to the prison. In the first interview sessions, their narratives referred to several crucial temporal moments in their lives, which they sometimes regretted. The moment they decided to come to India, the moment when they met their trafficker, the moment of doubt/fear while crossing over the border, the moment of arrest—all added up to their time in prison. The prison space, which was often in continuity with their experience of confinement and marginalisation in the homes and communities they had left behind, constantly reminded them of these times. They preferred to suspend memories of their experience of working as child labourers, sexual abuse, forced marriage, desertion by the husband, and domestic violence. They spoke of the time that lay ahead of them, time that was their own and that would be beyond the clutches of the prison, State, and home, and in which their dignity would be restored. Their conscious suspension of time did create ruptures in their narratives, but it told me that they were experiencing time differently. Hence, memory becomes an important tool in the construction and reconstruction of their everyday lived experience.

There were several ways through which Bangladeshi women prisoners tried to negotiate the monotony of their routine and structured everyday lives. One such way was by discussing rumours, and another was through forging relationships of love in prison. There were several rumours concerning the date on which they would be sent back to Bangladesh. They would often tell me that there was news that the West Bengal government was making efforts to send them back to Bangladesh soon; they believed that everyone in the state was proactively working towards sending them back, irrespective of whether they had completed their prison terms. These rumours provided them with temporary relief. Their desire to return home or be released from prison comes from their embodied experience of time. The rumours enable them to collapse their embodied time with the time of the state. However, the state functions with its own understanding of temporality, according to which an 'illegal' migrant woman has to go through the various stages of the criminal justice system. The police have a certain fixed time within which they need to produce the woman in court. The court needs to call an undertrial every fortnight to appear before it.

Prison terms need to be served for a certain fixed time. So time is defined for every stage through which the migrant woman needs to be processed.

What is not fixed is the time when they will be sent back to Bangladesh after they have completed their sentence. During the period between their completing their sentenced terms and actually being sent back to Bangladesh, they are known as *jaankhalash*, which literally translates to 'end of life'. In prison, this implied the end of prison life. Once a jaankhalash, the Bangladeshi women prisoners referred to themselves as 'free public', that they were roaming around in the prison as someone who is free and not as a prisoner. Ironically, there was no freedom for the women, except in a conceptual sense. This time as jaankhalash was the hardest to deal with for the prisoners, because it entailed an uncertainty for which the prison staff had no answers. No one seemed to know when these prisoners would be sent back to Bangladesh. Each officer waited for orders till they could process the papers for their release, and more often than not, things remained in limbo for everyone.

The Bangladeshi women prisoners resisted the stereotype of a female prisoner as merely a number and a body in prison, devoid of emotions and desires. Their bodily desires were constantly invisibilised because of a lack of opportunity to express themselves. 'Love' with both male and/or female prisoners was a way to make their bodily desires visible, through body tattoos, winks, gestures, and their gait. The looks and letters they exchanged with male prisoners alleviated their desires to an extent. 'Love in prison times' kept them alive and provided them with an excitement absent within the prison structure (see Mehta 2014a). Their expressions and feelings of love were not non-cognitive or non-structured. Rather, they were often strategised actions to revolt against or negotiate with the structures in the prison and the shackles of their married life.

As discussed above, the Bangladeshi women were constantly trying to understand and convey their everyday experience to me in terms of time—when she migrated, what time of the day she migrated, when she ran away from the brothel, when she was arrested, when she was sent to prison, when she got her sentence, for how long she had been an undertrial, how many days were left for the sentence to be over. And then they could no longer calculate 'time', as they did not know how much time they would have to spend in the prison as a jaankhalash. While the prison time is in itself arduous, they can calculate it till the date when their term officially gets over. What is primarily painful for them is their inability to calculate time as a jaankhalash. So from calculated time, they move to an ambiguous space of infinite time.

They cannot conceptualise their 'home' in terms of time. They were so busy calculating time in the prison that the time they had left behind is relegated to oblivion, and the time of their return remains blurred and at the level of mere anxiety. The pushing of the past into oblivion, as discussed above, may be a conscious effort to forget a violent past that had compelled them to leave their homes and country. Also, the image of a home in the future remains a blur because, *first*, they are not sure if their families will accept them or if they want to return to their families at all; and *second*, the time taken and the process for deportation was an uncertain one, ridden with challenges. Therefore, they kept referring to the time they crossed the border, as their time in prison is a consequence of that moment. This particular point brings us back to the 'space-time' context—both epistemologically and conceptually. The fact that they begin their narratives from post-migration events may be attributed to their location in the prison. It is possible that this conversation would have a different beginning in a setting outside the prison, or once they were released from prison. The prison as a site of research could be a reason why they begin their narratives from a point that will inform the researcher why they are meeting in prison. Had this research taken place in Bangladesh after the women's return post-imprisonment, the pegs of the narrative would have been different.

Where both space and time are *a priori* in the closed institution, it is up to the women to find meaning in that given space-time context that imagines the prisoner as only a 'docile' body. A female prisoner has to move beyond this given understanding of body, space, and time for her everyday survival. They do this by suspending time or by visualising a future time. The time in prison is negotiated through a love relationship with male prisoners and/or female prisoners, or by way of engaging with rumours. The present time, for the Bangladeshi women in prison, is in some senses constitutive of suspended time, future time, and 'love in prison times'.

Conclusion

The Bangladeshi women prisoners challenged spatio-temporal controls of the nation, prison, and home on their lives. They changed the course of the time imposed on them in the prison with the help of rumours and love. Both rumours and the self-expression of love gave them a virtual location outside the regimented space-time location of the prison. It helped them to transport themselves from the physical space and time of the prison to a world in which they can be in control of their lives. Prison, the physical space of their marginality, also became a space for resistance. Although they cannot change their physical surroundings, they negotiate with time and create a 'mental space', which is neither absolute nor transcendental, as it was for Decartes or Kant. It is an ambiguous and open mental space based on an embodied experience of time. This mental space constantly tries to negotiate with the nexus of democratic, capitalist, and patriarchal ideologies which are trying to disembody the prisoner through the maintenance of a normative moral order in various political, economic, cultural, and social spaces. The negotiations through 'love' and the role of rumours in imagining a 'future' call for a reformulation of the 'mental space' where mind and bodily experiences coexist.

Endnote

1. Parts of this section have been published in Mehta (2014b, 47–57).

References

Bandyopadhyay, M. 2010. *Everyday Life in a Prison: Confinement, Surveillance, Resistance*. New Delhi: Orient BlackSwan.

Bhatia, M., and V. Canning (eds). 2021. *Stealing Time: Migration, Temporality and State Violence*. Basingstoke: Palgrave Macmillan.

Bosworth, M. 1999. *Engendering Resistance: Agency and Power in Women's Prisons*. Aldershot: Ashgate.

Collins, P. H. 1986. "Learning from the Outsider Within: The Sociological Significance of Black Feminist Thought'. *Social Problems* 33 (6), S14–S32.

______. 1998. 'The tie that binds: Race, gender, and US violence'. *Ethnic and Racial Studies* 21 (5), 917–938.

______. 2000. 'Gender, Black Feminism, and Black Political Economy'. *Annals of the American Academy of Political and Social Science* 568 (1), 41–53.

Crenshaw, K. W. 1991. 'Mapping the Margins: Intersectionality, Identity Politics, and Violence against Women of Color'. *Stanford Law Review* 43 (6), 1241–1299.

Dorsch, S. 2013. 'Space/Time Practices and the Production of Space and Time. An Introduction'. *Historical Social Research* 38 (3), 7–21.

Foucault, M. 1977. *Discipline and Punish: the Birth of the Prison*. New York: Pantheon Books.

Goffman, E. 1961. 'On the Characteristics of Total Institutions'. In E. Goffman, *Asylums*, 1–124. New York: Anchor Books.

Grosz, E. 1995. *Space, Time and Perversion: Essays on the Politics of Bodies*. New York: Routledge.

Gupta, A., and J. Ferguson. 1997. 'Beyond "Culture": Space, Identity, and the Politics of Difference'. In Akhil Gupta and James Ferguson (eds), *Culture, Power, Place: Explorations in Critical Anthropology*, 33–51. Durham, NC: Duke University Press.

Haraway, D. 1988. 'Situated Knowledges: The Science Question in Feminism and the Privilege of Partial Perspective'. *Feminist Studies* 14 (3), 575–599.

hooks, b. 1989. 'Choosing the Margins as a Space of Radical Openness'. *Framework: The Journal of Cinema and Media* 36, 15–23.

Lefebvre, H. 1991. *The Production of Space*, Donald Nicholson-Smith (trans.). UK: Basil Blackwell Limited.

Massey, D. 1994. *Space, Place and Gender*. Minneapolis: University of Minnesota Press.

Mehta, R. 2014a. 'So Many Ways to Love You/Self: Negotiating Love in a Prison'. *International Feminist Journal of Politics* 16 (2), 181–198.

______. 2014b. 'The Mango Tree: Exploring the Prison Space for Research'. In K. Lumsden and A. Winter (eds), *Reflexivity in Criminological Research: Experiences with the Powerful and the Powerless*. London: Palgrave Macmillan.

Niranjana, S. 2001. *Gender and Space: Femininity, Sexualization and the Female Body*. New Delhi: Sage Publications.

Phadke, S., S. Khan, and S. Ranade. 2011. *Why Loiter? Women and Risk on Mumbai Streets*. New Delhi: Penguin Books.

Raju, S, (ed.). 2011. *Gendered Geographies: Space and Place in South Asia*. New Delhi: Oxford University Press.

Ranade, S. 2007. 'The Way She Moves: Mapping the Everyday Production of Gender-Space'. *Economic and Political Weekly* 42 (17), 1519–1526.

Ray, R. 2000. *Fields of Protest: Women's Movements in India*. New Delhi: Kali for Women.

Stanley, L., and S. Wise. 1983. *Breaking Out: Feminist Consciousness and Feminist Research*. London: Routledge.

Visweswaran, K. 1994. *Fictions of Feminist Ethnography*. Minneapolis: University of Minnesota Press.

Chapter 8

Governmentality and Contestations

Experiences of Women Recidivists in Mumbai

Mangala Honawar and Vijay Raghavan[1]

Criminological literature, since the 1980s, has focused on the concepts of 'criminal career' and 'career offender', suggesting discernible patterns in the criminal histories of offenders (Gottfredson and Hirschi 1986, 1988, cited in Gilfus 1992, 63). Yet, this literature centres almost exclusively around *male* offenders. Little attention has been paid to questions about the female 'criminal career', how that career begins, its contours, and how they define their commitments and identities in relation to criminality (Gilfus 1992, 63).

Studies on recidivism have not focused on women's own perceptions about their involvement in crime. This chapter is based on fieldwork among women offenders in the city of Mumbai. It explores the perceptions, experiences, and motivations of women offenders that lead them to enter and continue in crime. The study attempts to understand the nature or phenomenon of recidivism through a focus on women offenders in Mumbai.

This study is essentially exploratory in nature and uses the qualitative methodology. It explores the phenomenon of recidivism in the specific context of women's lives, articulating the research participants' perceptions of their pathways to crime having a record of more than one arrest over a three-year period. The study participants (undertrial or convicted) were located either in prison or in the community, depending on the status of their cases (on remand/chargesheet filed/charge framed/trial ongoing/judgment stage) at the time of data collection. The life histories of these respondents were developed through in-depth interviews. Purposive sampling was used as the sample being investigated was small. Within purposive sampling, maximum variation sampling was used to capture a wide range of perspectives, ranging from the typical to the most extreme in nature.

The sensitivities and intricacies associated with the commission of crime, and the perception that it is purely a legal issue have led to a limited understanding of women's pathways to crime. The criminal justice system, comprising law enforcement (police), adjudication (courts), and corrections (prisons), is not only involved in processing offenders, but also leaves a deep impact on the lives of the women offenders, who largely come from difficult situations. Thus, it was important to understand the impact of the criminal justice system on recidivism among arrested women in Mumbai. We draw on the idea of governmentalities and the negotiation of multiple subjectivities in order to understand the experiences of recidivists.

Women Prisoners in India

Women constitute 4–5 per cent of the prison population. According to *Prison Statistics India* (NCRB 2015), of the total population of 419,623 inmates, 401,789 are male and 17,834 are female.

Table 8.1 shows the occupancy of males and females in prisons in India.

A total of 374 women convicts with their 450 children, and 1,149 women undertrials with their 1,310 children were lodged in various prisons in the country at the end of 2015 (NCRB 2015).

Since the number of women in property offences was low as compared to men, the average male to female ratio being 96:4 (NCRB 2012, 2014), it was decided that the study would focus on women offenders above the age of eighteen and involved in offences including theft, pickpocketing, housebreaking, drug peddling, and trafficking, and women arrested under the prohibition law to capture

TABLE 8.1: Occupancy of Male and Female Offenders in Prisons in India

Convicts: 134,168 (32.0% of total inmates)	**Undertrials: 282,076 (67.2% of total inmates)**
Male: 128,428 (95.7% of total convicts)	Male: 270,160 (95.8% of total undertrials)
Female: 5,740 (4.3% of total convicts)	Female: 11,916 (4.2% of total undertrials)
Detenues: 2,562 (0.6% of total inmates)	**Others: 817 (0.2% of total inmates)**
Male: 2,490 (97.2% of total detenues)	Male: 711 (87.0% of total others)
Female: 72 (2.8% of total detenues)	Female: 106 (13.0% of total others)

Source: National Crime Records Bureau (NCRB) 2015.

the diversity of the phenomenon of recidivism. It is also relevant to mention that despite the vast difference in the male to female ratio, one cannot ignore the increasing trend in female criminality. This is clearly supported by the fact that the involvement of women in total cognisable crimes has seen a steady increase, from 3.1 per cent in 1990 to 4.1 per cent in 1995 to 4.7 per cent in 1996, and then to 5.8 per cent in 2006 to 6.2 per cent in 2010, and finally, to 10.2 per cent in 2014 (NCRB 1990, 1995, 1996, 2006, 2010, 2014). This may imply that the presence of women in the world of crime and repeat crime is not uncommon anymore, especially in the metro cities.

Efforts to understand the reasons for female criminality in India have ranged from sociological studies, to research from a social work perspective, to more popular work on profiling female criminals through literature and film. Some studies examine the social location of women and the impact of their caste-class status on the incidence of crime (Ahuja 1969; Bilimoria 1987). Others have traced women's criminal behaviour to illiteracy and to conflicts in their 'private' lives (Bajpai and Bajpai 2000; Chatterji 2009; Mishra and Gautam 1982; Prasad 1982; Sohoni 1989).

In focusing on the incidence of crime and on questions of whether women offend less and why, these studies tend to ignore the more critical questions with regard to the criminal justice system, and how the everyday practice of the power to punish shapes the experiences of women who traverse this system. The dominant trend of studies on women in crime in India has been to understand the causative factors; socio-demographic and personality characteristics; women as victims; women as accomplices in crime; and the prison as an institution of control, with only a passing reference to women recidivists. These studies do not adequately situate the issue within a critical discussion of the nexus between the family and the State. However, some studies have documented the experiences of women prisoners during their detention in police and prison custody as undertrials. Sahni's (1988) study noted that recidivists did not exhibit passivity and helplessness in relation to their processing by the criminal justice system. The experience of recidivist women is significant in problematising the dichotomy between the 'public' and the 'private' and the 'inside' and the 'outside'. Cherukuri's (2008) work in Chanchalguda prison in Hyderabad found that more than two-third of the population there had been convicted for dowry-related crimes. She identified dowry as a 'patriarchal enterprise'. Shankardass (2000) raised the most pertinent theoretical questions regarding women and crime in India, problematising 'male-stream' criminology and Western feminist criminology and the need to advance feminist criminological theories in India.

Recidivism

Recidivism in a criminological context can be defined as the reversion of an individual to criminal behaviour after s/he has been convicted of a prior offence, sentenced, and (presumably) corrected (Maltz 2001, 1). Another definition of recidivism, as observed by Maltz (ibid.), can be understood as a sequence of failures: failure of the correctional system to 'correct' the ex-inmate; failure of the ex-inmate's ability to live in a society; and failure of the society in reintegrating the ex-inmate within a law-abiding environment. Any attempt to make recidivism an operational concept must pay attention to the fact that recidivism is an interval time between two events: a release event and a failure event. The release event could be from incarceration, from parole supervision, from a halfway house, or from any other type of official custody (Carvalho and Bierens 2002, 971–972). Maltz's first definition puts the onus of reversion to crime on the individual, while the second definition is more comprehensive and lays the onus on the failures of the correctional system as well as of the society in reforming the individual.

Literature on recidivism highlights the reasons for and the surrounding contexts of recidivism. Social inequalities, racial discrimination, and bias in criminal justice processing have been found to be responsible for the high crime rates in the West (Langan 1985; Snowball and Weatherburn 2007; Roberts 2007). Another significant reason for recidivism could be repeated arrests due to the bias of the police against criminals, and the creation of a criminal record based on suspicion. Some recidivists are part of the universe of the professional criminals, who earn their livelihood through crime (Raghavan 2010, 108). Several studies establish that career criminals do not live exclusively in the underworld, but are part of both worlds, moving in and out of criminal and social networks, managing to stay afloat in both (ibid., 111).

The absence of substantive literature on recidivism among women offenders does not come as a surprise. Sociological studies of women's imprisonment, notwithstanding their contribution to a better understanding of the meanings of female incarceration, have for the most part reinforced notions of passive femininity and disregarded active subjectivities. Making a decisive break from an emphasis on discipline and control, a relatively new body of scholarship has emerged with a sympathetic and feminist perspective, aimed at investigating the relationship between agency and identity among women prisoners. Despite—or perhaps because of—their liberationist intent, these texts often situate agency on one side of the domination/resistance binary (Hoffman 1999), limiting women prisoners yet again to a single text or a normative definition of their identity.

However, in more recent times, in stark contrast to representations of female prisoners as passive, misguided, and helpless, implicit in the growing body of literature on women prisoners' resistance is a desire to comprehend how women manage to acquire and exert greater control over their own destinies. Drawing mainly on feminist and postmodern theories of subject formation (Butler 1990), contemporary criminological theorisations of women's imprisonment are undergirded by the assumption that women are able to reason and reflect on their circumstances, rather than being conditioned objects (Naffine 1996). While these theorists acknowledge that a majority of women prisoners are subjected to oppression inside and outside of prison, they also insist that it is necessary to consider prisoners agential subjects and understand power relations from the point of view of those subjects (Bosworth 1999; Shaw 1992; Smith 2002).

While prisons control and further subjugate women, they also promote traditional notions of femininity and reduce women to an infantilised status (Smith 2002). The purported elevation of female inmates as resisters is attributed to the way the very notion of femininity is negotiated and employed as a strategy of resistance (Bosworth 1999), and to the ways that inmates resist penal imperatives and negotiate self-interest (Corcoran 2007; Smith 2002). Such approaches are united insofar as they find a causal link between resistance and the negotiation of identity and power relations in prison.

Interactions and Experiences of Women Repeat Offenders within the Prison System

Practices of Control

Punishment regimes in women's prisons operate in close relation with the visible and invisible forms of social control.[2] The daily lives of women prisoners must be understood in conjunction with control, since control is the most defining moment in a prison. Prisons are a part of the larger societal network and replicate the societal ideologies of control over women (Cherukuri 2008, 90). The narratives below reinforce the ideas of surveillance and disciplining within the prison. One respondent in my study said:

> I was forced to confess to crime by the police. The constables, on the instruction of the senior crime police inspector, took me in a small room behind the police station and gave me electric shocks on my hands and legs till I gave in. The pain was unbearable and lasted for several days. After I was sent to prison, I asked the jailors to send me to the hospital for treatment, but they just ignored me.

Another woman respondent in my study shared:

> The police put me in lock-up and said they will teach me a lesson at night for committing theft. After 8 pm, one male police constable came near the lock-up with his phone and asked if I wanted to speak to my family. I readily agreed. He pretended to dial some number and came near the bars of the lock-up and started showing me porn videos. I spat on him, so he came inside and slapped me. All this happened in the presence of the woman police constable who was guarding the lock-up, but she didn't say a word. The constables take advantage of us because we cannot rebel against the police.

The threat of violence, the actual use of force and violence, the complicity of the authorities in such acts of violence, and the use of sexualised forms of humiliation and punishment are some of the ways of disciplining women inmates. Sometimes the women prisoners also use violence to defend themselves or their children, to escape from restraint, and in retaliation to abuse. The prison system perceives women's bodies as merely sites for sexual control and exploitation. Their sexual urges must be controlled, especially their behaviour with the male officers during their routine rounds or when they traverse the prison premises during their visit to the canteen, or *mulaqat* (weekly interview with family) or court. A third interview respondent shared:

> Recently, I am getting a stomach pain which is troublesome. I doubt if it is because of the powder, which is added to the food of all inmates, both men and women, to keep their sexual desire in check. The jailor told me, how else do you think women will be in control, no one can live without sex?

As the following respondent's narrative suggests, desire is also controlled by the assertion of normative ideas of heterosexuality through the prison community:

> I have become a topic of discussion in the prison. Here, the day starts and ends with my name. They think that I do dirty things with other girls in our group. So I was shifted to the new prison on the other side. What all can they stop?

The jailors do not openly talk about the prevalence of lesbianism, especially among women recidivists, since they are the ones who stay in the prison for longer periods or are 'frequent visitors' to the prison. There is, however, a resigned acceptance of the fact that they engage in lesbianism within their network of women, based on the stories that do the rounds in the prison. The presence of sexual encounters among women recidivists in prison raises another significant issue. For the women recidivists, the controls exerted by the prison staff are often similar to those exerted by their families. There is resistance by the women prisoners on this issue against the prison staff, who present the prison as a gendered space.

The staff tries to control such activities by breaking the networks formed among women prisoners by shifting some of them to a separate barrack. Such practices of separation reflect the repressive dimension of the State, with reform as an objective and strategy of governance. This opinion and perception of the prison staff with regard to women repeat offenders clearly reflect their bias against them. They are always labelled as doubly deviant, for breaking the law and for transgressing their gender roles. In addition to this, the high burnout levels of the prison staff results in less empathy and sensitivity towards prisoners, and hence they see no scope for reform or change in women prisoners.

More recently, in 2017, a woman inmate's death in one of the main prisons for undertrial women in Mumbai has brought to light the tough conditions under which women prisoners reside in jails. The event received extensive media coverage and political attention was drawn to the women prisoners' concerns. This incident brought to light the conflicts between the prisoners and prison staff over rationing of food, methods of interrogation and control, and groupism among the prisoners.

There is enough literature that highlights the fact that the prison is an institutional site of power, structured by essentialist notions of masculinity and femininity (Maycock and Hunt 2018; Sabo, et al. 2001). The prison retains a view of women as a homogeneous category and then attributes to this category stereotypical behaviours and emotions, which it then reifies through its *modus operandi* (Thornton 1996, cited in Quadrelli 2003, 134).

Bosworth (1999) notes that women do not endorse the feminine behaviour promoted by the prison; in fact, they endeavour to resist the restrictions placed on them on an everyday basis. Narratives about the impact of prison on recidivism reveal negotiations based on the formation of networks in prison, support from women gang-lords, informal control of inmates over the staff, the dual standards used by the staff vis-à-vis women recidivists, and prejudiced attitude against women inmates.

Controls, Persuasion, and Resistance

The resources of the prison as an institution are geared towards controlling men, primarily due to the high numbers of male prisoners, and the assumption that men are stronger, more violent, and in need of stricter control than women. Women's prisons are perceived as less problematic. However, research findings reveal that women are not really passive or disciplined. Women's prisons are rarely perceived as disordered, yet female prisoners are far from compliant (Bosworth 1999, 139). This fact becomes more evident when jailors address the difficult women as *beta* (child) in an attempt to persuade them to listen or comply with the prison rules. The prison staff realise that simply asserting their authority and adhering to formal rules would not be effective in maintaining order. Informal negotiations with some of the difficult prisoners are an important strategy.

While early studies of the prison culture (Clemmer 1940; Irwin 1980; Sykes 1958) tended to consider the deprivation and importation models as opposite ends of a spectrum, more recent studies have understood these as complementary rather than competing models. Such an *integrated model* might recognise that while inmates experience pains of imprisonment (deprivation), focusing exclusively on this fails to take into account the fact that inmate culture is constructed of conflicting personalities and prior experiences that are brought into the institution (importation). In addition to combining the concepts of the deprivation and importation models, integrated models may also include additional factors not considered by the initial models, such as family visits, the institutional environment, and the coping behaviours of inmates. A more sophisticated integration is possible through an examination of the reciprocal effects that the factors inherent in each of these models have on each other. It is thought that such variations of integrated models can help to clarify why different inmates respond differently to the inmate culture and to the overall prison experience (Dobbs and Courtney 2004).

Conversations with women offenders in prison revealed that some women not only refused to listen to the jailors, but they also did not even bother to respond to them. Some responded and then ignored them, while others made excuses not to comply with their requests. This was during their 'free time', when they were allowed to roam within the prison premises. The majority of women followed the time and rules of the prison during the daily routine, like tea, breakfast, lunch, dinner, *bandi* time (12 PM to 3 PM, when the prisoners are locked in barracks) and counting the total (total count taken before the prisoners are locked inside the barracks), as if they conform to the rules of the prison as an 'institution' but not necessarily to those of the prison staff.

The following instance from one of the author's field notes provides evidence of such instances of subordination. At one point the assistant jailors, who sat in the electrical room of the prison, called the women by their names and asked them to clean wheat. One of them responded: 'I am not here to clean wheat...I am here for bigger things.' She ignored the jailors and went to her barrack to sleep. The jailors sent another prisoner twice to the barracks on the first floor to call all the women to come and clean wheat. While some of them came at once, some others made excuses, saying this was their prayer time, and some just did not bother to come down at all. The jailors managed to get the work done with the women who had agreed to do it. They did not bother about the rest, which indicated their informal practices within the prison. In such situations, it was quite clear that women inmates subverted the rules of the prison, and there were 'heterogeneous, individualised responses to routinised life' (Bandyopadhyay 2010).

While it is apparent that women prisoners are under the control of the prison staff, the staff members too are under the informal control of the prisoners due to their numbers and their ability to come together as a challenging and daring force. There is an unspoken fear among the prison staff that if they behave rudely with the women, the women can unite and even dare to physically abuse the staff to teach them a lesson. The methods of surveillance as a tactic of governance (Foucault, cited in Bandyopadhyay 2010) are also indirectly used by the staff for their own protection.

Formation of Networks in Prison

Survival within the prison depends on the informal networks that women are able to create and sustain, both within and outside the prison. The recidivists are particularly dependent on their 'gangs' or work groups for safety and for support through the legal process. Some of the women interact only with their own group members. Due to the close association between them, they largely keep to themselves and do not allow others to be a part of their group.

When other women prisoners are around, they speak in low voices. One of them is usually the most dominant and dictates instructions to the group. Due to such associations, young women, especially those with no stable family outside, feel supported and protected by the group to which they belong. As one woman, who regularly commits thefts, said:

> My family has completely dismissed me. Apart from the thefts I committed, my life was also at threat at some point due to my involvement with a married man. There were attempts on my life twice, but I was saved as I got information beforehand and informed my lawyer. He has a good network with the police. He got me arrested and sent me to prison for my safety. Now I can think of some future options as my friends here have good contacts.

The group members have their contacts both inside and outside the prison. Their contacts include bar owners, agents who arrange for escorts for businessmen, gang-lords, police officials, lawyers, and others who are a part of the nexus in the criminal world. This demonstrates the complex and layered niches within which the prison as a system is positioned in society. Although prison is intended as a space to isolate an offender from her gang, it functions as a node in the larger networks of crime. This is due to the significant amount of time that women spend with each other in prison. The prison becomes a space of incubation of pathways to crime, rather than isolation from it.

Support from Gang Leaders

Prison conditions prove to be a major determinant of whether one is likely to become a professional criminal, since they provide an environment in which prisoners can socialise with each other. With prisoners being stuck inside such a small space for years, there is plenty to talk about, including various crimes and techniques. This often leads to the creation of gangs within prisons. Wacquant (2001, 111), based on his work in Europe, highlights that 'ethnically based street gangs and "super gangs" such as the Disciplines, El Rukn, Vice Lords... have taken over the illicit prison economy and de-stablised the entire social system of inmates, forcing a shift from "doing your own time" to "doing gang time"'.

Some of the women who have a strong hold over illegal businesses outside the prison are on the lookout for smart young girls to be part of their activities. Two such financially strong women buy favours from the young girls by getting them snacks from the canteen and helping them with their bail money. In return, they contact the confidantes of these women outside the prison.

One such woman is referred to as 'mummy', which is equivalent to the status given to a famous don, fondly referred to as 'daddy' (Bose 2016). Most women in prison are in awe of her due to her stronghold over even the prison staff. One of the women, who keeps her distance with them, shared:

> They all address her as Mummy and touch her feet. I don't. Some also work for her. They wash her clothes, utensils, and keep her space clean. In return, she pays them and buys them food from canteen. She has paid bail amounts for many such girls and they work for her business when they get released. I heard that [name of one of the inmates], who recently delivered a child, was not only bailed out by her, but also provided with accommodation. Now she works for her outside.

The prison has become a second home for some repeat offenders, who are aware of the weaknesses of the prison system and use them to their advantage. They continue to wield the authority and power they had outside the prison by collaborating with some corrupt members of the criminal justice system. Such collaborations not only protect them, but also enable them to use the prison as a recruitment ground to further their illegal work outside the prison. I situate the sense of agency among recidivists within such practices.

Perceptions of Women Recidivists

Dominant perceptions of women recidivists and their behaviour in prison are critical in framing how these women are treated.

The separation of prisoners is a key organisational practice. Bandyopadhyay (2010, 15) highlights that prison authorities distinguish between the 'habitual criminals' or the professionals and the first-time offenders. Accepting that the former group is likely to create problems, one officer pointed out:

> We are here to keep the habitual criminals in control. They are the clever ones. They are the ones who have come to prison before. They know the way around here. They can and do teach others a thing or two about living here and living well. The first timers learn from them. That is why it is essential to keep them apart. Security has to be tight because of them. (ibid.)

One of the jailors from our fieldwork articulated this prejudiced view of recidivist prisoners: 'Now look at her [pointing a finger towards one of the respondents]. Is she worried in life? These women have gone out of hand. You can't bring them back. They are our regular customers in prison and we treat them as such.'

Another jailor, who has seven years of experience in the prison department, joins in the conversation:

> See, madam. They have learnt the tricks of making easy and quick money. They can't work hard like us. Plus, they have multiple relations and addictions. How can they survive with a meagre income like us? Once they make a good amount of money, they enjoy their life. When their money gets over, they go in for another catch. It is a vicious cycle. They will never come out of it. Take it from me in writing.

In contrast, some of the women recidivists who are *regulars* in prison and are trusted are given certain privileges by the staff, such as a share of the special food that comes for some prisoners, getting an extra egg or fruit, permission to stay out during *bandi* (which gives them an extended sense of freedom denied to others), etc. They are given certain important responsibilities in prison, such as gathering the inmates and giving them instructions on work, assembling them for the total, taking care of the children of the prison staff, distributing food to the inmates, and most important of all, keeping activities in check to avoid violence among inmates. Such practices are a marker of their relationship with the authorities in prison and give them importance in the eyes of the prisoner community. Through such practices, the prison staff co-opt the women recidivists in the management of the prison.

A senior male prison official, who is responsible for the overall maintenance of the prison, says: 'Nearly 25 per cent of the women in our prison are repeaters.' He takes some names and says this one is an 'original'. He says that in the case of such women (women belonging to the Pardhi community), crime is in their blood. He mentions another woman and says that she has seventeen to eighteen cases against her. She also files cases in high courts against the decision of the lower benches. He says:

> These women commit thefts of Rs 3 to 4 lakh, then it is okay if they get arrested, they earn so much money without any hard work that it is okay for them to stay in prison. And once they come in the record of the police, it doesn't matter to them whether they commit crime or not, because the police implicate them in one case or the other. So they feel it is better to commit crime and come inside the jail than entering the jail without doing anything (crime).

The police and the prison staff who deal with repeat offenders see little scope for change in them. These findings concur with Massin's analysis of girls in Belgian reform schools between 1920 and 1975 (2015, 287). She found that women were either labelled rebels or were construed as victims and subdued girls, who had to be put on the right track.

Conclusion: Prison as a Contested Site

The prison is considered a formal organisation where practices are regulated within the legal framework of the prison manual. Although this structured life is a given, various everyday practices of the inmates, such as disobeying the jailors, the financially strong prisoners engaging the services of the poorer and weaker ones, physical closeness with other inmates, and remaining outside the prison barracks during bandi time (for those prisoners trusted by the staff), are expressions of the subversion of prison rules and regulations. Formal and informal practices within the prison coexist and merge in everyday prison practice.

Most women recidivists retain their 'selfhood' (some control over what one does or maintaining one's dignity) in most of their actions (Bandyopadhyay 2010, 140). These can be seen as strategies to cope with incarceration—bringing in a sense of normality to an otherwise branded pathological existence. Women recidivists form networks with actors within and outside prison (inmates, jailors, lawyers, agents, etc.) in the criminal justice system. This is a conscious effort to reclaim their lost agency within the prison. The spaces within prison that characterise an apparent isolation from society are actually nodes in the larger networks of crime, and are used as recruitment grounds to further the illegal work outside the prison. This shows that imprisonment facilitates a learning environment and reinforces recidivism, with the negotiations of women recidivists leading to the blurring of boundaries between the inside and the outside. The punitive prison conditions do not have a deterrent effect on the women, thus rendering the prison goals ineffective.

The prison staff, too, have a prejudiced attitude towards the women recidivists, believing that they are there to form illegal contacts and use them outside to make easy money. Prison officers see them as 'originals', implying that they were born to be criminals, and thus see no scope for reform in them. The staff in no way tries to reform women or prevent them from committing crimes.

The women recidivists and the staff, who enjoy privileges in the prison, do not question the practices of governance as long as they are able to manipulate the system to their advantage. The constant surveillance enforced on the inmates to control them is indirectly used to protect the staff from the collective resistance of the prisoners. Prison staff negotiate their authority to some extent and co-opt the women recidivists in tactics of prison management, within relationships of mutual respectability between themselves and the women recidivists.

Endnotes

1. This chapter is based on the doctoral thesis of the first author, which studied recidivism and its dimensions among women offenders in Mumbai, and the impact of criminal justice processing on recidivism among women.

2. Bentham's Panoptican stemmed from a regime of visibility, and it became Foucault's (1979) groundbreaking work. It was an architectural solution, optimising surveillance for factories, hospitals, schools, and prisons. The prisoners under surveillance are situated in cells located in a circle around a tower in the building's centre. While prisoners are unable to look into the tower, the surveillance agent is able to look into the cells. In such a setting, round-the-clock surveillance is not necessary to establish discipline. As Foucault argues, there is an implicit uncertainty of the timing and duration of surveillance. It is this uncertainty that makes inmates constantly experience the surveillant's gaze, and thus discipline (Baumgarten and Ullrich 2011).

References

Ahuja, R. 1969. *Female Offenders in India.* Meerut: Meenakshi Prakashan.

American Civil Liberties Union. 2004. *The Forgotten Population: A Look at Death Row in the United States through the Experiences of Women*. New York.

Bajpai, A., and P. Bajpai. 2000. *Female Criminality in India*. Jaipur: Rawat Publications.

Bandyopadhyay, M. 2010. *Everyday Life in a Prison: Confinement, Surveillance and Resistance*. New Delhi: Orient BlackSwan.

Baumgarten, B., and P. Ullrich. 2011. 'Discourse, Power, and Governmentality. Social Movement Research with and beyond Foucault'. Available at https://www.researchgate.net/publication/299398010_Discourse_Power_and_Governmentality_Social_Movement_Research_with_and_beyond_Foucault (accessed February 2022).

Bilimoria, R. 1987. *Female Criminality: An Empirical Study in Andhra Pradesh*. Lucknow: Eastern Book Company.

Bonta, J., B. Pang, and S. Wallace-Capretta. 1995. 'Predictors of Recidivism among Incarcerated Female Offenders'. *The Prison Journal* 75 (3), 277–295.

Bose, A. 2016. 'Daddy: The Arun Gawli Story'. Available at https://livingtotellatale.wordpress.com/2016/11/29/daddy-the-arun-gawli-story/ (accessed December 2021).

Bosworth, M. 1999. *Engendering Resistance: Agency and Power in Women's Prisons.* Aldershot, Brookfield USA, Singapore, Sydney: Ashgate, Dartmouth.

Bottos, S. 2007. *Women and Violence: Theory, Risk, and Treatment Implications*. Available at http://www.csc-scc.gc.ca/research/092/r198-eng.pdf (accessed November 2021).

Butler, J. 1990. *Gender Trouble: Feminism and the Subversion of Identity*. New York: Routledge.

Carvalho, R., and J. Bierens. 2002. *A Competing Risk Analysis of Recidivism*. Available at https://pdfs.semanticscholar.org/abe9/ae30caf10acd94cb4d6619873d44dfba445d.pdf (accessed November 2021).

Chatterji, S. 2009. 'A study of women who have been convicted of committing crimes against women in Nashik Jail'. M. A. Thesis, Tata Institute of Social Sciences, Mumbai.

Cherukuri, J. 2008. *Women in Prison: An Insight into Captivity and Crime.* Cambridge: Cambridge University Press.

Chockalingam, K. 1983. 'Recidivism among Adult Offenders'. *Indian Journal of Social Work* 44 (1), 81–86.

Clemmer, D. 1940. *The Prison Community.* New York: Holt, Rinehart & Winston.

Corcoran, Mary S. 2007. 'Normalisation and its discontents: Constructing the irreconcilable political prisoner in Northern Ireland'. *British Journal of Criminology* 47 (3), 405–422.

Denney, A., R. Tewksbury, and R. Jones. 2014. *Beyond Basic Needs: Social Support and Structure for Successful Offender Reentry*. Available at https://epublications.marquette.edu/cgi/viewcontent.cgi?article=1096&context=socs_fac (accessed November 2021).

Dobbs, R., and A. Courtney. 2004. 'Prison Culture'. In *Encyclopedia of Prisons and Correctional Facilities*, 720–724. Thousand Oaks, CA: Sage Publications.

Fili, A. 2013. 'Women in Prison: Victims or Resisters? Representations of Agency in Women's Prisons in Greece'. *Signs: Journal of Women in Culture and Society* 39 (1), 1–26.

Foucault, M. 1979. *Discipline and Punish. The Birth of the Prison*. New York: Vintage Books.

Gilfus, M. 1992. 'From Victims to Survivors to Offenders: Women's Routes of Entry and Immersion into Street Crime'. *Women and Criminal Justice* 4 (1), 63–89.

Gottfredson, M., and T. Hirschi. 1986. 'The true value of lambda would appear to be zero: An essay on career criminals, criminal careers, selective incapacitation, cohort studies, and related topics'. *Criminology* 24, 213–233.

———. 1988. 'Science, public policy, and the career paradigm'. *Criminology* 26, 35–55.

Government of India. 2003. *Model Prison Manual for the Superintendence and Management of Prisons in India*. New Delhi: Bureau of Police Research and Development, Ministry of Home Affairs. Available at http://bprd.nic.in/WriteReadData/userfiles/file/5230647148-Model%20Prison%20Manual.pdf (accessed November 2021).

———. 2014. *Report on the Evaluation of Crime and Criminal Tracking Network and Systems Project*. Ministry of Home Affairs, GoI. Available at https://mha.gov.in/sites/default/files/IIPA-Report-CCTNS.pdf (accessed November 2021).

Hoffman, D. 1999. 'Turning Power Inside Out: Reflections on Resistance from the (Anthropological) Field'. *International Journal of Qualitative Studies in Education* 12 (6), 671–687.

Irwin, J. 1980. *Prisons in Turmoil*. Boston: Little, Brown.

Johnson, R. 2011. '11 Stunning Facts about America's Prisons'. *Business Insider*, 23 July. Available at https://www.businessinsider.com/11-facts-about-prisons-2011-7?IR=T (accessed November 2021).

Krishnan, V. 2017. *Modernisation of Police Forces*. Available at https://prsindia.org/theprsblog/modernisation-of-police-forces (accessed December 2021).

Kruttschnitt, C., and K. Carbone-Lopez. 2006. 'Moving Beyond the Stereotypes: Women's Subjective Accounts of Their Violent Crime'. *Criminology* 44, 321–351.

Langan, A. 1985. 'Racism on Trial: New Evidence to Explain the Racial Composition of Prisons in the United States'. *Journal of Criminal Law and Criminology* 76 (3), 666–683.

Langan, P., and D. Levin. 2002. *Recidivism of Prisoners Released in 1994*. Special Report, Bureau of Justice Statistics, US Department of Justice. Available at https://www.bjs.gov/content/pub/pdf/rpr94.pdf (accessed November 2021).

Maltz, M. 2001. *Recidivism*. Orlando, Florida: Academic Press.

Massin, V. 2015. *Hearing the Voices of Delinquent Girls in Belgian Reform Schools (1920–1970)*. Available at http://www.academia.edu/19711665/Hearing_the_Voices_of_Delinquent_Girls_in_Belgian_Reform_Schools_1920-1970 (accessed November 2021).

Maycock, M., and K. Hunt (eds). 2018. *New Perspectives on Prison Masculinities*. London: Palgrave Macmillan.

Miller, S. 2005. *Victims as Offenders: The Paradox of Women's Violence in Relationships*. New Brunswick: Rutgers University Press.

Mishra, L., and B. Gautam. 1982. 'Female Criminality: Causes and Consequence'. *Readings in Criminology*, Souvenir Volume. Calcutta.

Naffine, N. 1996. *Feminism and Criminology*. Cambridge: Polity.

Narasappa, H., and S. Vidyasagar. 2016. *Access to Justice Survey 2015–16*. Bengaluru: DAKSH and EBC.

National Crime Records Bureau (NCRB). 1990, 1995, 1996, 2006, 2012–2014. *Crime in India*. Available at:
https://ncrb.gov.in/en/crime-india-year-1990
https://ncrb.gov.in/en/crime-india-year-1995
https://ncrb.gov.in/en/crime-india-year-1996
https://ncrb.gov.in/en/crime-india-year-2006
https://ncrb.gov.in/en/crime-india-year-2012
https://ncrb.gov.in/en/crime-india-year-2013
https://ncrb.gov.in/en/crime-india-year-2014 (accessed December 2021).

———. 2015. *Prison Statistics—2015*. Available at https://ncrb.gov.in/sites/default/files/PSI-2015-%2018-11-2016_0.pdf (accessed December 2021).

Neminski, M. 2014. 'The Professionalization of Crime: How Prisons Create More Criminals'. *Boston University Core Journal* 23, 81–83.

Penal Reform International. 2008. 'Women in prison: Incarcerated in a man's world'. *Penal Reform Briefing No. 3*. Available at https://cdn.penalreform.org/wp-content/uploads/2013/06/brf-03-2008-women-in-prison-en.pdf (accessed November 2021).

Pew Centre on the States. 2011. *State of Recidivism: The Revolving Door of America's Prisons*. Available at https://www.michigan.gov/documents/corrections/Pew_Report_State_of_Recidivism_350337_7.pdf (accessed November 2021).

Prasad, S. 1982. 'A study of women murderers in Tamil Nadu'. *Readings in Criminology*, Souveneir Volume. Indian Society of Criminology.

Quadrelli, C. 2003. 'Aberrance, Agency and Social Construction of Women Offenders'. School of Justice Studies, Faculty of Law, Queensland University of Technology. Available at https://eprints.qut.edu.au/15849/1/Carol_Quadrelli_Thesis.pdf (accessed November 2021).

Quinney, R. 1975. *Criminology: Analysis and Critique of Crime in America*, Boston: Little, Brown & Co.

Radhakrishnan, M. 2012. 'The Dynamics of Recidivism in Andhra Pradesh'. *Sociological Bulletin* 61 (3), 450–464.

Raghavan, V. 2010. *Youth Arrested in Extortion Cases in Mumbai City: Processes of Entry and After*. Mumbai: Tata Institute of Social Sciences.

______. 2014. 'Prison Reforms: Historical and Contemporary Perspectives'. In K. Jaishankar, T. Mukherjee, and P. Bharadwaj (eds), *Indian Prisons: Towards Reformation, Rehabilitation and Re-socialisation*. New Delhi: Atlantic Publishers and Distributors (P) Ltd.

Rath, B. 2017. 'Let's not take India's crime statistics seriously'. *The Wire*, 4 December. Available at https://thewire.in/government/ncrb-crime-statistics-india (accessed November 2021).

Roberts, E. 2007. 'Constructing a Criminal Justice System Free of Racial Bias: An Abolitionist Framework'. *Columbia Human Rights Law Review* 39 (1), 261–266.

Roebuck, J. B., and G. O. Windham. 1983. 'Professional Theft'. In G. P. Waldo (ed.), *Career Criminals*. New Delhi: Sage Publications.

Sabo, D., T. Kupers, and W. London (eds). 2001. *Prison Masculinities*. Philadelphia: Temple University Press.

Sahni, S. 1988. *Women Prisoners: The Remand and Under-trial Experience*. Mumbai: Tata Institute of Social Sciences.

Schwartz, J., and D. Steffensmeier. 2008. 'Nature of Female Offending: Patterns and Explanation'. In Ruth T. Zaplin (ed.), *Female Offenders: Critical Perspectives and Effective Interventions*, 43–75. US Department of Justice, Office of Justice Programs, 2e. Available at https://www.ojp.gov/ncjrs/virtual-library/abstracts/nature-female-offending-patterns-and-explanation-female-offenders (accessed December 2021).

Shankardass, R. (ed.). 2000. *Punishment and the Prison: Indian and International Perspectives*. New Delhi: SAGE.

Shastri, T. 1976. 'A Study of Women Prisoners and Their Families in Maharashtra'. *Social Defence* XII (46), 31–37.

Shaw, Margaret. 1992. 'Issues of Power and Control: Women in Prison and their Defenders'. *British Journal of Criminology* 32 (4), 438–452.

Sohoni, N. 1989. *Women Behind Bars*. New Delhi: Vikas Publishing House.

Smith, Catrin. 2002. 'Punishment and Pleasure: Women, Food and the Imprisoned Body'. *Sociological Review* 50 (2), 197–214.

Snowball, L., and D. Weatherburn. 2007. 'Does racial bias in sentencing contribute to indigenous overrepresentation in prison?' *Australian & New Zealand Journal of Criminology* 40, 272–290.

Spidle, E. 2017. 'Invisible and Incarcerated: Women in a Male-dominated U. S. Prison System'. *Honors Theses* 87, Union College. Available at https://digitalworks.union.edu/theses/87 (accessed November 2021).

Steffensmeier, D., and E. Allan. 1996. 'Gender and Crime: Towards a Gendered Theory of Female Offending'. *Annual Review of Sociology* 22, 459–487.

Sykes, G. M. 1958. *The Society of Captives.* Princeton, NJ: Princeton University Press.

Thornton, M. 1996. *Dissonance and Distrust: Women in the Legal Profession*. Melbourne: Oxford University Press.

Tiwary, D. 2016. 'Why India has a "low" crime rate'. *The Indian Express*, 12 January. Available at http://indianexpress.com/article/india/india-news-india/why-india-has-a-low-crime-rate/ (accessed November 2021).

Uma, P. 1993. *Impact of Correctional Programmes on Female Prisoners*. Chennai: Department of Criminology, Madras University.

United Nations Office on Drugs and Crime. 2010. *The Bangkok Rules*. Available at https://www.unodc.org/documents/justice-and-prison-reform/Bangkok_Rules_ENG_22032015.pdf (accessed November 2021).

United Nations. 2015a. *Standard Minimum Rules in Treatment of Prisoners (Nelson Mandela Rules)*. Available at http://www.unodc.org/documents/justice-and-prison-reform/Brochure_on_the_UN_SMRs.pdf (accessed November 2021).

———. 2015b. *Universal Declaration of Human Rights*. Available at http://www.un.org/en/udhrbook/pdf/udhr_booklet_en_web.pdf (accessed November 2021).

Wacquant, L. 2001. 'Deadly Symbiosis: When Ghetto and Prison Meet and Mesh'. *Punishment and Society* 3 (1), 95–135.

Part III

Humane Prisons?

Challenges of Governance

Chapter 9
Redesigning Women's Prisons for Correction

Upneet Lalli

Incarceration is one of the severest penal sanctions imposed by the State. It has consequences not only in terms of a loss of liberty, but also in social, psychological, and economic spheres. The consequences are more severe for women prisoners as they face greater social stigma than men for violating the criminal law and challenging gender norms. They continue to remain unseen and neglected as well as one of the most misunderstood sections of our society. Women prisoners are held in a system primarily designed and organised for men. Their numbers are also small, and consequently, their needs remain largely unmet. Drawing on my experiences as an administrator within the prison system in India, in this chapter, I critically analyse some of the underlying issues that women in prison grapple with. I also review the role of the State agencies that have a duty towards these women's safe custody and treatment.

Women inmates in all nations represent an estimated 2–9 per cent of the national prison population in around 80 per cent of the prison systems in the world (Walmsley 2015). According to a report on the World Female Imprisonment List (2017), there were more than 714,000 women held in prisons throughout the world, constituting 6.9 per cent of the global prison population. The report points out that the number of female prisoners has been increasing at a faster rate than that of male prisoners since the year 2000, with the number of women and girls in prison increasing by more than

53 per cent, compared to the male population increase of around 20 per cent.

There is now a growing awareness that the gender-specific needs of women prisoners have to be responded to. On 22 December 2010, the United Nations General Assembly adopted the *United Nations Rules for the Treatment of Female Prisoners and Non-Custodial Measures for Women Offenders*, also known as *The Bangkok Rules* (2010), which provided for the gender-specific needs of women in prison. They are milestones in terms of their recognition of some of the needs of women in prisons, and represent certain global aspirations with the common goal of improving the outcomes for women prisoners. The rules within international conventions cover issues ranging from the classification of women prisoners, to standards of healthcare, safety, and sanitation, hygiene, the treatment of female inmates' children, to non-custodial sanctions. Despite the growing awareness, the prison system still seems unprepared at the ground level for the increasing number of women in prison.

The State has a duty to keep prisoners in its safe custody. 'Prisons' in India is a state subject, as per entry 4 of List II of the Seventh Schedule to the Constitution of India. Therefore, the administration and management of prisons is primarily the responsibility of the state governments. There are wide variations in the prison systems of various states in the country. Article 21 of the Constitution of India, which guarantees the right to life and personal liberty, has been broadly interpreted by the Courts to encompass various rights of prisoners, including right to dignity and access to justice, emphasising the humanisation of prison conditions. There are provisions in the Criminal Procedure Code that specify how women will be arrested and detained. Women prisoners also have the right to equal protection of law and right to dignity. Imprisonment should also meet the requirements of effective rehabilitation and reintegration. In *Sunil Batra v. Delhi Administration (1980)*, the Court declared that a person in prison did not become a non-person.

A Committee was set up by Parliament in 1997 to review and monitor the measures taken by the Union government in the direction of securing for women equality, status, and dignity in all matters. It covered issues relating to women in detention as well. The Committee on Empowerment of Women (2001–2002) gave certain recommendations for women prisoners, which included issues like coloured uniforms for women convicts, separate kitchens for women inmates, provision of sanitary towels for women inmates, etc.

The Committee on Empowerment of Women (2016–2017), which presented its tenth report on *Women in Detention and Access to Justice*, observed that the problems that women encounter in contemporary prisons were connected to their experience of imprisonment as well as with reference to their pre-prison lives. Women prisoners had experienced victimisation, unstable family lives, school and work failure, and substance abuse. Mental health problems and social factors also contributed to their marginalisation and the increase in numbers across prisoners.

Despite the small proportion of women prisoners, the State must instate a gender-responsive system for governing the prison population. Women's biological needs, their family caring responsibilities, and their earlier victimisation in many cases combine to create incarceration experiences that may be quite different from those of men. Imprisonment is disproportionately harsher for women since practices within prison have for the most part been designed for men. The current system is inadequate to meet their requirements and needs to be redesigned keeping in view the various developments that have taken place. The philosophy of imprisonment has changed from confinement and deterrence to rehabilitation and reintegration. *The Nelson Mandela Rules* (2015)[1] emphasise upon the various programmes and treatments that need to be offered by the prison administration to support the social reintegration of prisoners.

Profile of Women Prisoners in India

As per National Crime Records Bureau (NCRB) 2016, the total prison population of India was 433,003. The number of women inmates in India has increased variably in the past few decades. In June 1997, there were 7,268 women held in prisons across the country and 77.85 per cent (5,658) of them were undertrials. The number of young children living with their mothers in prison was 885 in 1997 (NCRB 1997). In the year 2000, there were 9,089 women inmates, that is, 3.3 per cent of the total prison inmate population; the proportion rose marginally to 3.9 per cent in 2005, with 13,986 women inmates, and then at the end of 2010, the number of women inmates was 15,037 (4.1 per cent). The total population of women inmates was 18,498, that is, 4.3 per cent of the total prison population in 2016 (see Table 9.1).

TABLE 9.1: Prison Statistics in 2016

	Male	Female	Total	Percentage
Convicts	129,760	5,923	135,683	31.3%
Undertrials	280,770	12,288	293,058	67.7%
Detenues	2,953	136	3,089	0.7%
Others	1,022	151	1,173	0.3%
Total	**414,505**	**18,498**	**433,003**	

Source: NCRB 2016.

As observed, there has been an upward trend in the rate of women's imprisonment. Relationship problems feature strongly in women's pathways into crime. However, women offenders still constitute a smaller proportion than their male counterparts. In 2015, there were 3,398 women convicts out of a total of 74,821 life convicts in the country undergoing sentence for life imprisonment (NCRB 2015). This accounts for 4.5 per cent of the total prison population (including male and female offenders). A total of 325 convicts, including ten females, lodged in different prisons of the country were serving capital punishment at the end of 2015.

As can be seen from Table 9.2, the proportion of middle-aged women is almost 50 per cent to the younger age group of around 31 per cent of women prisoners. The prison regime has also to take into account the needs of all age groups. There are women who may

Table 9.2: Age-wise Distribution of Female Prisoners

Age Group	Convicts	Undertrials	Detenues	Others	Total	%
18–30 Years	1,387	4,325	41	100	5,853	31.6%
30–50 Years	3,146	5,967	83	44	9,240	50.0%
50 Years and Above	1,390	1,996	12	07	3,405	18.4%

Source: NCRB 2016.
Note: The female inmates' population also includes foreign female inmates.

be pregnant or nursing, middle-aged and older women (who may be mothers-in-law, in prison primarily for their daughters-in-law's death due to dowry demands), all of whom need to be cared for. In the course of my work as an administrator, I have come across women inmates who are visually impaired and some who are partially paralysed. What correctional programmes and interventions can be offered for such inmates?

Women's Prisons in India

The Justice V. R. Krishna Iyer Committee (1986) studied the condition of women in custody and recommended separate institutions for women offenders. Women convicts who are shifted to the women's prisons—which is sometimes only one in every state—may end up losing contact with their families. In the state of Uttar Pradesh, for instance, the women's prison is located in Lucknow and the convicts, when shifted there, may be almost 400 kms away from their homes. Hence, Rule 4 in *The Bangkok Rules* (2010) asserts that women prisoners should be allocated to prisons close to their homes or places of social rehabilitation. The need to update the *Model Prison Manual* (2003) was stressed by the Supreme Court in the Public Interest Litigation (PIL) on *Re: Inhuman Conditions in 1382 Prisons* (2013).

The new *Model Prison Manual* (2016), which serves as a benchmark to be adopted by all states so as to ensure uniformity in laws governing prisons, has incorporated *The Bangkok Rules* and made provisions in the chapter on women prisoners. As per Chapter XXIV, it is required that at least one women's prison be established in each state to ensure the safety of women prisoners and to guard them against any form of exploitation. The provision of separate enclosures for women inmates has also been proposed. Provisions for segregation, security, pregnancy, childbirth, and family care, healthcare, and rehabilitation for women prisoners have been covered in this chapter.

There are twenty exclusively women's prisons in India. Not every state has an exclusive prison for women. States like Haryana, Himachal Pradesh, and Madhya Pradesh do not have an exclusive women's prison, whereas Tamil Nadu and Kerala have five and three women's prisons, respectively. India has sixty-four open prisons, out of which only two are exclusively for women, that is, Yerawada Open Prison and the Women's Open Prison in Trivandrum (NCRB 2016). However, the Durgapura and Sanganer open camps in Rajasthan do take in a few women inmates (Gopinathan 2017). Women are not lodged in open prisons on grounds of 'protection', a practice which discriminates against women prisoners. In a PIL, *Sunil Kumar Gupta v. Government of NCT of Delhi and Ors.* (2017), the Delhi High Court questioned the discriminatory practice of denying the right of open prisons to women inmates by equating them with hard-core prisoners, who were at risk of escape and therefore not made eligible for a move to semi-open jails. The state of Delhi changed its rules to end this discrimination against women inmates. The semi-open prison for women in Delhi was opened recently, in June 2019 (Lakhani 2019).

Table 9.3 shows that except for Delhi, Bihar, Maharashtra, and West Bengal, there is no overcrowding in the exclusive women's prisons. However, some of the district jails or central jails where women are held are overcrowded in states like Chhattisgarh, Uttar Pradesh, Rajasthan, and Bihar.

Most of the women prisoners are poor, uneducated, and unskilled, and they come from marginalised sections of society. Around 122,984 out of a total 433,003 prison population, lodged in

TABLE 9.3: Women's Prisons in India

State/UT	Number of Women's Prisons	Total Capacity of Inmates	Inmate Population
Tamil Nadu	5	2,018	546
Kerala	3	272	142
Rajasthan	2	450	227
Andhra Pradesh	1	160	99
Bihar	1	83	110
Gujarat	1	210	100
Maharashtra	1	262	307
Odisha	1	52	25
Punjab	1	320	165
Telangana	1	250	218
Uttar Pradesh	1	420	265
West Bengal	1	300	366
Delhi	1	400	552
Total	**20**	**5,197**	**3,122**

Source: NCRB 2016.

various prisons in the country, were reported as illiterate, and 181,672 were reported to not have finished education till the tenth grade. These two categories accounted for 28.4 per cent and 42 per cent of the total prison population, respectively (NCRB 2016). Women entering and exiting the criminal justice system are incredibly disempowered. Women inherently have a lower status in society and the label of criminality places them far below the average woman. They also become objects of curiosity, and often, the ones who are well-known have the media following them every time they go to the court for their trial.

Gender roles also result in a particular stigma being attached only to women prisoners, which further contributes to their discrimination and oppression. For women charged with the murder of their husbands or children, life can almost come to a standstill, with no hope of redemption. Sometimes, due to patriarchal control, they are caught in a vicious circle and move from one imprisoned life to another. After their release, they are shunned, and some of them do not want to be released at all due to the fear of social ostracism. Most painful for them is when their families refuse to accept them. This is quite different in the case of male prisoners. Even men convicted for offences like rape may not be shunned in a similar manner by their families in comparison with women, who are seen to have defied social norms.

Access to Justice

Women inmates experience multiple layers of discrimination in all spheres of life, and particularly in the justice system. Most women inmates do not understand the legal proceedings. Free legal aid is mandated by the law, but the quality of legal aid is poor. Research in India has underlined that pre-trial detention is ordered in a significant number of petty cases and that prison costs could be considerably decreased if petty offenders were kept out of pre-trial detention. While bail is a right, pre-trial detention is sometimes not a function of the risk of absconding or obstruction of justice but rather a result of the economic condition, which prevents suspects from paying even small amounts of bail. Many a times, women undertrials report that their lawyers do not follow up with their cases. To add to their woes, they may not have someone to give a surety or money to deposit the bail amount as fixed by the court. Often, women who may have been granted bail are unable to furnish the surety, and hence remain confined inside. It is hoped that with the constitution of Undertrial Review Committees,[2] access to justice would improve for women inmates. Women are generally perceived as ignorant of the prison rules of remission, parole, and premature release. Legal help in this regard would alleviate their stress about their uncertain future. Rule 2 of *The Bangkok Rules* (2010) states that special attention should be paid during admission procedures for women and children. They should be provided with facilities such as contact with family, access to legal advice, and information about prison rules and regulations in a language that they understand.

Prison Staff

Prison staff is responsible for the safe custody and treatment of prisoners. The total female staff in the prisons of India, towards the end of 2016, for 18,498 women inmates was 5,150, and this included superintendents, deputy superintendents, assistant superintendents, medical staff, warders, and other correctional staff (NCRB 2016). Although prisons have been renamed as *sudhar ghar*s or correctional centres, the correctional staff strength is too inadequate. There were only thirty-four female probation and welfare officers, six psychiatrists/psychologists, and sixty-two social workers. There were only 314 women medical staff, which included medical officers, pharmacists, lab technicians, and other medical staff (ibid.). The ratio of women prisoners to medical staff was as high as 65:5 in West Bengal and 21:5 in Maharashtra. Delhi was the best placed, with a ratio of 2:6 (ibid.). Some states like Maharashtra and Tamil Nadu now have a provision for recruiting 33 per cent women staff, so the strength of women staff is increasing in these states, while other states have a shortage of women staff, especially at the assistant and deputy superintendent levels.

The low ratio of women staff has implications for the way women inmates are supervised and cared for. The author, while conducting training programmes for prison staff, has often found that prison staff invariably complain that women inmates are more troublesome and difficult to deal with as compared to male inmates. They are unaware of the emotional impact that imprisonment has on women. Hence, there is a greater need for gender sensitisation of staff, both male and female, so that they may effectively understand the issues confronting women prisoners.

The human element is important for bringing in reforms in the system. Rule 29 of *The Bangkok Rules* states:

> Capacity-building for staff employed in women's prisons shall enable them to address the special social reintegration requirements of women prisoners and manage safe and rehabilitative facilities. Capacity building measures for women staff shall also include access to senior positions with key responsibility for the development of policies and strategies relating to the treatment and care of women prisoners.

There were only twenty-eight women officers at the senior level, that is, at the superintendent level and above (NCRB 2016). The discussions with female staff during the various training programmes conducted by the author at the Institute of Correctional Administration, Chandigarh point towards gender biases and fewer opportunities for promotion at a higher level. In 2017, the first Conference on Role of Uniformed Women in Prison Service was organised by the Bureau of Police Research and Development (BPRD) to discuss and focus on the issues of women staff working in prisons. I was also associated with the conference. During the different panel discussions, the staff requested that separate toilets and changing rooms, crèches and child support facilities, and appropriate accommodation in prison premises be made available for the female prison staff. Some flexibility in working hours was also recommended for pregnant women officers. In the coming years, there will be more women in prison service and the system will have to be responsive to their issues as well.

Space for Women Inmates

Imprisonment confines an individual within a small, specified, controlled space for a prescribed time period. The space for women prisoners in central and district prisons and sub-jails, where both male and female prisoners are housed, is limited. Men and women occupy space differently. Male prisoners have greater opportunities to explore the prison space, which they utilise by visiting the prison canteen, temple, or library; working in the prison factory, farm, or office; attending classes or vocational training in other parts of the prison; and participating in sports. Women have minimal opportunities as they mostly remain confined to the barracks. The women's barracks are also quite small, just enough to accommodate them. Sometimes, there is no place to play games, no separate canteen, and women cannot visit the temple, library, or even the garden. For women within prisons, the space is constricted, allowing little or no opportunity to explore.

Seth (2004), in her study on the conditions of women in prison, pointed out the problem of overcrowding in the prisons of Punjab. The number of women prisoners was more than double the original sanctioned strength in all the jails. She reported that because of a lack of space in some prisons of Punjab, a number of women slept on the floor. In fact, the area in which women were kept was very small, leaving them with insufficient place to even walk. As a result, their muscles slackened and pain in the legs was common due to a lack of physical activity. During my visits to various prisons, I observed that smaller and limited spaces lead to frustration and conflict, which find expression in squabbles for some women, while the coping mechanism for others is withdrawal. The regular occurrence of squabbles normalises such conflictual interactions within the prison space, and women prisoners begin to accept them as part and parcel of their everyday life. During the research on the *Survey of Quality of Life of Women Prisoners*, I observed that many women inmates, while speaking about the cause of conflicts inside, used expressions like '*jahan do bartan honge to awaaz to hogi hi*' (wherever there are two utensils, noise is inevitable). One woman even said: '*ek chup sua such*'(keeping silent serves to avoid any dispute).

Overcrowding and Redesigning Space

There is a dire need to redesign prisons and prison regimes, as imprisonment affects women differently than it does men. While the number of women prisoners is increasing at a high rate, their needs and rights are not being fulfilled simultaneously. The women's barracks located within the main prisons are normally small and often located at the end of the prison, and that is all the area the women have to move around. There are no activity rooms and limited opportunities for self-development. Restrictions are placed on their visits to the prison library or prison canteen, located within the main prison complex. One prison had a bakery unit, and while women were keen to work there, only male inmates had the privilege of access to working there. Women inmates in India also have no space to claim as their own, in which to keep their personal belongings. Their bags and packets are kept near the sleeping berth or, in many prisons, hung on the wall, and there is no privacy. Disputes amongst inmates concerning the handling of personal items do arise. It is quite humiliating for women to change in the presence of others, particularly during menstruation.

Bhandari (2015), in her research on women prisoners in Rajasthan, found that 63.89 per cent women stated that their cells were overcrowded and 94.44 per cent women stated that there were no educational programmes conducted, or that they were unaware of any such programmes. It was also observed that 96.11 per cent respondents stated that there was no mechanism available for grievance redressal.

Indian prisons provide no space to display women's belongings, such as pictures and photographs. I was pleasantly surprised to see that in Dochas prison in Ireland, in prisons in the United Kingdom and in Boronia in Perth, Australia, the inmates had their own personal spaces where they displayed photographs of loved family members, and children's pictures and artwork. In fact, the Dochas prison was hailed as a beacon of progress (its very name means 'hope'). Accommodation is arranged in 'houses' catering to almost a dozen people. The prison management encourages the women to take responsibility for their lives and provides a better environment for self-exploration and independence. In India, open prisons provide this opportunity, but are limited in number for women inmates.

Security concerns continue to dominate prison architecture. Women inmates are considered to pose no serious security risk and there are very few instances of women attempting to escape; yet invariably the prisons housing them are designed with these security concerns as ordering principles. Prison architecture and regime are inclined towards the punitive end of the spectrum, with the focus remaining on security and control. The Government of India started the Modernisation of Prison Scheme in 2002–2003 for five years with an outlay of Rs 1,800 crore, and this gave a major thrust to strengthening prison infrastructure. The Union government and state governments contributed funds for this scheme with a cost-sharing ratio of 75:25. These funds were used for the construction of new prisons, expansion and renovation of existing prisons, construction of staff quarters, and increasing civic amenities in all existing prisons. The scheme was implemented in twenty-seven states and was extended for a further two years. Under this mega-project, 125 new prisons and additional barracks and prison staff quarters were added to the existing infrastructure (Ministry of Home Affairs 2011).

However, there was no engagement with the end users: the prisoners and the staff. The author has seen some new prisons, in which even the school area is all grills and bars. There was no creativity in the design and it totally lacked a humane approach. In fact, far too many iron bars had been used in one prison, and when we asked why, we were told that it was a measure to strengthen security.

There is a need to develop an 'architecture of hope', instead of making the environment too despondent. Why can women prisons not have a play area, where the women can find some outlet through physical activity? Studies show that green areas reduce stress, and when you care for plants and nurture their growth, it reduces violence and promotes well-being (Linden 2015). Having courtyards and gardens will be healing for the mothers and children as well. In India, there are no mother-baby units, which are common in European prisons. Sometimes mothers have been separated from their children and placed in solitary confinement cells. The author has seen the pre-release centre of Boronia, Perth, which offers support to low-security women prisoners and prepares them for reintegration into the community. They are housed in an environment which closely resembles life outside of prisons. There are cottages, green areas, a meditation centre facility, a café, and a mini store to purchase necessary items, all in a community-style setting, which recognises the diverse needs of the women in prisons.

Developing such a system requires a radical change in the philosophy of punishment and imprisonment. While designing and constructing new prison facilities, the prison administration should ensure that there is ample physical space, infrastructure, and equipment to provide high-quality rehabilitation. Modernisation activities, if properly organised, can increase rehabilitation opportunities for prisoners.

Mothering Role and Children

At the end of 2016, there were 1,942 children living in prisons with their mothers, who numbered 1,649 (convicted, undertrial, detenues, and other). This accounted for 8.9 per cent of the total female prison population. In 2016, a total of 400 women convicts with their 459 children, and 1,192 women undertrials with their 1,409 children were lodged in various prisons in the country.

Motherhood and imprisonment, and its consequences for dependent children, is a critical area of discussion. Different countries show a variation in rules permitting children to stay with their imprisoned mothers. In some countries like China and Russia, mothers are not permitted to carry their children with them inside the prison. In countries like Hungary, Japan, and Romania, children are allowed to live with their imprisoned mothers till the age of one year, whereas in South Korea and Nigeria, children can live with their mothers up to the age of eighteen months. In some countries like Eritrea, there is no age limit for children. A vast majority of countries allow women to have children with them up to the age of six (Robertson 2012). In India, the prison manual permits children to live with their incarcerated mothers until the age of six. Globally, the provision has always sparked debate: Should children be allowed to live with their imprisoned mothers at all? It is believed that allowing children to spend their formative years in prison would negatively impact their physical as well as mental development.

While some attempts have been made to frame policies for the children of prisoners, there is no focus on the rights of the mothers in prison. Both parenting in the coercive prison environment and the pain of separation from children have a host of adverse psychological consequences, on women prisoners as well as on children. Since women are detained in institutions that are designed primarily for men, there is limited flexibility for nursing mothers. Children are locked up with their mothers during lock-up time, even during the day. The incarceration of women can have an adverse impact on the children (Lalli 2013). Once a child turns six, s/he has to be produced before the Child Welfare Committee (CWC) as they fall under the category of a child in need of care and protection, in case there is no one to look after them as mandated by the Juvenile Justice (Care and Protection of Children) Act 2015. Separation from the child is equally traumatic for the mother, unless she is assured of the child's well-being and regular contact is maintained with the child. A study conducted by Chattoraj (2000) revealed the pathetic conditions and deprivations faced by the children lodged with their mothers in different prisons in India. The children were deprived of care and basic facilities such as education, health, nutrition, and recreation in the prison.

In *R. D. Upadhyay v. State of Andhra Pradesh & Ors.* (AIR 2006 SC 1946), the Supreme Court issued directions for the minimum standards of treatment of pregnant women and for the children of women prisoners living in prisons. The court ordered that before sending a pregnant woman to prison, the concerned authorities must ensure that the prison in question has the basic minimum facilities for child delivery as well as provisions for pre-natal and post-natal care for both mother and child. Other guidelines issued stated that any gynaecological examination of female prisoners should be performed in the district government hospitals. Another important direction was that pregnant women in jails should be allowed to give birth outside the prison facility (except in some extreme cases), to ensure that the newborn received proper care.

Further, in some cases arrangements were made for temporary release/parole (or a suspended sentence in the case of minors and casual offenders) to enable an expectant prisoner to deliver her baby outside the prison. Only exceptional cases constituting high-security risks could be denied this facility.

There have been some improvements, but the situation is still far from fulfilling any basic norms of humane prisons. As a result of the Supreme Court guidelines, crèches have been opened up within some of the prisons, and birth certificates are issued without mentioning the prison as the place of birth. There needs to be proper monitoring of the crèches and the conditions inside. A news item in *The Hindu* (20 May 2018) reported that forty-six boys and girls were living with their incarcerated mothers in prisons in Odisha. They had no access to court-mandated welfare, and were not going to school. Effectively, the children in prison also serve time along with their mother's sentence as they remain confined to the prison itself. Very few superintendents make the effort of letting the children go on picnics or see the outside world; this adversely affects their cognitive growth and development. The author has seen during her visits to various prisons that invariably, CWC members themselves do not visit the prisons regularly to look after the best interests of these children. In India, there is a need to emphasise non-custodial sentences for pregnant women and women with young children.[3]

Constricted Use of Time and Correctional Programmes

It comes as no surprise that many of the barracks lodging women have no clock or calendar. Time seems to stand still behind the high prison walls and iron bars. The only time that is of relevance seems to be that of lock-up and lock-out, the counting or *ginti* time, the time to go to court, or the day of the *mulaqat* (weekly meetings). The undertrials have their court dates, which they look forward to in the hope of early release. However, for them the period of detention is most uncertain and stressful. For the convicts serving life sentences (nearly 50 per cent of the inmates), time stretches on. There are no initiatives directed towards the constructive use of time inside the prison. The prison structure and routine govern the everyday lives of women prisoners. The work they are assigned conforms to female stereotypes and replicates household routine, with little creativity, which will not necessarily enable them to earn any livelihood after their release.

Spending sufficient time engaged in meaningful educational or vocational training activities or productive work forms what *The Nelson Mandela Rules* (2015) call the 'normal occupational life', which prison administrations should seek to establish. Leading a busy life in prison can help reduce the risk of depression and other mental health problems among the prisoners, and can enable them to lead an independent life afterwards. One of the effects of 'institutionalisation' is learned helplessness, especially seen in women inmates.

With no purposeful activity, prisons cannot be rehabilitative. As per the NCRB (2016), only 13.4 per cent inmates were imparted various vocational training by the jail authorities during 2016. Only 20 percent of the prisoners are involved in work programmes (Lalli 2015), and the percentage is much less amongst women prisoners. Hence, they mostly do not earn wages and even when they do, they are unaware of it. For instance, they do not know the wage rates or the rules regarding how they can use the money and when it can be withdrawn. Usually, they only know that the wages have been deposited in their accounts.

Correctional programmes for women in prisons should be more gender-sensitive, based on a risk and needs assessment. Further, only those staff who have strong interpersonal skills should deal with the prisoners, and necessary training should be given to the staff in this regard. Since women are the major care-providers for their children, there should be greater opportunities given to women with children, along with programmes for reintegration.

Safety, Security, and Dignity

In Indian prisons, only women staff are allowed in the women's barracks. No male staff can enter without a female staff being present. There are a number of safeguards to ensure the safety of women prisoners, and to avoid incidents of sexual abuse of women. The locks of the enclosures and barracks where women are confined are different from those in use in other parts of the prisons, so that there is no possibility of the keys for the locks of other enclosures being misused for opening the enclosures of women prisoners.

According to Amnesty International's report, 'Not part of my sentence' (1999), in countries like the USA, women prisoners have been subjected to a wide range of abusive sexual practices such as sexually coloured remarks and inappropriate touching by the male staff while being searched. The male staff also gaze at them when naked. According to Amnesty International's reports, in the US many women in custody have faced sexual assault at the hands of staff. According to Human Rights Watch, at least 15 per cent of incarcerated females in the US have been victims of sexual assault in prison. These assaults occur at the hands of prison staff and other inmates. Male staff are allowed to search women inmates, and their job entitles them to perform strip searches and have access to prisoners in their most vulnerable states. Prison officials are not the only perpetrators of sexual assault against female inmates. In the US, 'the rate of inmate-on-inmate sexual victimization is at least 3 times higher for females (13.7 per cent) than males (4.2 per cent)' (Piecora 2014). The cross-gender supervision accounts for prison sexual assaults against females (Piecora 2014). However, while there is no cross-gender supervision and search in Indian prisons, there have still been allegations of sexual misconduct in judicial custody.

In India, there is a silence on the issues of women inmates who have been the victims of abuse of power, and actions that have stripped women of their dignity. Some survivors of sexual abuse in prison, like Soni Sori, a Scheduled Tribe (ST) schoolteacher and warden, brought their experiences to public notice and demanded justice. She was arrested on charges of being an intermediary for the Maoists in 2011. While in detention, she was tortured and sexually assaulted by the police at the Dantewada police station in Chhattisgarh (*Soni Sori v. State of Chhattisgarh*, 2011).

Shamim Modi, a law professor, has narrated the ordeal of her arrest and detention amid a string of tribal protests. She was detained in a prison in Harda district of Madhya Pradesh in 2009, where a single room served as the women's ward. She spent twenty-two days in unhygienic living conditions and poor sanitation, with hostile prison staff and under constant threats, with little medical or psychological help. After twenty-two days, she was moved to a bigger prison in Hoshangabad, where prison guards searched her in an intrusive manner. In fact, her demand to see the *Model Prison Manual* was ignored. While recalling her experience in prison, she said, 'There is often so much abuse that you don't feel human, it can make you forget you ever had rights' (Jyoti and Nair 2017).

A newspaper report (*The Times of India* 2011) mentioned:

> [A] few women who served prison terms have alleged torture and inhuman treatment within the prisons across Tamil Nadu .... In this report, a woman inmate shared her distress and said, 'I was stripped naked by convict wardens in the presence of the jail wardens and other prisoners and abused both verbally and physically. It was a humiliating experience'.

Having male staff in charge of women inmates sometimes also results in stigma being attached to the women inmates, as there is a perception that these women have been abused by them. During an interview, one inmate expressed her fear that people would assassinate her character after her release from prison, as it is believed that they are sexually abused inside. This perception really needs to be changed.

The *Model Prison Manual* (2016) provides for restricted access to male staff inside the women's barracks. It mentions that the matron or the woman warder shall have custody of the keys of the wards and enclosures in which female prisoners are confined during the day. After the locking up, she will deliver the keys to the lady deputy/

assistant superintendent, who shall then lock them up in the key chest. The deputy / assistant superintendent shall hand over the keys to the matron or female head warder once again in the morning, at the time of unlocking. It also provides for suitable measures that may be taken (including the provision of alarm bells) to ensure minimum delay in opening the barracks in case of an emergency. More women staff who are trained and gender-sensitive can ensure that women in prison remain safe and are treated with dignity. The search at the time of entry needs to be done in an enclosed area, which is absent in many prisons. Any custodial violence should be strictly punished. Internal Complaints Committees, set up to deal with complaints of sexual harassment, should be proactive, and prison inmates should be made aware of the system.

Medical and Health Facilities

Various researchers have found that imprisonment has a negative impact on health (Bergh, et al. 2011; Douglas, et al. 2009). At the time of entry, health assessment is currently more in terms of just asking the prisoner if she has health problems and measuring her height and weight, rather than conducting a comprehensive medical examination. The number of doctors catering to women prisoners is also inadequate. In overcrowded prisons, skin diseases are common among inmates. Some of the provisions in *The Bangkok Rules* focus particularly on gender-specific health needs and preventive healthcare services. Rule 10, for instance, recommends that gender-specific healthcare services that are at least equivalent to those available in the community should be provided to women prisoners. Some other relevant rules related to health facilities pertain to preventive healthcare measures, including education and awareness on gender-specific health conditions.

Mental health is another neglected area. Many of the women inmates have been victims of domestic abuse and violence. Imprisonment further adds to the trauma, and an absence of counselling facilities makes them more vulnerable to mental illness. Depression, anxiety, and self-harm are common. Women prisoners suffer from mental health problems more than male prisoners do (Bergh, et al. 2011). The rhetoric about the 'empowerment' of women survivors of violence does not cover women inmates. Fears of intimidation, bullying, disbelief, isolation, separation from families and friends, and worries about how their children are being taken care of have a negative impact on the mental health of women prisoners. A study by the National Institute of Mental Health and Neurosciences (NIMHANS) on the mental health of women in Central Prison Bangalore found that 60 per cent of the inmates had mental disorders. Depression was a common problem. Emotional reactions during imprisonment ranged from denial, anger, withdrawal, and finally to an acceptance of their situation (Murthy and Parthasarathy 1998). Very few prisons are equipped with facilities for taking care of the mental health needs of women inmates. Counselling facilities are almost missing, and only non-government organisations are involved in such work in many prisons.

Mental health programmes in prisons should be related to oppressive situations such as domestic violence, which have led the inmates to offend and become victims as well as offenders. The Indian prison system needs to make a concerted effort to implement *The Bangkok Rules* and improve access to healthcare facilities in prisons across the country.

Grievance Redressal

When the processes of grievance redressal in prison are not in order, it leads to agitation and even violence. One such incident took place in Byculla prison in 2017. In June of that year, around 200 women inmates, including the accused in the Sheena Bora murder case, Indrani Mukherjee, scaled the two-storied Byculla prison's terrace and staged a protest over the death of a woman inmate inside the prison. It was alleged that the inmate had been beaten and sexually assaulted when she protested the shortage of food rations (Jyoti and Nair 2017). The women inmates alleged that no emergency medical aid was provided to her after she collapsed. Six members of the prison staff were arrested. After the incident, a committee headed by Members of Parliament was constituted to study the conditions of women's prisons. The committee visited the Byculla prison and observed that the living conditions of women in prison were terrible. The committee presented its report to the then Union Women and Child Development Minister, Maneka Gandhi, and recommended a separate prison manual for women prisoners, CCTV camera coverage, recreational facilities, and grievance redressal within a specified time (Kulkarni 2018). Unfortunately, prisons only come into focus when something goes wrong. An inquiry into the failure of the system should be followed by actions for improvement. If the suggested changes are not implemented, the status quo would continue. Women prisoners rarely use the complaint boxes inside prison, since many are unlettered and there is a pervasive lack of trust vis-à-vis the administration and their responses to complaints. In many prisons, the boxes are not even placed in the women's barracks. While researching custodial deaths in Punjab, the author found no complaints lodged by women prisoners with the Human Rights Commission at the national level. An effective grievance redressal mechanism and the creation of a congenial environment where prisoners feel safe to put forth their grievances would prevent violent expressions of dissatisfaction such as the one in Byculla.

Family Contact

Women draw their identity from the family and define themselves in terms of family relations, as a mother, wife, daughter, or sister. They lose these identities in prison, except in relation to other women inmates. In the case of women offenders, contact with the family is lost if they have transgressed the law, especially in those cases where they have murdered their spouses. The prison administration also recognises that family contact is important. The systems and practices that ensure the maintenance of family contact include the visiting system or *mulaqat*, furlough, parole, telephone calls, letters, and meetings with case partners or family members lodged in the same jail. These practices have various operational rules, which restrict their optimum utilisation. In most prisons, iron grills separate the inmates and visitors, so intimate contact with children and significant others is impossible, and in overcrowded prisons, audibility is poor. Many prisons have now improved their *mulaqat* rooms, and now the prisoners and their relatives can hear each other better as there are soundproof rooms and individual cabins equipped with speakers. An unintended consequence of the new prisons that have come up is their location: since they are situated far away from the city, families face difficulties in travelling to meet the prisoners. It increases the financial burden, which leads families to reduce their visits. Free transport may be provided from the local bus stands to enable easier access. Such practices will institutionalise family contact as a coping mechanism for stress.

In those cases where both the husband and the wife are in prison, there is no family meeting and bonding if they are lodged in different jails. Since there are strict regulations keeping male and female prisoners apart, children will have difficulty meeting both parents together, even when they are held in the same prison. Telephone facility is now by and large available in most prisons, and is quite successful in maintaining contact and getting news from the family outside. The author has come across some women inmates who often do not have the telephone numbers of family members. At times, the numbers are changed. Visits, either from the family to prison or from the prisoner to the family on temporary leave schemes (like parole, furlough, etc.), though not always possible, are the most direct ways of maintaining relationships. This is especially useful for women, who are stigmatised and often alienated from the family due to imprisonment.

Policy Interventions and Recommendations

Although there have been various committees on prison reform, the criminal justice system in India continues to be unresponsive to women's needs. Some recommendations pertaining to women inmates were made by the All India Committee on Jail Reforms (1980–1983), and then by the National Expert Committee on Women Prisoners (1987). The state of women prisoners and their young children in prisons today is still far from satisfactory. The recommendations of such expert committees have not been implemented in accordance with their visions. Scarce resources, a lack of will, and general apathy have resulted in a woeful neglect of women in prison.

To understand the importance of the various challenges faced by women in detention in their access to justice, the Committee on Empowerment of Women (2016–2017) presented its tenth report on *Women in Detention and Access to Justice*. It recorded the following observations. The committee tried to solve the problem of overcrowding in prisons through jail *adalats* (courts). A jail/prison adalat is a court held inside the prison by the Chief Judicial Magistrate, where cases of undertrials involved in petty offences, punishable up to three years, are disposed of. For women inmates facing problems in access to justice, the Committee suggested that the District Legal Services Authority (DLSA) should have access to all the details of prisoners through an Integrated Prison Software System, which can help in reducing the number of undertrial prisoners. More women lawyers should engage with DLSAs to facilitate access to justice for women prisoners. The Committee also suggested an interface with civil rights activists and noted that there was a shortage of doctors and paramedical staff. The Committee also recommended better healthcare and a need to have medical staff in the ratio laid down in the norms. It encouraged a structured approach to deal with women inmates.

The Bangkok Rules provide assistance to policymakers, legislators, prison staff, and administrators to meet the specific needs of women in the criminal justice system. These rules deal with the different needs of women in prisons in terms of providing assistance on different aspects of the prison system, such as healthcare, rehabilitation programmes, training of prison staff, protection of dignity during searches, protection from violence, aftercare, and visiting rights. While a major part of the rules has been incorporated in the *Model Prison Manual* (2016), these rules now need to be implemented in practice. Some of the areas in which reform is sought pertain to:

Prison Architecture and Design

Prison design needs to creatively balance safety and security concerns with a humane approach to the way spaces shape experiences. For instance, a separate wing for mother-child units, where mothers can be lodged with their children, can be a step in the right direction towards meeting the specific needs of childcare. Better *mulaqaat* rooms with provision for toys, which permit physical contact with children, is another way to redesign the prison space in sync with a humane approach. New prisons can have family units where children above the age of six can stay over weekends with their mothers. Open spaces allowing outdoor activities and walking paths and activity rooms will be conducive to rehabilitation.

Access to Healthcare

Basic access to menstrual products and medical care must be a priority. Doctors and paramedical staff in all women's jails, proper pre-natal and post-natal care for women inmates, hygienic conditions for pregnant and nursing women, and adequate nutrition for women and for the healthy development of their children are some essential aspects of prisoners' right to basic healthcare. Mental health, largely ignored under the current system, needs special attention. Attending to the mental health needs of inmates would involve screening them at the time of admission as well as providing them with continued support through counsellors during imprisonment. Appropriate services should be provided for women prisoners with psycho-social needs, especially those who have been subjected to physical, mental, or sexual abuse.

Appropriate Staffing and Training

A gender-specific approach to prison governance can be translated on the ground only when the staff receives adequate training towards this goal. Another way in which the specific needs of women may be addressed is through the appointment of more female staff members.

Reintegration

Classification, counselling, correctional programmes, and focusing on work that will enable the women to earn their livelihoods after release, such as skill development workshops and educational programmes, are essential components of the reintegration process. The government should also establish transit/short-stay homes for women who are released from detention, enabling them to stay with their children till they find permanent housing.

Open Prisons

At present, there are just two open jails for women inmates in the country. In *Sunil Kumar Gupta vs. Government of NCT of Delhi and Ors. W.P.(C) 7787/2017*, a PIL in the Delhi High Court challenged the guidelines in the selection criteria that exclude women prisoners from confinement in semi-open prisons and open prisons without any justification. Subsequently, the Delhi government changed its rules. Long-term female convicts could be shifted to open jails to enable better contact with their families, especially children, and help build their sense of responsibility. Open prisons make the transition to life after release easier.

Non-custodial Alternatives

Avoiding custodial sentences and pre-trial detention where possible will prevent many negative outcomes for both parents and children. At present, the Indian criminal justice system is still focused on incarceration as a response to all kinds of crime, and its thinking around alternatives to imprisonment is limited. The provisions of the *United Nations Standard Minimum Rules for Non-custodial Measures (The Tokyo Rules)* (1990) should guide the development of appropriate alternatives for different kinds of offenders, especially women offenders. Community sentences are an option, particularly with reference to offences that carry a sentence of less than a year's imprisonment. Short suspension of sentences in the case of women with caring responsibilities for children, community orders, probations and suspended sentences, and weekend furloughs are possible alternatives for a restorative justice framework (Lalli 2016).

Conclusion

Women prisoners are marginalised not only because women offenders and inmates are fewer in number, but also because there has always been a sense of complacency on issues surrounding women prisoners. Unfortunately prisoners—and women prisoners in particular—are not a priority for any government, as the former are typically poor, illiterate, and powerless. In addition, there is a prevailing attitude that prisoners deserve what they get. Despite several international conventions and rules around the rights of prisoners and local reports by committees advocating policy changes, the system has been unable to translate these ideals and recommendations into practice. *Prima facie* there is an intent to incorporate these global standards; however, this is always juxtaposed with overwhelming concerns for the safety and security of those outside the prison. This ambivalence is reflected in the neutral and homogenised approach to dealing with incarcerated women. Change is possible through a more humane and gender-sensitive approach, as discussed in this chapter. Such an approach will recognise the vulnerabilities of and damages caused by the incarceration of women.

Endnotes

1. United Nations Standard Minimum Rules for the Treatment of Prisoners, adopted and revised by the United Nations in the resolution A/RES/70/175, known as the Nelson Mandela Rules in 2015.

2. In *Re: Inhuman Conditions in 1382 Prisons*, the Supreme Court has directed the setting up of an Undertrial Review Committee in every district. It recommends the release of undertrial prisoners and convicts who have undergone their sentences or are entitled to be released from jail due to bail or remission granted to them. The committee is headed by the District and Sessions Judge, and members include the Superintendent of Police, Prison Superintendent and Secretary, District Legal Services Authority (DLSA), who meet every month and review the cases of undertrial prisoners.

3. As per Rule 64 of *The Bangkok Rules*:

> Non-custodial sentences for pregnant women and women with dependent children shall be preferred where possible and appropriate, with custodial sentences being considered when the offence is serious or violent or the woman represents a continuing danger, and after taking into account the best interests of the child or children, while ensuring that appropriate provision has been made for the care of such children.

References

Ahuja, R. 1969. *Female Offenders in India*. Meerut: Meenakshi Prakashan.

Amnesty International, 1999. *'Not Part of my Sentence': Violations of the Human Rights of Women in Custody*. Amnesty International. Available at https://www.amnestyusa.org/pdf/custodyissues.pdf (accessed November 2021).

Barik, S. 2018. 'Behind bars: Incarcerated mothers and their innocent children'. *The Hindu*, 20 May.

Bergh, B. J., A. Gatherer, A. Fraser, and L. Moller. 2011. *Imprisonment and Women's Health: Concerns about Gender Sensitivity, Human Rights and Public Health*. Europe: World Health Organization.

Bhandari, A. 2015. 'Socio-Legal Status of Women Prisoners and their Dependent Children: A Study of Central Jails of Rajasthan'. *Social Crimonol* 3 (1).

Chattoraj, B. N. 2000. *Children of Women Prisoners in Indian Jails*. New Delhi: LNJN National Institute of Criminology and Forensic Science, Ministry of Home Affairs, Government of India.

Committee on Empowerment of Women (2001–2002). 2001. *Women in Detention*. New Delhi: Ministry of Home Affairs.

______. (2016–17). 2017. *Women in Detention and Access to Justice*. New Delhi: Lok Sabha Secretariat.

Corston, B. 2007. *A Review of Women with Particular Responsibilities in the Criminal Justice System*. London: Home Office.

Douglas, N., E. Plugge, and R. Fitzpatrick. 2009. 'The Impact of Imprisonment on Health—What Do Women Prisoners Say? *Journal of Epidemiology and Community Health* 63 (9), 749–754.

Gopinathan, S. 2017. 'Gender bias behind bars: Why are there so few open prisons for women inmates?', *The Ladies Finger*, 7 October. Available at https://www.firstpost.com/india/gender-bias-behind-bars-why-are-there-so-few-open-prisons-for-women-inmates-4119575.html (accessed December 2021).

The Indian Express. 2017. 'Why women prisoners denied open jail benefit: HC to Delhi Govt', 4 September. Available at https://indianexpress.com/article/india/why-women-prisoners-denied-open-jail-benefit-hc-to-delhi-govt-4828734/ (accessed November 2021).

Jyoti, D., and R. Nair. 2017. 'Tales from former inmates: What life is like in a women's jail in India'. *Hindustan Times*, 26 July.

Kulkarni, P. 2018. 'Prison reforms in the offing for female inmates across India'. Available at https://punemirror.com/pune/prison-reforms-in-the-offing-for-female-inmates-across/cid5147265.htm (accessed February 2022).

Lakhani, Somya. 2019. 'At first semi-open jail for women, Tihar inmates get taste of life outside'. *The Indian Express*, 17 June. Available at https://indianexpress.com/article/delhi/at-first-semi-open-jail-for-women-tihar-inmates-get-taste-of-life-outside-5783542/ (accessed November 2021).

Lalli, U. 2013. 'Mitigating the Plight of Incarcerated Mothers in India'. In G. Eljdupovic and R. J. Bromwich (eds), *Incarcerated Mothers: Oppression and Resistance*, 93–105. Canada: Demeter Press.

______. 2015. 'Transposing Mandela blueprint for prison reforms'. *The Tribune*, 10 August.

______. 2016. 'Reimagining Prisons: Restorative Justice and Some Issues for Indian Prisons'. In P. S. Jaswal, G. I. S. Sandhu, U. Lalli, and S. Jain (eds), *Victim Compensation and Restorative Justice*, 9–22. Punjab: Rajiv Gandhi National University of Law.

______. 2018. 'Let prison walls be permeable to outside world'. *The Tribune*, 24 November.

______. 2019. *Survey of Quality of Life of Women Prisoners*. Institute of Correctional Administration, Chandigarh.

Linden, S. 2015. 'The Rise of Green Prison Programs'. Available at https://www.psychologytoday.com/us/blog/socially-relevant/201508/the-rise-green-prison-programs (accessed November 2021).

Manjoo, R. 2014. *Special Rapporteur on Violence against Women*. Report, UN Women. Available at http://www.unwomen.org/en/docs/2014/5/special-rapporteur-on-violence-against-women-a-hrc-26-38 (accessed November 2021).

Ministry of Home Affairs, GoI. 2011. *Scheme of Modernisation of Prisons*. Available at https://mha.gov.in/sites/default/files/SchemeMP-131011_0.pdf (accessed November 2021).

Murthy, S., and R. Parthasarthy. 1998. *Manual on Mental Health Care for Women in Custody*. Bangalore: NIMHANS, and New Delhi: National Commission for Women.

National Crime Records Bureau (NCRB). 1997. *Prison Statistics India*. New Delhi: Ministry of Home Affairs.

______. 2015. *Prison Statistics India*. New Delhi: Ministry of Home Affairs.

______. 2016. *Prison Statistics India*. New Delhi: Ministry of Home Affairs.

Office of the United Nations High Commissioner for Human Rights. 1990. *United Nations Standard Minimum Rules for Non-custodial Measures (The Tokyo Rules)*. Available at https://www.un.org/ruleoflaw/files/UNITED~2.PDF (accessed November 2021).

Parveen, S. 2008. *A Study of Condition of Women Prisoners and Their Children in Eastern U.P. Jails*. New Delhi: National Commission of Women.

Piecora, C. 2014. 'Female Inmates and Sexual Assault'. *Jurist: Legal News and Commentary* 15 September. Available at https://www.jurist.org/commentary/2014/09/christina-piecora-female-inmates/ (accessed November 2021).

Robertson, O. 2012. *Collateral Convicts: Children of Incarcerated Parents. Recommendations and Good Practice from the UN Committee on the Rights of the Child. Day of General Discussion 2011*. Geneva: Quaker United Nations Office. Available at http://www.quno.org/sites/default/files/resources/ENGLISH_Collateral%20Convicts_Recommendations%20and%20good%20practice.pdf (accessed November 2021).

Seth, J. 2004. *Shattered Lives: Women behind Bars: Report on the Assessment of the Conditions of Women in Detention in the State of Punjab*. New Delhi: National Commission for Women.

The Times of India. 2011. 'Ex-women prisoners say conditions bad, inmates tortured', 8 March.

United Nations Office on Drugs and Crime. 2010. *The Bangkok Rules: United Nations Rules for the Treatment of Women Prisoners and Non-Custodial Measures for Women Offenders with their Commentary*. Available at https://www.un.org/en/ecosoc/docs/2010/res%202010-16.pdf (accessed November 2021).

———. 2015a. *Doha Declaration on Integrating Crime Prevention and Criminal Justice into the Wider United Nations Agenda to Address Social and Economic Challenges and to Promote the Rule of Law at the National and International Levels, and Public Participation*. New York: United Nations.

———. 2015b. *The United Nations Standard Minimum Rules for the Treatment of Prisoners (the Nelson Mandela Rules)*. Available at https://www.unodc.org/documents/justice-and-prison-reform/GA-RESOLUTION/E_ebook.pdf (accessed November 2021).

Walmsley, R. 2015. *World Prison Brief: World Female Imprisonment List*. London: Institute for Criminal Policy Research.

———. 2017. *World Prison Brief: World Female Imprisonment List*. London: Institute for Criminal Policy Research.

Case Laws

R.D. Upadhyay v. *State of Andhra Pradesh and Ors.*, AIR 2006 SC 1946.

Re: Inhuman Conditions in 1382 Prisons, W.P. (C) No. 406 of 2013.

Soni Sori v. State of Chhattisgarh, 201114 SCC 658.

Sunil Batra v. Delhi Administration, AIR 1980 SC 1579.

Sunil Kumar Gupta v. Government of NCT of Delhi and Ors. WP(C) 7787/2017.

Chapter 10
Impact of Pre-Trial Detention on Women

Madhurima Dhanuka

Women prisoners are more prone to suffering from anxiety due to incarceration, which gets escalated when there is little or no social contact with their family members who give up due to social stigma.

Parliamentary Committee on
Empowerment of Women

According to the International Centre for Policy Research (ICPR), more than 714,000 women are held in penal institutions throughout the world, either as pre-trial detainees or as sentenced prisoners (ICPR 2017). While this is a small proportion of the general prison population worldwide, Penal Reform International (PRI) reports that the number of women prisoners across the world has increased by 53 per cent since 2000 (PRI 2018).

At the end of 2018, there were 19,242 women prisoners in India, which constituted 4.1 per cent of India's prison population (NCRB 2018). Women prisoners in India have increased at a higher rate (111.7 per cent) than the increase in the number of prisoners (71 per cent), which is interestingly double the rate of increase across the world (CHRI Analysis 2020).

Women prisoners constitute a vulnerable group in prisons, which necessitates that legislators, policymakers, adjudicators, and prison management ensure that their specific needs are taken into consideration while framing and implementing policies. It must also prompt them 'to look more carefully at whom we imprison and ask, in every case, why we imprison and what we expect prison to achieve' (Heard 2017).

The United Nations Rules for the Treatment of Women Prisoners and Non-Custodial Measures for Women Offenders (Bangkok Rules) 2010 highlight the particular risks for women in detention. In the commentary to the rules, it states:

> Women, especially those who are illiterate, poor, those who have been violently victimised and who are the primary carers of their children and families, feel particularly vulnerable on first admission to prison. They are often unaware of their legal rights, are extremely distressed about what is happening to them and what impact that will have on their children. (Bangkok Rules 2010)

Moreover, women prisoners are predominantly incarcerated for minor, non-violent, property or drug-related crimes (Heard 2017). Vulnerable and economically disadvantaged, women are increasingly likely to be detained pre-trial, due to their inability to afford bail or the services of a lawyer (United Nations Office on Drugs and Crime 2008). The impact of pre-trial detention on women, including the economic, social, and mental impacts, are in most cases greater than that on men.

This chapter delves into the vulnerabilities of women prisoners in India and deliberates the various impacts that imprisonment has on them. It further documents recent studies and reports on these issues, and based on an evaluation of these, puts forth recommendations for reducing the use of pre-trial detention for women prisoners.

The issues raised and inferences made in this chapter are based on interactions with women prisoners confined in various prisons in West Bengal and detailed discussions with prison officers, medical officers, legal aid authorities, and other experts in the field over the last decade. These interactions were made as part of initiatives to ensure effective access to legal aid for women prisoners through legal aid camps, legal awareness camps, and as part of campaigns organised by legal services institutions for women prisoners.

Women in Pre-Trial Detention in India[1]

There are 19,242 women prisoners in India, 68.4 per cent of whom are undertrials. There are only twenty-four women's prisons among the 1,339 prisons that exist across India, although in several other prisons female prisoners are confined in separate enclosures, with the capacity of these enclosures ranging between two to several hundred, depending on the category of prisons. And 1,732 women prisoners are accompanied by their children (less than six years of age) in prison.[2]

The geographical spread of women prisoners varies across the country. Uttar Pradesh has by far the highest number of women in prison (4,053), followed by Maharashtra (1,602), Madhya Pradesh (1,509), and West Bengal (1,479). The Union Territories, apart from Delhi (530), have a particularly low number of women in prison.

In terms of the period of detention, the majority of women spend anywhere between a few months to a year in pre-trial detention prior to release or conviction. The majority of women (48.9 per cent) are aged between thirty to fifty years. A large proportion of women are in prison for murder, followed by those accused or convicted for dowry deaths.[3]

Women Prisoners and their Vulnerabilities

The *Handbook for Prison Managers and Policymakers on Women and Imprisonment*[4] states a number of reasons for the intensity of the vulnerabilities of women prisoners, which include:

(a) Post-release stigmatisation, victimisation, and abandonment by families.

(b) Gender-specific healthcare needs that cannot be adequately met.

(c) High likelihood of having caring responsibilities for their children, families, and others.

(d) The extreme distress caused by imprisonment to women, which can lead to severe mental health problems or exacerbate existing problems.

(e) Challenges they face in accessing justice on an equal basis with men.

A majority of the women accused or convicted of crimes are from poor and marginalised sectors of the community; or they are unlettered and unaware of their legal rights; or they have no economic means to hire a lawyer. These factors place them in an even more vulnerable position, where they may not comprehend the legal proceedings and be manipulated into giving or signing statements which may not be conducive to their defence. For example, a mentally ill Indian woman unknowingly pleaded guilty to an offence under the Foreigners Act 1946 as a Bangladeshi national, whereas in reality she hailed from a small town in Assam. Women also face physical and sexual abuse in police and judicial custody, whereby force is exerted to make them confess to offences not committed, or sexual favours are asked or demanded in lieu of lenient treatment.

In recent interviews conducted with women prisoners, as part of a campaign by the National Legal Services Authority (NALSA),[5] the level of ignorance seen among women prisoners was astounding. They were unaware of the particulars of their cases, and did not know whether they had lawyers to represent their case. Their nonchalant response was: 'Our family must have hired.' And these were not just new entrants; even those who had been in prison for years had similar responses. This ignorance makes women more vulnerable, and is indicative of the imminent need to provide special attention to women prisoners.

Women's Prisons

Women's prisons, including women's enclosures, differ from those of men in several aspects. They are often smaller. They are assumed to have fewer security needs. The inmate-staff relationships are informal. There are few physical violence incidents reported. Children are permitted to stay with their mothers till the age of six. However, given the low proportion of women prisoners, women's prisons are often not equipped with gender-specific amenities. This is despite recommendations by numerous committees to that effect.[6]

In addition to a robust policy that governs the establishment of prisons that are sensitive to the gender-specific needs of women, there is also an imminent need to ensure that all rules regulating the management of prisons are gender-sensitive. Even though the *Model Prison Manual 2016*, prepared by the Bureau of Police Research Development (BPRD), Ministry of Home Affairs, India, contains a separate chapter on women prisoners, these provisions lack a gender-sensitive approach to the governance of women's prisons, and in particular women's enclosures in largely male-dominated prisons, which are more prevalent.

Impacts of Pre-trial Detention

While women prisoners constitute a vulnerable group in themselves, those undergoing pre-trial detention entail a higher degree of vulnerability. The majority of women undergoing pre-trial detention need not be in prison at all, as many are charged with minor or non-violent offences and do not pose a risk to the public. Further, bail laws also have a specific provision permitting the grant of bail to women on account of their gender.[7] Many may actually be victims themselves, but are imprisoned as perpetrators of crimes instead. This happens quite often in cases of trafficking.

Given their smaller numbers, historical position in society, and the attitude of society towards them, the impact of pre-trial detention on women occurs at multiple levels. Issues such as separation from families, mental and emotional health problems, issues related to pregnancy and childcare, violations of human rights, limited knowledge of legal processes, and limited access to healthcare and other services are faced by all women prisoners.

Social Impact

The stigma of incarceration often impacts women more than men, and the consequences can frequently be irreparable. Women have traditionally been the sole caregivers for their children and homes, and their absence can have devastating effects on the entire family. Additionally, being incarcerated can often mean severance with family ties. Many women reported that their families feel ashamed to acknowledge them as family members during their stay in prison, or even after their release from prison. Their husbands often remarry, and children are kept away by family members. More often than not, the family fails to accept them back upon release. This leaves them stranded post-release, affecting their reintegration and rehabilitation. Many women prisoners complained of a lack of knowledge of the whereabouts of their children, and seek assistance to contact them. In some cases, even when they knew where their children were, they expressed their despair at not having seen or spoken to them for years.

Economic Impact

Monetary considerations impact women in more than one way. There is often a reluctance to set aside funds for a woman detainee's legal representation as she is seen as the non-earning member of the family. In some cases, there is even reluctance to post bail for her. For detainees who were the earning members of their families, the loss of income can mean a lack of education for their children or inadequate means for their proper upbringing. Further, even short periods of incarceration can lead to reduced chances of re-employment, despite being acquitted later on. As discussed earlier, during the visits, made as part of the NALSA Campaign,[8] many women prisoners were unaware of whether they had a lawyer and relied completely on their families to hire lawyers. Many of them did not know the status of their cases, and in some instances, even the details of the charges framed against them.

Health Impact

Prisons across geographies offer limited or poor healthcare facilities. For most, even basic hygiene amenities such as sanitary napkins can be inadequately available, thus making women prisoners vulnerable to infections and diseases. Additionally, most prisons do not segregate prisoners suffering from contagious diseases from the general population, further increasing the risk of health-related issues for women. The impact on pregnant or lactating women can be worse. Lack of proper pre-natal and post-natal care can adversely affect both the mother and child. Even with these vulnerabilities, pregnant and lactating women continue to be detained at the pre-trial stage.

Impact on Dignity

Impacts on the dignity and self-confidence of women prisoners are often deep-rooted and irreparable. Throughout the criminal justice process, women face the risk of further abuse, violence, and humiliation—from the police, prison officers, and fellow prisoners. For many women, custody means ill-treatment, threats of rape, touching, 'virginity tests', being stripped naked, invasive body searches, and insults and humiliations of a sexual nature or even rape. There are also instances of women prisoners being forced into giving sexual favours for preferential treatment, or even for basic services they are entitled to within the prison. In a recent study conducted in Haryana's prisons (Abbas and Dhanuka 2018), women prisoners narrated their harrowing experience of being strip-searched for mobiles in a jail in Gurugram. They shared that many of them cried for days after the searches were conducted. It left deep scars on their minds.

Psychological Impact

A day spent in custody without one's children and family, and being subjected to humiliation during searches can lead to severe mental trauma. A lack of, or inadequate, mental healthcare facilities is observed commonly across prisons. The lack of counselling and psychological help in prison often leads to serious mental health conditions. This adversely affects the reintegration of detainees post-release.

Impact on Children

A large number of children stay with their mothers across the prison system. They are confined for no fault of theirs, but merely because they have accompanied their mothers in the absence of alternate caregivers. While there are arguments in support of children younger than six years staying with their mothers, they do not negate the impact of incarceration on children. Even a short period in prison may have damaging and long-term consequences for the children. It subjects them to a prison environment without having committed an offence, increases their vulnerability to child abuse, and keeps them away from other members of the family. Moreover, interaction with other hardened criminals can often have a negative influence on children. The lack of proper arrangements to address their education needs, particularly in prisons located in smaller cities or remote areas, leads children to suffer more. Similarly, their dietary needs are often not met. Children in their growing years must be provided a balanced diet, which is rarely adequately available in prisons, even in those located in bigger cities.

Measures to Reduce the Impacts of Pre-trial Detention

The ill-effects of incarceration on women prisoners have been widely documented by governments, civil society organisations, and researchers, each of whom has provided a plethora of recommendations to promote the realisation of their rights. Yet the number of women prisoners seems to be increasing across the country as well as worldwide. This section summarises some important recommendations of recent reports. It further provides suggestions that can inform the future policies of governments and prison departments.

National Expert Committee on Women Prisoners (Justice Krishna Iyer Committee, 1987)

This committee was set up 'in order to identify the gaps in and drawback of existing facilities and services and to evolve a more humane policy towards humane offenders' in 1986. Among other terms of reference, the Committee was mandated to 'suggest legal, administrative and organisational measures for ensuring fair, humane and effective handling of women offenders at various stages of the criminal justice process'.

In its report, the Committee highlighted that the

> numerical factor has turned out to be a hindrance to the development of progressive action to ensure custodial and processual justice to women. Their statistically meagre numbers have become a basis for continued neglect and discrimination against them at all stages of the criminal-correctional process.

In its final report, the Committee laid down several recommendations on both policy and implementation changes, some of which are particularly relevant in the context of pre-trial detention. These are:

(i) To develop policy guidelines on the arrest, interrogations, search, and detention of women; bail and sentencing; pre-sentence investigations; use of socio-legal counselling; psychiatric services; and scientific classification in the pre-trial and conviction process.
(ii) Presence of legal aid cells for women in every police district.
(iii) Diversion of women offenders to separate and specialised trial processes and to non-institutional correctional options.
(iv) Formulation of a National Policy on Custodial Justice to Women and creation of a statutory autonomous body

named the National Authority on Custodial Justice to Women (NACJW). Among the functions of this body was the promotion of preventive and habilitative action for women offenders, as well as spotting and highlighting unjust procedures.

(v) Creation of specialised women's courts or *mahila nyayalayas* to provide a specialised mechanism of criminal justice to women. These courts were viewed as adjuncts to existing courts and could entail an expansion of jurisdiction of family courts, created in lieu of the pendency in court cases that affect women more adversely than men.

(vi) Holding of *nari bandigrah adalats* (courts in women prisons) along the lines of mobile judicial camps as an immediate modality for rendering speedy redress to women in custody. These *adalats* (courts) were to be conducted on a district-wise or cluster basis so as to cover all prisons and non-prison custodial institutions.

R.D. Upadhyay vs. State of Andhra Pradesh 2006

In *R.D. Upadhyay vs. State of Andhra Pradesh & Others*,[9] the Supreme Court of India observed:

> [C]hildren, for none of their fault, but per force, have to stay in jail with their mothers. In some cases, it may be because of the tender age of the child, while in other cases, it may be because there is no one at home to look after them or to take care of them in absence of the mother. The jail environment is certainly not congenial for development of the children.

While acknowledging some positive steps taken in this regard, the court noted that 'a lot more is required to be done in the States and Union Territories for looking after the interest of the children' (ibid.). It went on to issue guidelines to ensure the holistic development of the children of women prisoners inside prisons, as well as of pregnant prisoners. A few of these guidelines also touched upon preventing the use of unnecessary and prolonged pre-trial detention of women prisoners:

(i) As far as possible and provided a woman prisoner has a suitable option, arrangements for temporary release/ parole (or suspended sentence in case of minor and casual offender) should be made to enable an expectant prisoner to have her delivery outside the prison. Only exceptional cases constituting high security risk or cases of equivalent grave descriptions can be denied this facility.

(ii) The Courts dealing with cases of women prisoners whose children are in prison with their mothers are directed to give priority to such cases and decide their cases expeditiously.

(iii) The State Legal Services Authorities shall take necessary measures to periodically inspect jails to monitor that the directions regarding children and mother are complied with in letter and spirit.

Women in Detention and Access to Justice, August 2017, Report of the Parliamentary Committee on Empowerment of Women, India

Realising the significance of the various challenges faced by women in detention, the Parliamentary Committee on Empowerment of Women selected this subject for detailed examination and report to the Parliament in 2014–2015. The subject was further reselected during 2015–2016 and 2016–2017. The final report on the subject was adopted by the Committee in August 2017, and it highlighted some prudent concerns regarding women in detention in India. Interestingly, in an action-taken-document prepared by the Parliamentary Committee on this report in August 2018, the Government of India was said to have accepted and acted upon 83.33 per cent of the total recommendations given.

The report emphasised that even though the criminal justice process does not differentiate between genders, its slack attitude has made women more vulnerable, both as undertrials and convicts. It observed that 'women in prison have experienced victimisation, unstable family life, school and work failure, substance abuse and mental health problems' (Parliamentary Committee 2017). In the context of measures to reduce the use of pre-trial detention for women prisoners, it suggested the following:

(i) Conscious policy to not overcrowd prisons by finding alternative methods of dealing with non-criminal offenders and petty criminals: This was based on the premise that women prisoners facing charges of grave, professional, and violent crimes were outnumbered by suspected drug offenders, ticketless travellers, railway chain-pullers, and a variety of other non-serious offenders. The Ministry of Home Affairs was asked to impress upon the police force to desist from unwarranted arrests.

(ii) Need for focused care of women prisoners: The Committee opined that as women undergo emotional and psychological trauma, which is more pronounced than that encountered by male prisoners, there is an urgent need to address this. Thus, it recommended the filling of various vacancies in prisons to ensure focused interventions by counsellors, psychiatrists, welfare officers, and other experts to allay the mental anxieties of women prisoners, and ensure a more gender-sensitive prison management.

(iii) Specialised training: The Committee recommended that personnel handling women prisoners should be provided with emotional intelligence training and special attitudinal change training to develop a positive attitude towards women prisoners, in order to meet their specific needs.

(iv) Role of non-governmental organisations (NGOs): The committee recommended the regular visits of NGOs to jails. Greater access to and open communication with the prisoners should also be provided in the context of financial assistance, rehabilitation, legal aid, etc.

(v) Access to legal aid: The Committee recommended that more women lawyers be engaged by legal services authorities to facilitate women prisoners' access to justice. It also favoured concerted efforts to rope in legal volunteers to render assistance in drafting applications, affidavits, and other legal procedures.

Women in Prisons in India, June 2018

This report was undertaken by the Ministry of Women and Child Development, Government of India, to study the condition of women in prisons in India and inform action for improvement. The report recommended the establishment of a National Commission for Prisons, as recommended by the Mulla Committee, in order to provide a national perspective on prisons. It laid down a number of recommendations on the use of non-custodial measures for women offenders, and measures to reduce the undertrial populations in prisons.

On non-custodial measures, it was recommended that imprisonment be used as a last resort. Alternative punishments to imprisonment should be given priority, especially in the case of non-heinous and non-violent crimes committed by women. It was further suggested that women should either be incarcerated in open jail facilities or consideration should be given to non-custodial measures such as community service, housing in shelters run by independent agencies, admission to rehabilitation facilities, etc. Emphasis was placed on the liberal use of mechanisms such as bail, plea-bargaining, free legal aid, non-penal fines, probation, etc., to avoid the incarceration of women. The report also encouraged the use of community-based correction programmes, which were stated to have positive effects on the reform of women offenders at a fraction of the human and financial costs of imprisonment.

On reducing the population of women prisoners, with regard to convicts, it was suggested that decisions regarding early release and parole be taken more favourably vis-à-vis women. It was also suggested that legal aid cells in prisons facilitate applications by women prisoners wanting to appeal for their release. Conditions under Section 433A of the CrPC, which does not allow a person to be released until s/he has served out at least fourteen years of their sentence (in cases where s/he has been sentenced to life imprisonment for an offence in which death is a punishment, or where her/his death sentence has been commuted to life imprisonment), should not apply to women.

On reducing the population of undertrial women prisoners, it was recommended that states should activate the provisions available for the release of undertrials on an urgent basis. It further suggested that an amendment be made in Section 436A of the CrPC to allow earlier release of female prisoners on completion of one-third of their maximum possible sentence. It further emphasised the need to operationalise the Under Trial Review Committees, and ensure that a maximum time frame is decided for the release of women prisoners after bail is granted, but surety is not produced. It also encouraged conducting lok adalats in prisons for the delivery of speedy justice, especially in the cases of petty or non-violent offences.

The report also delved into the issue of awareness, and suggested that awareness should be generated among the general public so family members/relatives of undertrials may also assist inmates in securing an early release. It also recommended that provisions of legal aid be implemented, with linkages with district and state legal services authorities.

The report had a few specific recommendations for pregnant prisoners. This included the need to make arrangements for temporary release for the delivery of babies in a hospital outside the prison, and for information about the pregnancy to be made available to the court to enable it to grant bail where appropriate, or modify the detention order where deemed necessary.

On health concerns, the report recommended that both the physical and mental health needs of women prisoners be addressed regularly, and women prisoners be allowed access to doctors and psychologists as and when needed.

The reports mentioned above have highlighted the physical, emotional, and social consequences of pre-trial detention on women. These reports include not only specific references to the issue of pre-trial detention while documenting issues faced by women prisoners in India, but also provide recommendations for decongesting prisons and addressing issues linked to pre-trial detention.

The impact of pre-trial detention on women offenders is both acute and enduring. It is imperative that steps be taken to reduce the use of pre-trial detention for women and also reduce the impact that imprisonment has on women. Towards this end, the Central and state governments must necessarily prioritise the implementation of recommendations laid down in the reports discussed above. The key aspects that warrant immediate attention and action by functionaries, including the judiciary, state governments, legal services institutions, prison departments, etc., are listed below:

Efforts to Reduce the Use of Pre-trial Detention for Women

Such efforts should include the exploration of alternative, non-custodial measures in the case of petty or non-heinous offences; framing of a liberal bail policy in which the bail amount is proportional to the economic condition of women offenders, and for avoiding the custodial sentencing of pregnant and lactating women; ensuring prompt and effective access to legal aid at all stages of the criminal process; ensuring the effective implementation of statutory bail provisions, in particular Section 436A of the CrPC that specifies the maximum term for pre-trial detention; considerations for the setting up of special courts/benches, including prison courts, for prioritising the disposal of cases of women offenders; and for ensuring the effective functioning of the Under Trial Review Committees, which are mandated to review the cases of all undertrial prisoners every quarter.

Efforts to Reduce Negative Impacts of Imprisonment on Women

Efforts towards this should include a review of admission procedures by state prison administrations to ensure that women prisoners are informed about the details of their cases; prison rules and the prison regime; means to communicate with their families, particularly children; and procedures to access legal aid services. State prison administrations should take effective measures to ensure that women prisoners are respected and their dignity protected during personal searches. In particular, they should ensure that such searches are carried out by women staff who have been properly trained in appropriate searching methods, in accordance with established procedures. They should also explore alternative screening methods, such as scans, to replace strip searches and invasive body searches, in order to avoid the harmful psychological and possible physical impact of invasive body searches. It is further necessary that prison administrators make efforts to ensure that women prisoners are communicated with through the assistance of the probation officer or other relevant authorities about the whereabouts of their children, and procedures to effectively communicate with them.

The prison administration should ensure that the initial health screening of women prisoners includes a comprehensive screening to determine their primary healthcare needs. They should also ensure that women prisoners' requests for examination or treatment by a woman physician or nurse are accepted. It is also important for prison administrators to ensure that women prisoners are provided with sufficient sanitary napkins at the beginning of every month, and that regular check-ups are undertaken to ascertain their reproductive health needs. All such efforts might prove futile unless the prison administration ensures that all staff assigned to work with women prisoners receive training related to the gender-specific needs and human rights of women prisoners.

It is also important for courts to ensure that women prisoners are allocated, to the extent possible, to prisons close to their homes.

Legal services authorities and prisons must liaise to conduct camps for women prisoners to raise awareness on legal processes, as well as on cleanliness and hygiene. Further, it is important that individualised, gender-sensitive, trauma-informed, and comprehensive mental healthcare and rehabilitation programmes be made available for women prisoners with mental health needs in prison.

Conclusion

Pre-trial detention is challenging and difficult for all persons, but particularly so for women. The detainee immediately loses her freedom, and is also at risk of losing her family, home, job, and community ties. What makes the situation worse is that many of those held in pre-trial detention get their charges withdrawn due to lack of evidence, while others are acquitted at trial. Unfortunately, the damage is already done, having started from the moment a person is incarcerated.

The social, economic, physical, and psychological impact of imprisonment on women, and particularly on children who stay with their imprisoned mothers, makes pre-trial detention an ineffective, and often damaging, solution to offending by women. This necessitates that the government and policymakers prioritise efforts to ensure that pre-trial detention is used as a last resort for women. Difficult though it may sound, constant and sustained efforts can achieve this.

Endnotes

1. Data provided in this section is sourced from NCRB 2018.
2. Indian laws permit women to keep their children till the age of six years in prison with them. See also *RD Upadhyay v State of AP* AIR 2006 SC 1946.
3. The high percentage of women accused of dowry-related offences is a cause for worry, as it is noticed that there are rampant arrests of entire households in the event of dowry deaths or domestic violence. However,

the author has refrained from discussing this issue here as it merits a larger discussion on both the legal and practical aspects.

4. https://www.unodc.org/documents/justice-and-prison-reform/women-and-imprisonment.pdf (accessed November 2021).

5. The author was a member of one of the teams constituted under NALSA's Campaign for Enhancing Legal Services to Women Inmates and their Accompanying Children in West Bengal, wherein she interacted with more than 200 prisoners of one prison. See https://nalsa.gov.in/sites/default/files/document/Campaign_for_enhancing_Legal_Services_to_Women_inmates_and_their_accompanying_children_in_prisons.pdf (accessed November 2021) for more details.

6. Over the years, the Government of India has established various committees to study and suggest improvements in prison conditions, such as the All India Prison Reforms Committee 1980–1983 and the National Expert Committee on Women Prisoners 1987. More recently, the Parliamentary Committee on the Empowerment of Women also prepared a report on this issue.

7. Section 437, Code of Criminal Procedure 1973.

8. NALSA's Campaign For Enhancing Legal Services to Women Inmates and their Accompanying Children 2018.

9. AIR 2006 SC 1946.

References

Abbas, S., and M. Dhanuka. 2018. *Inside Haryana Prisons*. New Delhi: Commonwealth Human Rights Initiative.

Bureau of Police Research and Development. 2016. *Model Prison Manual*. New Delhi.

Heard, C. 2017. *Female Imprisonment Worldwide*. Available at http://blogs.bbk.ac.uk/events/2017/12/14/female-imprisonment-worldwide/ (accessed November 2021).

Institute for Criminal Policy Research (ICPR). 2017. *World Female Imprisonment List*. London: School of Law of Birkbeck, University of London, 4e.

Government of India. 2018. *Women in Prisons in India*. New Delhi: Ministry of Women and Child Development.

National Crime Records Bureau (NCRB). 2000. *Prison Statistics India*. New Delhi: Ministry of Home Affairs, Government of India.

———. 2018. *Prison Statistics India*. New Delhi: Ministry of Home Affairs, Government of India.

National Legal Services Authority. 2018. *A Campaign for Enhancing Legal Services to Women Inmates and their Accompanying Children*. New Delhi.

Parliamentary Committee on Empowerment of Women. 2017. Women in Detention and Access to Justice. New Delhi.

Penal Reform International (PRI). 2018. *Global Prison Trends 2018*. London: PRI.

United Nations Office on Drugs and Crime. 2008. *Handbook for Prison Managers and Policymakers on Women and Imprisonment*.

Committees/Programmes and Cases

All India Prison Reforms Committee, 1980–1983.

Code of Criminal Procedure, 1973.

National Expert Committee on Women Prisoners (Justice Krishna Iyer Committee Report). 1987.

R. D. Upadhyay vs State of Andhra Pradesh AIR 2006 SC 1946.

United Nations Rules for the Treatment of Women Prisoners and Non-Custodial Measures for Women Offenders 2010.

Chapter 11
CULTURE THERAPY IN PRISON
Trials and Tribulations

B. D. SHARMA

Journeying into the Prison

My journey in the Police Service began in 1980 with training at the National Police Academy, Hyderabad. After the training, I was allotted to the West Bengal cadre, where I served in various capacities in the field as Superintendent of Police (SP) of different districts and also as Deputy Commissioner of Police in the Calcutta Police. Most of these assignments were extremely sensitive and tough. One of my most challenging assignments was a five-year stint (on deputation) in the Border Security Force (BSF), which took me to difficult areas like Jaisalmer and Jammu (including the sensitive and volatile Rajouri-Poonch sector) on the Indo-Pakistan border. Here, living in the midst of cross-border firing and shelling, the gradual erosion of human sensibilities and respect for human life and dignity became central to everyday survival.

On my return to the cadre in 2005, I learnt that I had been posted as Inspector General of Prisons in the State Jails Department. However, when the official order came, it described my posting as Inspector General of Correctional Services. This perplexed me. I had spent almost twenty-five years in police service and yet this terminology was alien to me. Upon enquiring further, I learnt that a new law governing prisons in the state, the West Bengal Correctional Services Act 1992, had been enacted and implemented since April 2000, and that was the reason for the new terminology.

The new law had some very positive provisions aimed at the correction and rehabilitation of offenders as the main objective of the prison system. The law now designated jails as 'correctional homes'. It was ironic, bordering on a contradiction for me—that while in the past my work as a police officer entailed making arrests and ensuring the imprisonment of people accused of various kinds of offences for as long as possible, my responsibility now was to facilitate their 'correction'.

Experiences with Prison Life

I was the typical police officer, who never gave a thought to prisons and prisoners. Till that time, in my entire career spanning twenty-five years, I had only visited a jail once. That was fifteen years ago when, as SP of Murshidabad district and curious to see the inside of a jail and the condition of the prisoners lodged there, I visited the local central jail. It was an incognito visit to the Berhampore Central Jail through a personal request to the jail superintendent, with no prior announcement made to either the prison staff or the prisoners in order to avoid any possibility of the latter lodging a complaint in the court against the SP's visit to 'terrorise' them.

The visit was a revelation as I was used to seeing shabby and stinking lock-ups in police stations, where those arrested were placed in the confines of a single, unhygienic, and cramped cell. With the jail superintendent as my escort, I had walked around the sprawling campus of the jail, which housed vast dormitories accompanied by facilities such as playgrounds, recreation halls, and a hospital. I was surprised to find amenities such as a garden of flowers, a garden for vegetables, and a separate area for farming, where a variety of crops was grown by the prisoners themselves. Being no exception to the general mindset of the police in those days, such facilities being extended to prisoners seemed unnecessary and ludicrous, as I believed that criminals did not deserve such pampering.

I was wrong. I realised this during my tours of correctional homes after joining as Inspector General of Correctional Services, which gave me the opportunity to view the wretched life in Indian prisons. I saw from close quarters how prison brutalises and dehumanises the prisoner through a monotonous, stereotyped, and unchanging daily routine. This can only result in a 'maddening idleness', leading to suffering in silence. The suffering and torture is accentuated further in the case of those serving life sentences. This vast idleness pervaded all correctional homes, with more than two-thirds of the prison population comprising undertrial prisoners, who were not supposed to be given any 'labour' as per the rules unless they asked for it. Even convicts had hardly any work as most 'jail industries' were in disuse, or had been closed down due to inefficiency or a lack of funds. Coupled with this, and related to it, was the problem of mental illness among prisoners, both convicts and undertrials.

Just before my joining, a torrid debate had ensued throughout the country following the hanging of Dhananjoy Chatterjee at Alipore Central Correctional Home, Kolkata in August 2004 for the rape and murder of a teenaged girl. The morale of the inmates lodged in correctional homes was at its lowest. The general public was baying for the blood of the offenders, and the majority insisted that incarceration and the resultant harsh punishment of inmates was in the interests of society. These public debates shaped my understanding of the complex balance between incarceration and the associated deprivation of freedoms on the one hand, and the needs and demands of the larger society on the other.

My interactions with women prisoners and staff further enhanced my understanding of prison life. Conversations with them convinced me that in the case of women prisoners, multiple specificities of culture, power structures in the family, economic marginalisation, societal inequities, abuse, resistance, and sexuality together formed an important context for their imprisonment. Some of the crimes committed by these women against their family members were embedded in the patriarchal family structure, where the power dynamics played out in intimate relations, shifting the gaze from the individual to the larger social structure. In the case of women, unfortunately, gender shaped the punishments meted out to them by the State.

The condition of women prisoners was worse than that of male prisoners in many ways. They were pushed into one corner in a small enclosure carved out in the prison as an afterthought. This was because most prisons were initially not designed with women in mind, and historically, female criminality has not received much attention from prison administrators or the State.

This placing of the female enclosure or female ward within the larger prison was done only to meet the requirements of regulations that came into force from time to time for the women inmates.

Culture as Therapy

In a short span of time, I was convinced that reformation and rehabilitation of the inmates was the lowest priority of the Prison Department. In such a scenario, I used to constantly think of how to devise an appropriate tool to bring about the 'spirit of correction' in my correctional homes. This compelled me to attempt a balance between the provisions of the West Bengal Correctional Services Act 1992, the preservation of liberty, inculcation of dignity, and the sensitive societal concerns about crime. This is when I conceived the idea of using culture as therapy for the inmates. It could act as occupational therapy for prisoners by keeping them busy and also as cognitive behavioural therapy, resulting in their psychological well-being through an inner positive change in keeping with the spirit of correction.

First Step: Selection of Inmates

I took the first step towards the crystallisation of my thoughts and gradual evolution of the concept of culture therapy while visiting Berhampore Central Correctional Home in Murshidabad District on 23 July 2006. I had earlier worked as SP of Murshidabad and had a friend, Pradip Bhattacharya, who was a theatre director of renown. I invited him and his troupe to the correctional home during this visit to stage a performance for the inmates. It was during this visit that I requested Pradip to organise a production-oriented theatre workshop for the inmates, to which he readily agreed. I could not have imagined the hurdles I was to face in the completion of such a project involving the inmates, and especially the difficulties in getting women inmates to participate in the play.

Pradip selected around fifty inmates after a talent hunt, all of whom were initially men. Everybody thought that it was going to be a men's affair. But I insisted that women inmates should also participate equally in the project, and so he worked on selecting a few women prisoners. The fact that the initial response to the workshop was lukewarm and that most inmates had to be cajoled into participation came as no big surprise. Despite the initial reluctance, he managed to convince each one of them separately. Motivating them was a daunting task, given that the majority of them were barely literate. I cautioned the superintendent to make Pradip conversant with the variety of jail regulations and the unwritten codes of conduct that reigned supreme within the four walls of the jail, as he was to operate within the boundaries of the jail regulations.

Negotiating Prison Rules

After the final selection of the inmates for the workshop, the director visited the jail every day for almost a month and interacted with them. He met the male inmates in a specified room and women inmates in yet another room in the female ward as per the rules of the jail, which forbade interaction between the two sexes. He was informed that the jail code prohibited excessive personal interaction between the staff of the jail and the inmates, and the jail administration also informed him about the strict hierarchical structure in place. It was important for him to understand that his point of contact was at the highest level of jail administration, in this case the jail superintendent, and that any deviations from the jail routine for the theatre production could only be considered at this level.

We also requested him to show discretion about some important facts concerning the mental health of the prisoners in general and the convicts in particular. The range of mental health issues, which varied from common depression to schizophrenia and acute depression, sometimes drove inmates to attempt suicide. Pradip, after all, had to know what he was dealing with. Keeping these things in mind, we asked him to be prepared to face the occasional erratic behaviour from the inmates. Their behaviour could take the form of sudden emotional outbursts, caused by inner frustrations and pent-up anger. We also asked him to avoid discussing the inmates' pasts, especially any details of the crimes they had committed and which had led to their incarceration, since this could trigger a sense of guilt and disrupt their emotional stability.

I would get intermittent feedback regarding the progress of the workshop, along with a few anecdotes, as the days flew by. As I sat reading my mails one August morning, Pradip called up to tell me that he had the perfect play in mind. When I heard his suggestion, I was both surprised and sceptical. '*Tasher Desh*?' I asked in disbelief, 'Tagore's *Tasher Desh*?' My apprehension lay in the fact that the intellectual theme of this play could get easily lost in the abyss of incomprehensibility unless rendered skilfully. The participating actors were largely unlettered or semi-literate, who would be performing as part of an in-house production of Berhampore Central Jail for the first time in front of an audience. I assumed there was a possibility that the participants would either not understand the subtle themes of the text, or would be unable to translate it into a performance. In addition, *Tasher Desh* required an elaborate set, a wide range of props, and a large number of costumes for the large cast. Moreover, as this was a play penned by Tagore, the tiniest of mistakes would not go down well with our Bengali sensibilities. However, the director reassured me that he and his team would be able to pull it off. He had come up with the idea of the play while conducting the workshops for the inmates, and felt that Tagore's

Tasher Desh best described the prison system. Much like in the play, the inmates were just numbers in a deck of cards, while the prison administration played the role of the Ace, the King, and the Queen.

The Principle of Separation

While in the initial days of the workshop the male and female participants had practised separately, the male prisoners had to now rehearse along with the female inmates to stage the play. As the majority of female participants were barely literate, we took the decision to help them brush up on their knowledge of the Bengali language by holding group classes and providing them with study materials. It was the director's confidence in the project that motivated me.

At the pre-production stage, we hit a roadblock. Many of the female actors came from conservative backgrounds, and this became a problem. For instance, in some cases the family members back home controlled their actions even while they were lodged in the prison. This became evident once they reverted to their earlier stance and backed out of the production altogether, after having been cajoled into joining. The superintendent and the director decided to speak to the family members of the participants on the 'interview' dates when they visited the jail to meet the inmates. Through persuasion, the superintendent managed to convince the families of the women, and thus they could once again be coaxed into joining the workshop.

Language

Amongst the other problems that we faced were those of inhibition and lack of confidence of the participants. Their reticence must be seen in the context of their social background, upbringing, poor education, and isolation from their families. Many of them suffered from depression as they failed to cope with their inability to fulfil their familial obligations, duties, and responsibilities. The biggest challenge came in the form of dialect. The rural dialect of some of the participating inmates had always been one of the major concerns. The way they spoke was very different from the conventional Bengali spoken in urban areas. After much discussion with the director on this matter, we came to the conclusion that it would be best to not insist on trying to correct their natural diction just to appease the purists. Any attempt at superimposing a diction that did not come naturally would make the entire exercise artificial. It would take away their spontaneity and natural mannerisms, which had come forth during the workshop and which certainly added a distinct flavour to the entire production. After all, Tagore's work belonged to the masses, irrespective of their social or educational backgrounds, and it was bound to be interpreted in several ways. We agreed to go ahead with the experiment and take a gamble, even at the risk of offending the conservatives.

Protesting Staff Unions

And then came an entirely different type of roadblock in the form of a protest by the jail staff unions, which refused to cooperate with such a project. They said that it violated the rules of the West Bengal Jail Code. There is an age-old stipulation in the Jail Code of West Bengal vide Rule 949, which provides that 'no female prisoners shall, on any consideration, be allowed to leave the female enclosure of the jail except for release, transfer or attendance at Court or under the orders of the Superintendent for any special purpose' (Government of India 1967, 284). Superintendents, although given these discretionary powers, never really made use of them to allow male and female inmates to mingle due to various apprehensions. The conservative interpretation of this provision by prison officers thus came in the way of the equal participation of female inmates in various cultural and personality development activities inside the jails.

The guarding staff soon realised that regular rehearsals meant extra duty hours for them, and started sending me memorandums through their two recognised unions, asking for a review of the policy regarding the allowing of such workshops. It was no wonder, then, that these two rival unions were united in opposing my venture. It was perhaps difficult for the jail staff to accept the idea of such a project because they had become used to wielding unparalleled control over the inmates inside the four walls of the prison. They now felt this power slipping through their fingers. The same inmates they were used to ordering about would be reciting Tagore's poetry, singing his songs, and performing in his play. Through the workshop, they were in the process of developing and exhibiting their capabilities in front of the prison staff. The staff feared that with exposure to a creative, intellectual, and interactive space, they would be unable to keep the inmates under their complete control ever again. Their resistance was symbolic of this fear of an impending loss of control.

I was, however, adamant about going ahead with my decision, at the cost of displeasing the officers and staff. The stipulation had been made for the protection and privacy of the female inmates and could not be allowed to come in the way of their development and empowerment. Strict implementation of this provision would lead to discrimination against female inmates, and their exclusion from equal developmental opportunities. I issued the necessary directions in writing to the superintendent, allowing the female inmates to attend rehearsals along with the male inmates in order to be equal participants and beneficiaries of all cultural activities for their development and empowerment. They should, however, be accompanied by the female guarding staff. Prior to that, I held several meetings with the state-level leadership of the two unions to convince them about the steps I had taken.

Women are now allowed to participate equally in various production-oriented workshops under the culture therapy programme alongside the male inmates in West Bengal. The female guarding staff, however, accompanies them during their participation in such activities, both inside and outside the jails. The female inmates thus participate in every single public performance of plays, musical programmes, dance dramas, recitation performances, etc., alongside the male inmates on equal terms under the culture therapy programme. This step has brought about a qualitative change in the lives of the female inmates.

Interpersonal Issues among Prisoners

Ironically, just as I had successfully dealt with the resistance from the prison officers and staff, the inmates started posing problems of various kinds. There was a sense of jealousy among the male inmates who were not participating in the production. The participants had been exempted from the labour that they had been sentenced to for the duration of the workshop. This did not go down well with the non-participants, who considered it unfair that mere participation should accord the actors such a privilege. Some of the female inmates, many of whom were from Bangladesh and could not be a part of the workshop because of the uncertainty regarding their duration of stay in prison, taunted those taking part by calling them *natakwalis* (those who engage in drama, often used in a derogatory way). It was their way of protesting the special treatment shown to the participants.

In the case of some female participants, resistance from their family members continued. For instance, an inmate who had been persuaded after a lot of cajoling to take part in the workshop suddenly stopped coming to rehearsals. Upon enquiry, it was found that during a visit to the jail, the male members of her family had threatened her with dire consequences if she took part in the workshop. We had to allay the fears of the family members with regard to the 'loss of honour' that they associated with her participation in the *natak* (play).

As we dealt with one issue after the other successfully and fixed the date for an in-house performance in November 2006, the project received a major blow that threatened to halt the experiment altogether. Anita Banerjee, an inmate who had been rehearsing for the important role of queen in the play, suddenly backtracked just before the in-house performance. She was doing extremely well and had impressed the director with her talent. Hence, her refusal to act in the play at this juncture was quite frustrating for all of us. A round of enquiries revealed the reason behind her refusal. Anita was serving a life sentence along with her brother-in-law, Suman, for the murder of her husband. While in prison, Anita had taken Suman's permission to join the workshop, which had perhaps been given without an understanding of the full ramifications, including a stage performance for the entire jail. He refused to allow her to perform now. Anita feigned illness and had the jail doctor refer her to Kolkata's Presidency Jail hospital for treatment so that she would not be compelled to participate in the play under any circumstances. Now the director had no option left but to ask his wife, an accomplished actor, to fill in for the in-house show abruptly abandoned by Anita.

Motivations and Emotional Bonds

With the problems came some pleasant surprises from the inmates themselves. The case of Chandana Mondal was simply spectacular. This 40-year-old housewife from Bahadurpur, under Gajole Police Station of Maldah district, was a shattered person when the workshop began. She had been awarded the death sentence for the murder of her husband after her son testified against her in court. Going by the accounts provided by the superintendent and other prison officers, Chandana was a 'disturbed person', who needed psychiatric treatment as the officers felt that she showed suicidal tendencies. When we discovered that music was her hobby, we thought of asking her to participate in the workshops.

We could not have imagined the extent to which the workshop changed her life. As she began attending the workshop, we noticed changes in her behaviour. The director, who initially had reservations about her participating in the workshop, was impressed with her to such a degree that he decided to give her the all-important role of queen in *Tasher Desh*.

Incidentally, it was at this time that Chandana was given a second lease of life when the death sentence awarded to her was commuted to life imprisonment. She subsequently confessed to her crime and was extremely repentant.

Chandana had become our beacon of hope. She had reinforced our faith in theatre as an integral part of culture therapy. We were convinced of the motivational power of such a theatre workshop in bringing about a positive attitude in the minds of the inmates.

As things progressed, emotional bonds started forming during the course of the workshop. It was perhaps inevitable, given the circumstances inside the jail and the kind of emotional vacuum that existed. After all, emotional security is almost non-existent inside jail, especially in the case of life convicts, who do not know when, if at all, they will be released. Despite the resistance, the workshop also brought forth interesting connections that challenged societal stereotypes of masculinity and femininity, as well as those stigmatised as deviant. For instance, the workshop led to the development of intimate relationships between inmates, who were often from different castes, classes, and religious backgrounds. The news of bonding between men and women in the workshop came as no surprise to me. The attraction between a Muslim girl, Runa, and Budhadeb, a Hindu, became the talking point of the jail. There were reports of another relationship that also cut across religious barriers, between Sudarsan Bera and Rupsana Khatun, both talented actors.

These so-called 'scandalous' incidents provided the staff unions a ground on which to rake up the issue and demand once again that the workshop be called off. The exasperated superintendent threw up his hands and threatened to discontinue the workshop unless decorum was maintained. The inmates were so involved in the workshop by then that it was they who requested a meeting with the superintendent and other officers to individually assure them and the director that they would refrain from any activity that was not permitted by the jail code. The situation was settled, and while these relationships persisted, they stayed away from anything that would 'appear to be objectionable' within the provisions of the jail code.

The In-house Show

When the play was ready, we decided to hold an in-house show in the jail campus on 26 November 2006. The director wanted the show in the evening, but the superintendent disagreed, citing security grounds. When I entered the Berhampore Central Jail on the afternoon of 26 November for the in-house show, the entire place appeared charged with a rare positive energy, which I had not seen before. It was a festive occasion. On the sprawling sun-washed courtyard ringed by the dull red-brick cells and wards of the jail, more than 1,000 inmates, both men and women, had gathered for a very special event. They had been seated on three sides of the open-air stage for the performance. Their excitement was tangible. Buntings hanging from the trees and colourful masks plastered on the tree trunks made for an elegant backdrop to a white-washed concrete 'stage'. The stage was a pleasant mix of a rural setting nestled amidst ample greenery and grace, enveloped with still more masks and buntings. Backstage, a group of inmates was togged out in sequined costumes, sponge masks, and green and black stilts.

I was pleasantly surprised to see the district magistrate, district judge, and superintendent of police amongst the audience. They had been invited by the jail superintendent. The performance, which lasted one hour and fifteen minutes, left us completely speechless. A spark of life had been injected into the otherwise dreary existence of the inmates. While addressing the audience, I was emotional. I committed to taking the prison theatre out into the society. Having worked in the department for almost a year and having become fairly conversant with the rules and regulations of prison life, I knew full well that it was not possible to take the prisoners for a public performance outside the jail premises. In prison history, as far as I knew, there was no such precedent.

Performing Outside the Prison Walls

From then onwards, my work in the office was interspersed with my attempts at exploring possible instances of prisoners anywhere being taken out for a public cultural show. I spoke to prison officials in other states. I spoke to old-timers who had served in the jails, including retired prison officials whom I would meet often, searching for a ray of hope. I left no stone unturned in trying to find one such precedent, which I could cite in my proposal to the government. However, I always drew a blank. The minister-in-charge of the Correctional Services Department had been very appreciative of the theatre workshop, but denied permission for a public performance. As I grappled with this problem, I thought of using the provision of parole as a possible solution. 'Parole' is the conditional release of a prisoner temporarily, for a special purpose, before the expiry of a sentence on promise of good behaviour. Parole is usually granted to convict prisoners, allowing them to go home to be with their families, or attend to emergencies. If parole can be granted so prisoners can go home, then why can it not be granted for a public performance?

I discussed this issue with senior officials, who were not very confident initially, but nevertheless agreed that it was not outside the realm of possibility. I presented this idea to the minister-in-charge. He was apprehensive of taking such a big risk. Getting police clearance for the performance and dealing with the possibility of the escape of convicted prisoners were the major concerns.

People were curious about my work, and many also cast aspersions on my intentions behind engaging with prisoners in this manner. But I resolutely pursued the idea of a public performance. Hope came through a friend, Bhaskar Layek, a West Bengal Civil Service officer, in the chief minister's office. He advised me to put up my proposal to Tapan Bandyopadhyay, then director, Culture, who was a civil servant as well as a prolific writer and literary figure of renown in the state. He suggested that I write a proposal, clearly outlining the legal and security concerns in including the play in the forthcoming *Rabindra Janmotsav* theatre festival in the month of May 2007. This proposal was accepted in March 2007.

The first public performance of *Tasher Desh* by the prisoners was held on 17 May 2007 at Rabindra Sadan, Kolkata. We decided to put up the troupe at the Presidency Correctional Home of Kolkata, which was situated very close to Rabindra Sadan and had both male and female wards. The artists were transferred from Berhampore to Kolkata on 16 May, a day ahead of the performance, in accordance with routine procedures of transfer of prisoners.

The security arrangements were detailed and enormous. The presence of the chief minister at the event and the unprecedented instance of having so many prisoners outside prison walls at a particular venue, which had to be made secure, were critical elements of the security protocol. The experience of the Kolkata Police in this regard was limited. Their encounter with prisoners was restricted to transporting them from prison to courts, and escorting them on parole. No wonder, then, that they had practically converted the venue, Rabindra Sadan, into a fortress. The police *bandobust* (arrangement) at a cultural event made a number of spectators sceptical. However, despite these deterrents the auditorium was nearly full by the time the programme began.

Apart from the Chief Minister of West Bengal, the occasion was graced by the minister for jails, minister of the Public Works Department, the Mayor of Kolkata, other political dignitaries, and renowned personalities from academic, cultural, social, and philanthropic fields. The prisoners also had an opportunity to interact with the chief minister when, in a rare gesture of openness, he went to meet them backstage. To my mind, this left an indelible impact on them—the chance given to those perceived as utterly powerless to converse with someone in power.

With the customary ringing of three bells, the curtains went up. The background music and chorus infused the auditorium, as the actors enacted the play in their rustic intonation. Their performance was flawless and cast a spell on the audience. When the curtains swished to a close, there was a stunned silence before the theatre resounded with thunderous applause. It appeared to me at that moment that we had heralded the implementation of the spirit of the historic judgment of the Supreme Court of India in the case of *Sunil Batra vs Delhi Administration* (AIR 1980 SC 1579), which states that 'anyone's conviction for a crime does not reduce the person into a non-person and that all other freedoms including the freedom to minimal joys of self-expression and to acquire skills and techniques tailored to the limitations of imprisonment belong to him'. In this particular case, the Supreme Court of India has clearly established the right of prisoners to such cultural activities.

As a prison officer, I knew that history had been made. This show had an encore in Rabindra Sadan and in Berhampore a few months later, to a similar ecstatic audience reaction to a similarly flawless performance.

Extensions

There was no looking back after that first public performance by prisoners at Rabindra Sadan, Kolkata. I gradually added recitation, music, dance, *jatra* (a popular folk-theatre form in Bengal), art, and sports as new disciplines to be taught to the prisoners for their reformation and rehabilitation through cultural performances, painting exhibitions, and sport events outside the correctional homes. When I established an art gallery at the Alipore Central Correctional Home after starting a painting and sculpture workshop there, the women prisoners at Alipore Women's Correctional Home also requested for a similar workshop in their prison, which was promptly granted. In fact, we had the second state-level painting exhibition in 2009 at Alipore inaugurated by a very talented prisoner, Piu, a young woman who had really excelled in painting in the course of the two years that she attended the workshop.

I formed the West Bengal Correctional Home Residents Sports Club for the promotion of sports in correctional homes, and for facilitating the participation of prisoners in mainstream sports events as well as state-level competitions. When the male prisoners' kabaddi team was performing extremely well, even reaching the semi-finals in the State Kabaddi League, the women prisoners in Alipore Women's Correctional Home demanded that they too be allowed to participate in the State Women's Kabaddi Championship. And within a couple of months, they were training and participating in the state-level Kabaddi League and Championship. Simultaneously, many women prisoners who took part in the culture therapy enrolled for and appeared for the Secondary and Higher Secondary examinations, like some male prisoners.

It was upsetting to see that some women inmates could not give their best to the culture therapy project due to the emotional stresses specific to women. Aparajita, an enthusiastic and talented participant in the culture therapy programmes, was always stressed as her mother-in-law did not allow her children to come and visit her in the correctional home. Aparajita had been sentenced to life imprisonment after being accused of conspiracy in the murder of her husband. We could not help her as the mother-in-law was the custodian of the minor children. Aparajita was acquitted by the High Court after spending thirteen years in jail, and is now working for a non-government organisation, actively helping the prisoners.

The culture therapy gradually became a movement. The prisoners, including women prisoners, also went out of the state for performances. And it was always on parole and without any police escort. Over the course of the past ten years, more than 400 such outings of prisoners have been organised throughout India. Women prisoners have been equal partners in these cultural performances.

A Prisoners' Welfare Fund for the collection of funds through these cultural performances emerged as a by-product of the culture therapy programme. We used the funds to provide post-release support to the prisoners for rehabilitation; for financial support to prisoners who pursued education in the jail; as scholarships to the meritorious children of prisoners who were back home, living in the community; for subsistence to the family members of prisoners in case of abject poverty; for meeting the expenses of medical treatments of their family members; for financial assistance at the time of the prisoners' daughters' weddings; for organising cultural and recreational activities and sports in the correctional homes;

and for the publication of magazines, journals, and books written by the prisoners. It is, therefore, a unique instance of self-help by prisoners while in incarceration, which imparts a unique sense of human dignity to them. And women inmates were equal partners in this endeavour. More than a crore has been raised by prisoners from these public performances towards the West Bengal Prisoners' Welfare Fund during the past ten years.

Intimate Relations and Denial of Rights

The experiment with culture therapy raised the issue of emotional security of women. Participating in these activities sometimes enabled men and women to engage in intimate relationships, despite the constraints of prison rules and the jail code. An instance of this was seen in the intimacy between Rupsana Khatun and Sudarsan Bera, both life convicts in different cases. Their relationship led to some dramatic developments but culminated in a tragic ending, in spite of the very bold and courageous stand taken by them and some support from me, which bordered on irregular violations of some age-old rules of the prison department. My support for these prisoners was guided by larger humanitarian concerns. Rupsana was acquitted by the Supreme Court, which allowed her appeal and set aside the judgment of the lower courts in April 2011. She sent me an application for arrangements for her rehabilitation and permission to live in the correctional home for some time as she had nowhere to go, which I allowed. A few days later, Rupsana and Sudarsan submitted separate petitions for permission to get married under the Special Marriage Act 1954, and even signed the Notice of Intended Marriage in the presence of the superintendent and his officers. Her distant family members in Maldah, however, put pressure on her to return home, which she had to submit to. She submitted another petition to me, asking to be sent to her maternal uncle's house in Maldah, which we allowed. This sent Sudarsan Bera into acute depression and the correctional home authorities had to work hard to deal with the repercussions for quite some time after her release.

The relationship between Runa and Budhadeb, however, lasted for several years. They finally got married on 1 May 2018 outside the correctional home at Berhampore while on parole granted by the Inspector General of Correctional Services. The two of them have applied for transfer to the open-air correctional home at Lalgola, where the state government has provided for family cottages for convicts. However, they have not been transferred to the open-air correctional home yet, despite both being due for such a transfer. In a similar instance, another very talented woman convict, Chaitali Dolui, sentenced to life imprisonment along with her husband Sahadeb Dolui, has not been transferred to an open correctional cottage, although her husband has been sent to another open-air correctional home, albeit without a cottage facility because there seems to be no such precedent.

The cases of Runa, Rupsana Khatun, and Chaitali Dolui are painful reminders of the discrimination that women prisoners face in the matter of open prison opportunities. I left the Department in 2011. A lot of work has since been done towards the care, protection, and rehabilitation of women prisoners and their children in the correctional homes of the country. However, nothing has been practically done to extend the facility of open prisons to our women inmates, which is not only unfair as it denies them equal opportunities on par with male prisoners, but is also an obstacle to their rehabilitation. It requires a new and open mindset on the part of correctional officers to extend the facility to women prisoners liberally. We may also need to amend the rules for the purpose of women's open prisons. If women prisoners are not in a situation where they can live with their families (a number of them are imprisoned for crimes in the family) in the open prison, we may have to change the rules.

The women can perhaps be accommodated in specially-built open prison facilities alongside the regular correctional homes to address the issues concerning their protection and security. We may also think of having some jail cottage industries in these campuses.

Kerala and Maharashtra have shown the way in this respect, where the state governments have established open prisons for women.

The few inmates in the Kerala open prison, which lies within the prison complex of the Central Prison Thiruvananthapuram, live in a facility that is more like a ladies' hostel. Family members are allowed to visit them twice every month. They earn wages by running a cafeteria, growing organic vegetables, poultry farming, stitching, etc., which are slightly more than the daily wages they used to earn while being lodged in the regular prison. The Maharashtra open prison at Pune is larger than the one in Kerala, and therefore more women inmates can have access to the benefits of an open prison.

If women prisoners could become equal partners in the culture therapy programme and various other activities in the jails of West Bengal without ever endangering the security of prisons or prisoners, the facilities of open prisons can be extended to them for their rehabilitation on par with male prisoners without jeopardising any security codes.

Concluding Reflections

The paths and manoeuvres taken in the culture therapy project signify my journey as a prison administrator and activist. It is this project that enabled me to see how two apparently divergent roles could be reconciled. The gradual acceptance of the project of a cultural performance and its extension into the fields of sports and visual arts marks a lesson in implementing the spirit of correction. Such a project has the potential for scalability as it brings together the prison administration, the activist, the social worker, and the prisoner within the boundaries of prison rules.

Reference

Government of West Bengal. 1967. *The West Bengal Jail Code: Rules for the Superintendence and Management of Jails and Subsidiary Jails in West Bengal*, Volume 1. Calcutta: West Bengal Government Press.

Chapter 12
Where Do We Go from Here?
Re-examining Incarceration as a Response to Crime

Penelope Tong

The question, 'Where do we go from here?' assumes relevance in several contexts. It becomes relevant when looking at life from the standpoint of a prisoner, and more so a woman prisoner, given the baggage that society has strapped on to her. It becomes relevant when we realise that incarceration is the almost sole penal consequence that is accorded by the criminal justice system, but that incarceration alone does not fulfil the targeted goals of justice and deterrence, or the more specific goals of the prison department, namely *sudhar aur punarvasan* (reform and rehabilitation). It becomes relevant when we see that theoretical perspectives are moving from penal proportionality to social justice (Bureau of Police Research and Development 2003a; Foucault 1975), but that the department and frontline personnel are still directed by a retributive justice approach.

This chapter deals with the question of 'Where do we go from here?' from the perspective of women prisoners within the larger context of rehabilitation and reintegration. It reflects on positions vis-à-vis the targeted goals of the justice system. It draws from my experiences as a social work practitioner and my work with women undertrial prisoners in central and district prisons in two districts of Maharashtra. I was part of an initiative that aimed to understand the issues and concerns related to criminal justice processing, custody, psychosocial factors connected to crime, and processes of re-entry, rehabilitation, and reintegration of prisoners. Social work with women prisoners for almost two decades thus forms the backdrop of this chapter.

According to the Bureau of Police Research and Development (BPRD), post-conviction assignments to one of the prison industries form the basis of rehabilitation programmes in India (BPRD 2003b). Moreover, rehabilitation has been perceived as something that can possibly be completed during the duration of custody itself. In this context, the prison system homogenises the custodial experience and the time that may be needed by a person for rehabilitation. This is evident in the fact that there are no programmes or structures for the post-release phase. There is also a conspicuous absence of professionals who are trained to handle the complexities of crime and reintegration, both within prison and outside it, in the post-release period. Additionally, the neglect of factors such as social and economic disadvantage, experiences of exploitation, trauma, exclusion, etc. (Foucault 1975; Scott and Codd 2010), and their implications for routes in and out of crime do not figure in the programmes. This endeavour at correction is considered effective when there is individualisation of punishment, because of the extent to which it is able to engage with the body and soul of the perpetrator. This clearly cannot be achieved through the mere and unvarying application of a prison sentence in response to a particular form of crime (Foucault 1975).

The post-prison period is deemed outside the jurisdiction of the criminal justice system. This raises the concern of fixing responsibility, when reoffending takes place following the completion of a prison sentence. It is clear that neither the prison as a department, nor the larger criminal justice system as a whole, takes concrete responsibility for the rehabilitation and reintegration of prisoners after their release. In the case of undertrials—and sometimes even convicted prisoners—voluntary-sector organisations who come into prison take on the task of reaching out to prisoners as individuals and groups through various programmes aimed at facilitating reformation and rehabilitation (Bharadwaj 2008; Vadiraj and Gopal 2011).

The prison as a department (in Maharashtra) does not usually involve itself in these processes during the period of custody, and more so following the release of the inmates. The prison staff often disregard, discount, or distance themselves from the work of civil society organisations, who come to the prison with a rehabilitation agenda, and disagree with programmes that seem indulgent or unnecessary from a strictly security and custodian point of view. It is also not unusual for the prison staff to opine that investing in prisoners in the hope of reforming them is a wasted effort, and that the need in fact lies with those who have been criminally victimised. Persons accused and convicted of crime are clearly regarded as being of an immoral and self-indulgent character. In these circumstances, rehabilitation, or even steps in that direction, are not likely to translate into ground-level programmes. Academicians and practitioners function in parallel directions without dialogue, and criminal justice functionaries and civil society organisations perceive each other as opponents, rather than as collaborators.

A review of and reflection on the efficacy of the existing prison programmes in India and their contribution to the curtailing of crime and recidivism are in order. It is an indisputable fact that our society is unclear about the appropriate response to crime, and the criminal justice system is inclined towards harsh and retributive reactions (Scott and Codd 2010). There is a need to review and reflect on where the journey started and where we are now. An introspection of such a nature would facilitate discussion and deliberation on a question that needs reopening, namely: Where do we go from here in relation to our responses to crime?

Incarceration as a Response to Crime

The Indian Penal Code (IPC) categorically prescribes punishment as the consequence to committing an act delineated as an offence. This is specified in Section 2 of the Code, which says, 'Every person shall be liable to punishment under this Code and not otherwise for every act or omission contrary to the provisions thereof, of which he shall be guilty within India' (IPC 1860). The punishments include death, imprisonment for life, rigorous imprisonment, simple imprisonment, forfeiture of property, and fine (ibid.).

Imprisonment and fines continue to be the most commonly prescribed punishments in the IPC, with fines being the sole punishments in extremely minor cases, but are otherwise an alternative or adjunct to imprisonment. Imprisonment remains the solely prescribed alternative if the offender is unable to pay the fine. The IPC (Amendment Bill 1979) had proposed alternatives to imprisonment that included community service, disqualification from holding office, payment of compensation, and public censure. These ideas were also expressed in the recommendations of the All India Committee on Jail Reform (1980–1983), headed by Justice Mullah, who recommended that the preamble to the IPC should include that the objective of punishment was the protection of society, not simply through the isolation of offenders, but through their reformation and rehabilitation. The committee also recommended that there could be alternatives to prison sentences, and the application of differing forms of imprisonment, namely simple and rigorous, be removed. However, the amendment bill lapsed, and the Law Commission of India did not incorporate the recommendations in their 156th report (BPRD 2003a). Community service later became an alternative with several restrictions, which limited its utilisation to persons below the age of eighteen years, to cases where the maximum sentence was less than three years, with conditions on the upper and lower limits of the duration of the service, and contingent on the court's being satisfied about the suitability of the accused for community service (Government of India 2003).

According to sentencing philosophy and jurisprudence, penal consequences are contingent on whether the offence is considered as one against society or against an individual. Offences against society are seen as warranting a publicly and judicially pronounced penal consequence in the form of punishment. Crimes that are prohibited by law, and more so those considered 'heinous', are thus understood as warranting a punishment, even if there is a settlement and understanding arrived at by the parties concerned. The State, who is the guardian of the citizen, then becomes liable to execute the punishment. The goals of sentencing are therefore envisioned as retribution, incapacitation, specific deterrence, general deterrence, rehabilitation, or restoration, either independently or in combination (Radhakrishnan and Sikri 2014). However, there is currently no sentencing policy or guideline in India that could direct the choice and rationale for the particular forms of sentences. Sentencing policy guides and directs the practice of sentencing, whereas an absence of the same makes the sentence contingent on the inclination and orientation of the judge, and thus subject to a higher degree of variation in discretion (Kameswari and Nageswara 1999; Niruphama 2007; Radhakrishnan and Sikri 2014). Judges K. S. Radhakrishnan and A. K. Sikri wrote: 'In any case, it cannot be denied that the purpose of punishment by law is deterrence, constrained by considerations of justice' (Radhakrishnan and Sikri 2014, Sub-section 19). Nonetheless, they go on to say: 'Punishment, whatever else it may be, must be fair and conducive to good rather than further evil' (ibid.).

Incarceration continues to be the routinely used, singular, State-imposed consequence of violating a law, with the apparently simplistic understanding that the penalty of incarceration, and its capacity for deterrence and rehabilitation, will be punishment enough to reduce crime. The logic underlying the principles of proportionality guide sentencing practice. Accordingly, more severe crimes are matched with more severe sentences, and vice versa (Van Ginneken 2016). Some interesting findings that came out of Van Ginneken's study (ibid.) indicate that it is not necessarily the objective and duration of the sentence that count as punishment, but the subjective experiences of the person receiving the sentence. She found that a community-based sentence was more challenging for persons who lived in deprivation, while imprisonment was more distressing for persons who had a greater stake in conformity. The study highlights the fact that using the principles of proportionality and equal treatment to offenders without considering the individual impact of the sentences on them may not serve the purposes that they are intended for. It is therefore necessary to factor in the subjective experiences of severity in sentencing if they are to communicate retribution or influence reformation. It also means that incarceration is not necessarily more stringent than community-based alternatives. This is hence contrary to the general belief and expectation that the severity of the sentence/punishment has a positive relationship with deterrence. Proportionality may thus not necessarily be a useful sentencing principle (ibid.).

Trends in criminal justice administration have shown a steady rise in not only the numbers of persons who have been incarcerated, but correspondingly also in the number of prisons (Coyle 2002; Jacobson, et al. 2017; NCRB 2016). According to *Global Prison Trends* 2017, there has been an overall and continuing decrease in crimes of violence and property globally between the years 2003 and 2013 (Penal Reform International 2017). Nonetheless, the report observes that there has been no corresponding decrease in the use of imprisonment worldwide. In fact, it points to an almost 20 per cent increase in the global prison population since 2000, in comparison to an approximately 18 per cent increase in the general population. These figures are assumed to be lower than the actual figures because of the non-availability of data from all countries, and the likelihood of persons detained in police custody not being factored into prison populations (Walmsley 2017, as cited in Penal Reform International 2017).

The three most recent editions of the *Prison Statistics India* report show a marginal but steady incline in the total number of prisoners in the country, with the numbers being 411,992 at the end of 2013, 418,536 at the end of 2014, and 419,623 at the end of 2015. There was also an increase in the number of custodial institutions, namely central prisons, district prisons, sub-jails, women's prisons, borstal schools, open jails, special jails, and others. At the end of 2013, there were 1,391 institutions under prison departments across the states. In 2014, the number was 1,387, and in 2015, it was 1,401 (NCRB 2014, 2015, 2016).

It would undoubtedly be useful to take another look at the increasing numbers of prisoners and prisons and examine whether this steady rise could be attributed to the absence of preventive social policy, increasing rate of crime, the neglect of non-institutional options, or all three of them together and more. An examination of trajectories and trends in the use of imprisonment shows that one of the factors that have contributed to an increased extent of incarceration is the adoption of more punitive policies and the subsequent expansion of the scope of imprisonment by widening the net of crime and criminalisation, introducing legislations like the 'three strike sentencing' provision,[1] lowering the age of criminal responsibility for serious offences, and according imprisonment to those unable to pay fines (Coyle 2002; and Boekhout Van Solingen 2010 and Hungarian Helsinki Committee 2016, as cited in Jacobson, et al. 2017). The extent to which a country incarcerates its offenders is thus largely contingent on the choices and positions that a nation takes vis-à-vis its response to crime, and not necessarily on the actual rate of crime (Coyle 2002).

The *Global Prison Trends 2017*, while referring to a general increase in incarceration globally, has highlighted regional variations between South America, Southeast Asia, and West Asia, showing significant increases at the rates of 64 per cent, 40 per cent, and 33 per cent, respectively, since 2006. In Asia, the prison population rose by 29 per cent between 2000 and 2015, while there was an increase of only 18 per cent among the general population (United Nations Economic and Social Council 2016, as cited in Penal Reform International 2017). A noteworthy fact in this regard, as brought out in the report by the United Nations Office on Drugs and Crime (UNODC) in 2014, is that while women prisoners continue to remain a minority at under 10 per cent of the total prison population globally, their numbers have been increasing more rapidly than male prisoners across countries and continents, as indicated in statistics right from 1977 (United Nations Economic and Social Council 2017, as cited in Penal Reform International 2017).

Close to almost three centuries later, prisons have not had the deterrent effect that they are visualised to have (Jacobson, et al.

2017), and despite prisons, we still have crime. This is clearly evident in the fact that prison populations are on the rise, and so are the number of prisons (Coyle 2002; Jacobson, et al. 2017). This can also be illustrated by the presence of habitual/repeat offenders, who continue to return to prison despite frequent imprisonment, and the first-time entrants to prison who become repeat offenders. This certainly becomes a reason for taking stock and reconsidering our responses to crime.

Women in the Primarily Incarceration-oriented Justice System

According to *Prison Statistics India 2015*, there are a total of 419,623 prisoners. Of these, 401,789 (95.7 per cent) are male and 17,834 (4.3 per cent) are female (NCRB 2016). While there may be some common factors that cut across persons in prison, be they male or female, certain circumstances visibly pertain to the fact of being female and in prison.

Statistics indicate that women prisoners form an insignificant part of the total prison population. Nonetheless, this becomes a disadvantage at the outset, as their needs tend to go unacknowledged, infrastructurally neglected, and even disregarded within a male-dominated system. Opportunities for maintaining personal and menstrual hygiene become particular concerns in the case of women prisoners as they are connected to the differential need, availability, and access to water and toiletries. Pregnancy, childbirth, lactation, and maternal and child health also call for attention (Government of India 2018). The developmental and educational needs of children inside prison with their mothers (Government of India 2018; Sahni 1989), as well as those left outside (Prayas 2002) are concerns that are very closely intertwined with the arrest, sentencing, and incarceration of women, and continue to call for attention (Government of India 2018; Sahni 1989). While incarceration stigmatises and ostracises all those subjected to it, the impact is far more severe for women, who invariably have low levels of education and livelihood skills and who find that family and societal support are withdrawn following their incarceration (Committee on Empowerment of Women 2017; Foucault 1975; Government of India 2018; UNODC 2014; Van Ginneken 2016). There is clear evidence showing that women's offending is linked with marginality and attempts to cope with poverty (Liddell and Martinovic 2013; Penal Reform International 2017; UNODC 2014).

In the course of my experience with social work practice, I have found that the private, familial, and domestic domain and decisions around them have an impact on crime and the incarceration of women. This domestic scenario could include circumstances such as being forced into a marriage, love relationships, physical/sexual abuse, differences over a desire to pursue education, demise of a significant parent, the entry of a step-parent and subsequent changes in position within the family, behaviour that is perceived as conventionally unacceptable for a woman, disability, and desertion by or demise of male members on whom the woman was economically, emotionally, and socially dependent. In addition, women often shoulder the responsibility of supporting the family, despite these debilitating circumstances. These often contribute to the woman's initial movement out of and away from conventional domestic living arrangements, and onto pathways towards increased vulnerability, crime, and imprisonment.

These processes are also affected by women's place in society, which plays a role in their low levels of formal education and job skills. Women are generally imprisoned for offences related to a source of income, such as drug peddling, prostitution, cheating, theft, or offences associated with violent relationships (Brennan, et al. 2010; Simpson, et al. 2008). Offending is thus often related to earning, supporting families, and escaping from violence, and social situation (Brennan, et al. 2010; Liddell and Martinovic 2013; Simpson, et al. 2008). The non-availability of alternative support structures increases women's vulnerability. In this context, their encounters with the alert, welcoming, and supportive criminal networks become a viable option. Inadequate information regarding the support systems available in an emergency or a crisis compounds the situation of women prior to the crime, as well as at the time of release.

A focus on women prisoners and the complexity of their experiences will enable us to reorient the lens through which we view the primarily incarceration-oriented justice system. These considerations of women prisoners' lives are common knowledge, but appear to be obscure and do not get translated into revised criminal justice responses. Some of these have been highlighted below.

The Progressive Exclusion of Already Susceptible and Vulnerable Persons

Most people in prison, whether convicted persons or undertrials, have stories of emotional, economic, and social struggle. Incarceration, and the processes that go with it, are not aimed at recognising or acknowledging the same, and in fact contribute to intensifying the marginalisation and alienation. The situation of women is particularly emphasised within this context, given their history of subordination, discrimination, and violence, and the gender roles that society expects them to play in order to receive acceptance. Many women who come to prison on charges of murdering their husbands have experienced violent and abusive marriages that were not acknowledged or recognised during the several years that the violence prevailed. Furthermore, the woman becomes the only one to bear the brunt of her action because of the commission of the eventual crime, while the antecedents to the crime fade into the background. This is compounded by a process of continuing exclusion, both in prison and post-release.

The process can be illustrated through the following example. In one instance, a woman, along with her three children, was removed from her marital home following continuing discord in the relationship with her husband and marital family. Her natal family did not want to take responsibility for her and her three children, who were under the age of six years. She thus remained outside the home for a long time as she attended the divorce proceedings in court and awaited its outcome. On the day of the final decree, she allegedly picked up her 2-year-old son and threw him out of the court window, killing him in the process. She was incarcerated thereafter, and her two other children accompanied her. No one visited her during her time in prison, and she had no contact with the outside world. She appeared resigned and did not relate to anyone very much. In the course of the next year or so, she had to give up the only family that she had, her children. One child had crossed the age up to which she was allowed to be with her mother, and was returned to her father, who had remarried by then. The other child also had to be relinquished by his mother because she had been diagnosed first with tuberculosis, and eventually with schizophrenia. The woman passed away in a civil hospital sometime later, after what seemed like a long and solitary journey of trauma and exclusion.

While there may be many other nuances to this case that were not visible through the above account, and while other cases of other women may have varying circumstances attached to them, the reality of women in prison is that the journey of exclusion often begins long before the actual incarceration, and that incarceration often seals the doors to re-entry.

Many women, for whom the path to reintegration is not visible, take recourse to ex-prisoners as the next best option to family. However, these relationships often turn out to be exploitative and the women continue to remain within the frame of susceptibility. Women located outside a social structure remain in a continuing struggle, and this is yet another essential consideration when attempting rehabilitation and reintegration.

Family is a critical factor in reintegration (Haney 2002; Sumter, et al. 2012; UNODC 2014; Visher, et al. 2004), and has a significant role to play in countering the processes of exclusion that are generated by incarceration. If family and its potential for reintegration are not addressed appropriately, it could further the exclusion that women experience. However, it is often not given the place or the attention that it warrants within prison programmes in India. There is a need to gather data and understand the range of family circumstances that women in prison come from, and to work through the several intricacies and nuances that constitute relationships that could either foster re-entry or further alienation. Currently, there are weekly visits for undertrial prisoners and monthly visits for convicted prisoners, alongside intra-prison visits by co-accused family members, a pre-assigned number of letters which are screened, and a stipulated number of telephone calls (in prisons that offer this facility). However, there are several constraints, such as the non-availability of documents to prove the relationship between family members and the prisoners, the distance that families might have to travel, the costs involved, and relationships that are disturbed and need more than a stipulated space and time for visiting to heal.

Women are also often in various phases in their relationship with their families. A basic categorisation of women's circumstances with respect to their families, based on my experience as a practitioner, has been presented below in order to highlight their potential relevance in criminal justice programmes.

WOMEN WHO ARE AN INTEGRATED PART OF FAMILIES In these cases, the woman is still integrated with the family, and the family is integrated with the community. The family and community are not associated with crime. The offence is often committed within the circumstances of a more or less singular exigent incident (pregnancy/abortion, need for school fees/books for children, salaries not being paid on time, financial difficulties, some form of necessity, mental illness, etc.). The women in this category have often come in contact with the criminal justice system for the first time, and feel intimidated by the incarceration and criminal justice processing. Family support, while existent, may be temporarily withdrawn, but restored later. Women in these circumstances tend to remain aloof from other prisoners, and are interested in returning to their families and willing to make amends. There is no indication of any earlier crime history among these women.

Women Still within Families, but with Weak Bonds In these cases, the woman is still recognised as part of the family. The family is integrated with the community, and the family and community are not associated with crime. The woman has a history of non-compliance with familial/societal norms, maladaptive behaviour/petty offences, or delinquency, which has largely been informally dealt with. The family is unsupportive and inclined to disconnect.

Women within Families that are Familiar with and Accepting of Crime In these cases, the woman is integrated with the family. The family is familiar with crime, and in some cases, even integrated with a community that is also in crime. They have experienced a history of marginalisation, exclusion, living on the fringes of the mainstream community, an absence of opportunities for integration/legal livelihood, etc. The woman is a contributing member of her family, but she, her family, and often the community that they immediately belong to exist on the fringes of the larger mainstream social structure that they are a part of.

Women who have Taken on the Responsibility of Supporting Economically Constrained Families, and have Accepted Illegal Means of Livelihood that the Family may or may not be Aware of, While Either Continuing to Live with the Family or Moving Out In these cases, the focus is on the earning capacity of the woman and the perceived absence of other possibilities. There is difficulty with entry into alternative sources of income, which require re-training and do not offer the same income. In these cases, it appears that the woman forgoes her social position and existence for her own economic independence and for the sake of her family.

Women who are not within a Family/Institution In these cases, the woman may have moved out of the family structure because of abuse, strained relationships, and forced compliance with familial/societal norms (marriage, wanting to further education, other aspirations, etc.). Women who had lived in an institution may have moved out, either because they had attained majority or because they had difficulty adapting. The death of family members who were accepting of the woman, and intolerance and hostility from other family members could have also resulted in the woman's alienation from her family. It often appears that there is no scope for reconnection, as communicated by either the woman or the family, or both.

The above circumstances have serious implications for reintegration and need to be factored into prison programmes if the goals of prison and criminal justice are to be endeavoured towards. This is more so because even social welfare and other developmental services tend to exclude women who have been released from prison because they are perceived as a risk to work with or accommodate. Given the pathways that many women who have crossed the boundaries of legality have had to navigate through, incarceration often seems to be yet another experience that contributes to the process of marginalisation.

While rehabilitation and reintegration are the allegedly stated purposes of imprisonment, several countries bar convicted persons from acquiring public-sector jobs. Hungary and India are among some of the countries with such laws (Czafit and Kollo 2015, as cited in Jacobson, et al. 2017). Can systems of arrest, incarceration, conviction, and sentencing then be seen as processes which foster reformation, rehabilitation, and reintegration, or do they in fact serve to promote stigmatisation, labelling, anti-social sentiments, and exclusion?

PRISONS ARE CHARACTERISTICALLY DOMINATED BY THE POOR AND MARGINALISED It is an unquestionable reality that indigenous populations, migrants, ethnic groups, and the poor are disproportionately represented among prison populations (Bharadwaj 2008; Mauer 2004; Scott and Codd 2010; Vadiraj and Gopal 2011; Visher, et al. 2004). Research that undertook an examination of the histories of imprisonment of ten nations across five continents expectedly found variations in their prison populations. However, the variations could not be linked with any single factor, but instead appeared to be connected to the predominant features of the society, such as its political milieu, economy, structural characteristics and inequalities, and threats, both real and perceived (Jacobson, et al. 2017).

The high prevalence of the poor and marginalised in prisons points to the need for an examination of the extent to which laws and procedures may be anti-poor/marginalised, placing underprivileged groups at a disadvantage and at a higher risk of arrest, and the likelihood of a longer duration in prison. Many laws still remain oriented towards the rich, and we do not recognise that so-called 'violations of the law' are often a fallout and manifestation of social and economic inequalities (Scott and Codd 2010).

Any scrutiny of the offences, whether they be organised crime, theft, cheating, trafficking, or sexual abuse, reveals that their roots lie in social and economic inequalities, marginalisation, exclusion, and patriarchal practices.

Our prisons undoubtedly lodge women who are seeking to improve their economic conditions, but have not had access to, or been able to connect with, the appropriate means to do so. The high rates of illiteracy and living conditions that become visible from home visits are clear indications of the life situations of many women in prison. However, experience from practice indicates that while economic inequality makes the social environment more conducive to crime, there are varying situations that make women more vulnerable. One group that becomes visible comprises women who have left home at an early age and have had to fend for themselves. These women are often stuck within the cycle of criminal justice processing and the world of illegality. The following case is unfortunately representative of many women, who have left home as children either because they ran away or in order to build up their lives, but who continue to exist on the margins of the economic structure.

Ragini, like many others, started picking pockets as a young girl in her early teens, after she had run away from home and met a mentor, who taught her to pick pockets and snatch chains. She initially operated with a group and then went on to operate independently, gradually but steadily acquiring the label of a habitual offender. She later went on to marry a man she met on her way to and from court, who was connected to a gang. He died shortly after and she was on her own for a while. However, her continued arrests and incarceration led her to meet another man, who peddled drugs for a living. He was later accused of murder, and was murdered himself thereafter.

Yet another set of women are those who have been in crisis situations as adults and have not found legal sources of support. These women are largely either on their own or single mothers with the responsibility of children, or are women who have had to take on family responsibilities following widowhood, or those in the process of dealing with the alcoholism or substance addiction of spouses or children. This seems to be another path for economically disadvantaged women, and one sees how women move from struggling with a difficult life situation to meeting other people who have a source of livelihood within a crime space, and then eventually becoming established within that space. I have met women who got into drug peddling after seeing the improvement in the economic status of other women who had also taken it up. This process had resulted in the development of pockets within communities, where there was acceptance of this means of livelihood. It had also extended to future generations, and in the course of my practice, I have seen the arrest of three generations of women from the same family on charges of drug peddling. However, operating within an illegal space has high risks, costs, and strings attached, which make staying within the occupation difficult, but probably easier than getting out of it. Nonetheless, the women are most often unable to gain economically from the exercise due to the legal and psychological costs involved, and often continue to live in economic backwardness and disadvantage.

The Prioritising of Custodial Security over Rehabilitation

Security in custody is undoubtedly of consequence, both for the community at large and for the inmates, staff, and all those who are directly and indirectly affected. It certainly needs due attention and investment. However, there is often the likelihood of security being emphasised at the cost of an equivalent investment in prisoner-focused development and rehabilitation (Vibhute 2006). Security has been found to frequently supersede focus on the dignity of the inmate due to assumptions that prisoners are dangerous or violent. This is more so when the prison is short-staffed, when there is apprehension about the possibility of faltering on adequate security, and when there has been insufficient training, which could lead to an over-reliance on tighter security (Penal Reform International 2013).

An overarching concern with security could adversely affect the treatment of prisoners, and more so women prisoners, who have to undergo humiliating searches in order to prevent breaches in rules.

Security is also the overarching concern in decisions about whether health and mental health conditions get specialised medical attention or testing, which are only available at a facility outside the prison.

The information taken at the time of entry is also more focused on security and custodial concerns and less, or not at all, on factors that would need to be addressed or considered in the light of re-entry into the community following release (Sumter, et al. 2012). Ironically, upholding a prisoner's dignity has been found to be more conducive to order in prison and to rehabilitation as well, and an impersonalised and disproportionate concern with security while neglecting the individual and his/her dignity has been found to lead to disorder and resistance to staff authority and legitimacy (Liebling 2011, as cited in Penal Reform International 2013).

Security also takes priority in the case of availing of parole and furlough (a form of leave that the convicted prisoner is entitled to after the completion of a third of the sentence). A procedural requirement of a no-objection certificate from the police prior to sanctioning parole or furlough seems to be of greater significance than certification about how prison programmes have impacted the person. Women are often at a disadvantage when it comes to availing bail and other forms of temporary release because of an absence of social support from the outside, especially for follow-up of the same.

Nonetheless, prisons in India are visibly defined by custody and security and not correspondingly by programmes that address criminal behaviour and related factors. This apparently is also the concern that guides and directs the constant flow of accused persons to prison during their pre-trial period, as can be seen in the choice of incarceration as the preferred response for ensuring security. Alternatives such as release on personal bond, release following admonition, granting of the benefit of probation with or without supervision, and community service alternatives to imprisonment are very sparingly used. Notwithstanding the need for security, if prisons are to fulfil the stated goals of reformation and rehabilitation, security has to be a focused consideration in the face of real or threatened risks to security, and not an indiscriminate end in itself.

The Fluid Status of Undertrial Prisoners

The prison population is categorically defined by their status as either undertrial or convicted. During the year 2015, there were 134,168 convicted prisoners, which comprised only 32 per cent of a country-wide total of 419,623 prisoners. Undertrial prisoners numbered 282,076, or 67.2 per cent of the total prison population (NCRB 2016).

While the prison department takes on the responsibility of the convicted population, undertrials remain in an indeterminate position. The effects of incarceration, often for extended periods of time, include stigmatisation, a disruption of their lives, having their families affected by the arrest, etc. Even the often strong likelihood of their being innocent of the crime goes unrecognised and unattended to. An undertrial who is acquitted, or whose sentence is set off against the time spent in prison, slips through the system, taking with her/him the experience of arrest and incarceration, processing by the criminal justice system, disconnection from family, exposure to crime and other prisoners, etc.

The experience of committing a crime or being accused of a crime, and of arrest and imprisonment thereafter, calls for immediate attention even during the undertrial period. The fact that many women enter prison after traumatic experiences further emphasises this need. The experience of a young mother who was imprisoned could provide an example of one of several circumstances that accused prisoners, and particularly women, are confronted with.

Having experienced domestic violence from a husband who eventually got into an extra-marital relationship, Malini, a woman in her mid-twenties, left her home, intending to take her life. She took along her two children aged below five years, and an unborn child. She attempted suicide by jumping into a nearby river along with her children. Her two children drowned, but she survived. Needless to say, she was arrested for the murder of her children. When she came to prison, she was disoriented, distraught, and traumatised. She could not come to terms with the unforeseen path that her life had taken, and remained steadfast in her desire to die. This situation had been compounded from the start by the fact that she had no natal family from whom she could draw strength or recourse, and she was placed in an even worse situation after her arrest and imprisonment. Her husband, who had also been arrested and later released on bail as he had no direct involvement in the murder, also saw her as the perpetrator and wanted to distance himself from her. The absence of any alternative family support, and the birth of the child that she was pregnant with, who had also survived the suicide attempt, added to her dilemmas and the uncertain future that confronted her. Malini's husband, who had lost his other children and had discontinued his extra-marital relationship thereafter, responded positively to the new baby and wanted her. He gradually became willing to consider reuniting with his wife, although he ironically saw her as a threat to his child. Malini, who could see no other option for her newborn child and herself, and for whom there was no other conceivable and socially acceptable identity besides that of a married woman, also considered the prospect of returning to her marital home, and eventually did do so.

The processing of convicts does not currently include attention to collateral damages, but the prison department does consider them their responsibility for the duration of the sentence, and convicts do become a part of a programme, no matter how minimal.

The Effects of Incarceration

While incarceration was aimed at setting something right, the question that remains is whether its budgetary and human costs outweigh its benefits. It is evident that incarceration does more to estrange a prisoner from society through its stigmatising effects than it does to enable reintegration. It has a higher capacity for incapacitating the prisoner than for rebuilding capabilities that will allow them to return to the mainstream (Haney 2002). It brings distance into existing social relationships and creates spaces for entry into relationships that sometimes feed off social exclusion. It creates near permanent labels for the individual, which carry with them the risk of exposure and rejection from potential employers, relationships, and opportunities (Mauer 2004).

Foucault observes that prisons, by their very nature and character and the 'unnatural existence' that they foster, the violent constraints that they impose, and the abuses of power that they allow for, in fact contribute to a sense of injustice, anger, and a movement away from a sense of guilt (Foucault 1975).

For women prisoners, prison either closes doors to integration, or provides alternative relationships that do not necessarily facilitate the woman's development. Attention to the needs of women, both while in prison and post-release, becomes imperative. Many women have no idea about where they will go following release and need access to safe alternatives. This definitely brings one back to the question of who benefits from incarceration, given the high cost to the nation and the evidently low benefit to society (Coyle 2002).

The Under-utilisation of Incarceration Periods for Preparation of Reintegration

Most people who become prisoners will invariably be released at some point, and will be a part of the community again (Sumter, et al. 2012). This is a fact that needs to be kept in mind at the commencement of incarceration and right through its duration. However, the period of incarceration is perceived almost purely as a distinct entity and a consequence of the offence, and not as part of a process that seeks to address the context of the crime and the root of the problem that caused the offending behaviour. It also does not address the time spent in prison in relation to the often inevitable post-release period (Haney 2002; Sumter, et al. 2012).

In light of the needs of women prisoners, programmes in prison clearly do not take cognisance of the fact that different categories of women have different characteristics and intervention needs. The question of whether a woman is an undertrial prisoner or a convict takes greater priority in deciding how she will spend her time in prison, and factors such as whether she has gone through the experiences of violence and abandonment, or has recently killed her child or family member, are of less consequence. Similarly, a woman who has herself experienced being trafficked but is now in the role of trafficker would have different intervention needs from a woman who has just been trafficked, but has been arrested for being an illegal immigrant. This is also the case in a myriad other situations confronting those in prison. All women prisoners, for that matter, get processed in an administratively routine manner, with the only delineation being made on the basis of whether she is awaiting trial or has been sentenced. Even after sentencing, attention is not paid to the individual circumstances of the case.

We thus continue to focus on whether a prisoner is an undertrial or convict, and neglect addressing other, more critical questions of whether the person is a new entrant to prison, whether she is emotionally distressed or affected by the offence and incarceration, and whether she has acknowledged the offence or is denying it.

Incarceration is evidently not an effective method for addressing repeat offenders, and in cases where the offence has become a source of livelihood. In light of the fact that most women are arrested for property offences, there is a need to examine how this is addressed in prison, as offending associated with property often has stronger roots in economic struggles and is much more resistant to change, as livelihood has been relearned and has now become a way of life. Change, therefore, requires a lot more working through.

Similarly, one can question whether punishment through incarceration is likely to address issues related to the commission of crimes that have resulted from conflict, emotions, psychological disturbances, and the like.

Prisoner re-entry is a critical factor in the whole process, and programmes in prison can do much to influence the nature and experience of re-entry (Sumter, et al. 2012). A study on the challenges of re-entry found that prisoners who had participated in programmes during the custodial duration were able to cope with re-entry better than those who had not. The same study found that one-third of the respondents returned to prison within six months of their release. The offenders who returned to prison were found to be younger, with earlier and extensive criminal histories, and with a background of drug and/or alcohol abuse both prior to prison entry and even after release (Visher, et al. 2004). The study findings point to the significance of prison programmes and their relation to the post-release period, highlighting the need for these realities to be factored into such programmes. A study by Sumter, et al. (2012), which explored offender perceptions of their re-entry needs, indicated five areas: education and vocational training, cultural programmes, recreation, faith-based initiative, and life skills training. While educational and vocational programmes were seen to facilitate livelihood post-release, culture, recreation, faith-based programmes, and life skills were perceived as necessary for coping, both inside prison and post-release. Jobs, the stigma arising from incarceration, and concerns about familial relationships seemed to be areas of significance for the respondents (ibid.).

In their tenth report, the government-appointed Committee on Empowerment of Women chose to study the issues of women in detention and access to justice during 2014–2015, and then again during 2016–2017. On inquiring about the welfare of women prisoners and the opportunities available for them to contact their families, the Ministry of Home Affairs informed the committee that: 'Regular contact with family members is one of the greatest stress busters for any inmate, more particularly, for women detenues and undertrial prisoners and they are allowed to meet their family members more often than the convict inmates' (Committee on Empowerment of Women 2017,13).

The ministry also informed the committee about the existence of a welfare officer in prison, who coordinated the work of the welfare unit, helped inmates to adjust to the institutional environment, supported the dependents and families of prisoners in addressing problems, identified resources both inside and outside prison in order to meet the correctional needs, and facilitated pre- and post-release preparation and engagement. The welfare officer is also expected to play a role in the orientation and classification of prisoners, in maintaining an understanding between inmates and the administration, and also in facilitating discipline and security. Nonetheless, it was brought to the attention of the committee that not all positions of welfare officers had been filled (Committee on Empowerment of Women 2017, 22).

The role of the welfare officer as outlined above shows much clarity about the needs of prisoners. However, there is a gap in implementation. Besides, including prison discipline and security within the role of the welfare officer could in fact compromise her/his effective functioning.

Re-examining the Idea of Rehabilitation, Re-entry, Reintegration, and Restoration

Prison Statistics India 2015 has a chapter on the best practices in prisoner welfare and rehabilitation, where it has been categorically stated that the reformation and rehabilitation of offenders is 'the ultimate objective of prison' (NCRB 2015, 339).

When referring to the rehabilitation function of prisons, the report speaks about vocational training as the primary medium of rehabilitation in Indian prisons. In fact, it appears to be the only programme and it clearly aims at enabling productive occupation during the custodial duration, providing a source of income, and developing skills for a future post-prison livelihood. The report further speaks about the capacity of gainful work in correcting the psyche of prisoners, developing a 'responsive and respectful attitude' towards society, building self-confidence and self-esteem, and directing prisoners towards 'honourable livelihoods'. Training was largely given in carpentry, weaving, tailoring, and agriculture. Other forms of training included handlooms, soap and phenyl making, canning, etc. (NCRB 2016).

Other efforts to facilitate rehabilitation have also included improvements in prison infrastructure and conditions; addressing the needs of children in prison with their mothers; sensitisation and training of prison personnel in correctional administration; developing opportunities for education, sports, recreation, culture, and spirituality; developing contact with prisoners' families; legal aid services; establishment of public-private partnership-oriented manufacturing and other commercial units in prison; developing access to citizenship documents such as Aadhaar cards (Unique Identification), bank papers, and insurance papers; and other measures related to improved prison management (ibid.).

Nonetheless, crime is about victimising and re-victimising. It is also about a personal struggle and a journey. The knowledge of having to fend for oneself and feelings of anger, hostility, injustice, and revenge form the backdrop to crime, and are also present in the employment of incarceration as a response to offending.

Among prisoners, there are those who feel deeply remorseful about the crime, the stigma, the effects on their lives, and the fact of being in prison. There are others who neither acknowledge nor talk about it, but are visibly distressed by their imprisonment. There are yet others who categorically deny having committed the crime, either initially or for a long period, or never acknowledge it to anyone. Still others identify with the crime and are unwilling or unable to think of an alternate life (Tong 2017).

Given the above context, when undertaking the task of reformation and rehabilitation, it would certainly be necessary for the criminal justice system to expand its purview of intervention to comprehensively encompass programmes aimed at (*a*) overcoming histories, (*b*) addressing psychological/psychiatric states, (*c*) facilitating personal and professional development, (*d*) enabling coping with social conditions/circumstances, and (*e*) preventing recidivism.

The Need for Change in the Prison Agenda

The rationale behind the retention of prison as a critical space within the criminal justice system has been subject to considerable scrutiny, debate, disagreement, and even an eventual alteration in its stated purpose (Foucault 1975; Scott and Codd 2010). While the journey from a penal position to a correctional/reformative/rehabilitative focus, to the more current inclination towards social justice, certainly shows promise, it remains to be seen how much of the essence and spirit of the changing positions have actually percolated into practice.

It was back in the mid-nineteenth century that 'delinquency', as it was referred to then, began to be regarded as something that could not be located solely within the person committing the 'delinquent' act, but had to be extended to the society that s/he was located within (*A'Humanitaire,* August 1841, as cited in Foucault 1975). This was because of society's inability to provide for basic human needs, and opportunities for all. The understanding of delinquency was primarily altered from its misperception as being the lot of the poor to recognising it as an outcome of the repression they suffered at the hands of the influential. The Fourierists rejected the notion of a 'criminal nature' and explained crime as being contingent on a 'play of forces' linked to the 'class that they were born in', which enabled their movement towards 'positions of power' or, alternatively, to prison (*La Phalange*, 1 December 1838, as cited in Foucault 1975).

Within the Indian context, questions about the departmental position vis-à-vis the purpose and scope of prison, the current programmes, the functionality of existing structures, the implications for women prisoners, and responsibility for reintegration continue to call for attention. The prison department has functioned within a retributive framework for almost two centuries, and will continue to do so if the larger criminal justice system does not take the initiative for reform. Factors such as the creation of newer laws, all calling for increased incarceration, can only contribute to a steady supply of prisoners. This will in turn continue to feed into the already voluminous population of economically and socially disadvantaged custodialised undertrials. The overcrowding becomes a drain on resources and negatively impacts prison conditions and other service structures such as legal aid, which further impacts prisoners negatively (Coyle 2002; Jacobson, et al. 2017). This increases the likelihood of greater discipline and law and order, making the overall custodial environment and experience unhealthy (Coyle 2002). The prison programme, which covers only convicted populations, continues to exclude undertrials, and their rehabilitational needs remain unattended and unaddressed. The burden on the prison staff has repercussions for their relationships and the treatment of prisoners (Coyle 2002).

The opening of prisons to development-sector organisations and their subsequent entry into prisons has changed the prison environment to the extent that prisoner issues are now receiving more attention. Issues that were not addressed earlier (children left outside, follow-up with lawyers, aftercare, etc.) are now getting attention (Bharadwaj 2008; Vadiraj and Gopal 2011). However, this continues to remain at a micro-level, with more attention to urban prisons and less to more rurally located prisons. Furthermore, a variety of programmes are being brought into prison, depending on what the organisation can and wants to offer. This collectively amounts to a fragmented, diverse, and subjective set of services. The prison department and personnel also see these services as needing to be monitored, in order to ensure that they do not contravene prison norms and rules. In this endeavour, there might sometimes be cooperation, while other instances will be met with non-cooperation. However, the prison staff still thinks that development-sector organisations are soft targets for the inmates, while the organisations believe that the prison administration may not be as receptive as desired. A process of requesting, negotiating, and explaining is what often precedes interventions by voluntary organisations.

Conclusion

The discourse on the reformation and rehabilitation of offenders is not new. Several committees and reports on criminal justice and prison reform, including the All India Committee on Jail Reform headed by Justice Mullah (BPRD 2003a), the Committee on Reforms of Criminal Justice System headed by Justice Malimath (Government Of India 2003), and the more recent committee on the draft national policy on criminal justice, headed by Madhava Menon (Ministry of Home Affairs 2007), have all made their recommendations. However, it is likely that two aspects may need greater understanding and investment. One is a more functional and operational understanding of the terms 'reformation' and 'rehabilitation', their nature, and what they entail. The second factor is the need to establish who is responsible for rehabilitation, as there is no one directly responsible for reintegration and reoffending as of now. This mandate needs to be given to a particular department if there is to be any in-depth work in this area. The prison department could be considered for this task, because otherwise, their role will remain limited to the implementation of custodial programmes without being accountable for their contribution and relevance to the lives of released prisoners. Their approach to rehabilitation will also remain confined to industries within prison.

The prison department and development-sector organisations currently function parallel to each other, with a palpable discomfort between the two. There is much scope for complementary and supplementary roles and synergy in the endeavour towards rehabilitation and reintegration.

A politically initiated re-examination of the provisions of incarceration as the primary response to being accused or convicted of crime is critical if we are to fulfil the goals of criminal justice. Furthermore, the prison department's opinions on and experiences of reformation and rehabilitation need to be documented and drawn on. Discussions that are both internally and externally facilitated need to take place periodically in an effort to enable a sharing of experiences, thoughts, and ideas, as well as an intermingling of positions taken by prison personnel, development-sector organisations, and academicians.

Endnote

1. The three strikes sentencing law in some states in the USA aims to increase the sentences of offenders previously convicted of two or more violent crimes or serious felonies, and limits their chances of receiving punishment other than a life sentence.

References

Bharadwaj, P. 2008. *Community Participation in Prisons: A Civil Society Perspective*. New Delhi: Commonwealth Human Rights Initiative. Available at http://humanrightsinitiative.org/old/publications/prisons/community_participation_in_prisons.pdf (accessed November 2021).

Brennan, T., M. Brietenbach, and W. Dieterich. 2010. 'Unravelling Women's Pathways to Serious Crime: New Findings and Links to Prior Feminist Pathways'. Louisville, Kentucky: American Probation and Parole Association.

Bureau of Police Research and Development. 2003a. *Implementation of the Recommendations of All-India Committee on Jail Reform (1980–83)*. Vol. 1. New Delhi: Ministry of Home Affairs.

______. 2003b. *Model Prison Manual for the Superintendence and Management of Prisons in India*. New Delhi: Ministry of Home Affairs. Available at http://bprd.nic.in/WriteReadData/userfiles/file/5230647148-Model%20Prison%20Manual.pdf (accessed November 2021).

Committee on Empowerment of Women (2016–2017). 2017. *Tenth Report: Women in Detention and Access to Justice*. New Delhi: Lok Sabha Secretariat. Available at http://164.100.47.193/lsscommittee/Empowerment%20of%20Women/16_Empowerment_of_Women_10.pdf (accessed November 2021).

Coyle, A. 2002. *Managing Prisons in a Time of Change*. London: International Centre for Prison Studies. Available at http://www.prisonstudies.org/sites/default/files/resources/downloads/managing_prisons_0.pdf (accessed November 2021)

Foucault, M. 1975. *Discipline and Punish: The Birth of the Prison*. New York: Vintage Books.

Government of India. 2003. *Committee on Reforms of Criminal Justice System: Report*, Vol. I. New Delhi: Ministry of Home Affairs.

______. 2007. *Report of the Committee on Draft National Policy on Criminal Justice*. New Delhi: Ministry of Home Affairs.

______. 2018. *Women in Prisons: India*. New Delhi: Ministry of Women and Child Development.

Haney, C. 2002. 'The Psychological Impact of Incarceration: Implications for Post-Prison Adjustment'. Los Angeles: University of California-Santa Cruz. Available at https://www.urban.org/sites/default/files/publication/60676/410624-The-Psychological-Impact-of-Incarceration.PDF (accessed November 2021).

Jacobson, J., C. Heard, and H. Fair. 2017. *Prison: Evidence of its Use and Over-use from Around the World*. London: Institute for Criminal Policy Research. Available at http://www.prisonstudies.org/sites/default/files/resources/downloads/global_imprisonment_web2c.pdf (accessed November 2021).

Kameswari, G., and V. Nageswara Rao. 1999. 'The Sentencing Process: Problems and Perspectives'. The Indian Law Institute.

Liddell, M., and M. Martinovic. 2013. 'Women's Offending: Trends, Issues and Theoretical Explanations'. *International Journal of Social Inquiry* 6 (1), 127–142.

Mauer, M. 2004. 'Thinking About Prison and its Impact in the Twenty-First Century'. Fifteenth Annual Walter C. Reckless Memorial Lecture, Ohio State University. Available at https://www.sentencingproject.org/wp-content/uploads/2016/01/Thinking-About-Prison-and-its-Impact-in-the-Twenty-First-Century.pdf (accessed November 2021).

National Crime Records Bureau. 2014. *Prison Statistics India 2013*. New Delhi: Ministry of Home Affairs.

______. 2015. *Prison Statistics India 2014*. New Delhi: Ministry of Home Affairs.

______. 2016. *Prison Statistics India 2015*. New Delhi: Ministry of Home Affairs.

Niruphama, R. 2007. 'Need for Sentencing Policy in India'. Paper presented at the Second Critical Studies Conference: 'Spheres of Justice'. Available at www.mcrg.ac.in/Spheres/Niruphama.doc (accessed November 2021).

Penal Reform International. 2013. *Balancing Security and Dignity in Prison: A Framework for Preventive Monitoring*. London: Penal Reform International. Available at https://cdn.penalreform.org/wp-content/uploads/2013/11/security-dignity-v8-final_for-web.pdf (accessed November 2021).

______. 2017. *Global Prison Trends 2017*. London: Penal Reform International. Available at https://www.penalreform.org/resource/global-prison-trends-2017/ (accessed November 2021).

Prayas. 2002. *Forced Separation: Children of Imprisoned Mothers (An Exploration in Two Indian Cities)*. Mumbai: Prayas, Tata Institute of Social Sciences.

Radhakrishnan and Sikri. 2014. Narendra Singh vs State of Punjab & Anr, March 2014.

Sahni, S. 1989. 'Women prisoners: The remand and undertrial experience'. Ph.D. thesis, Tata Institute of Social Sciences, Mumbai.

Scott, D., and H. Codd. 2010. *Controversial Issues in Prisons*. Maidenhead: Open University Press.

Sevdiren, O. 2011. *Alternatives to Imprisonment in England and Wales, Germany and Turkey: A Comparative Study*. Heidelberg: Springer-Verlag.

Simpson, S., J. Yahner, and L. Dugan. 2008. 'Understanding Women's Pathways to Jail: Analysing the Lives of Incarcerated Women'. *The Australian and New Zealand Journal of Criminology* 4 (1), 84–108.

Sumter, M., E. Monk-Turner, and J. Rougier. 2012. 'Offenders Perceptions of Reentry Needs in Trinidad and Tobago: An Exploratory Study'. *International Criminal Justice Review* 22 (3): 297–308. Available at http://citeseerx.ist.psu.edu/viewdoc/download?doi=10.1.1.872.2640&rep=rep1&type=pdf (accessed November 2021).

Tong, P. 2017. 'The Other Side of Murder'. *Indian Journal of Social Work* 78 (4), 651–674.

Vadiraj, S., and A. Gopal. 2011. 'Social Work in India's Criminal Justice Institutions: Needs, Experiences and Challenges'. Case Study: Series 1. Sir Dorabji Tata Trust and Allied Trusts. Available at https://www.tatatrusts.org/upload/pdf/social-work-india-criminal-justice-institutions.pdf (accessed November 2021).

Van Ginneken, E. F. 2016. 'The pain and purpose of punishment: A subjective perspective'. Working Paper, The Howard League of Penal Reform. Available at https://howardleague.org/wp-content/uploads/2016/04/HLWP-22-2016.pdf (accessed November 2021).

Vibhute, K. 2006. *Open Peno-correctional Institutions in India: A Review of Fifty-Five Years, Experiences and Expectations*. Max Planck Institute for Foreign and International Criminal Law. Available at https://pure.mpg.de/rest/items/item_3014411_1/component/file_3014412/content (accessed November 2021).

Visher, C., N. Lavigne, and J. Travis. 2004. *Returning Home: Understanding the Challenges of Prisoner Reentry. Maryland Pilot Study: Findings from Baltimore*. Washington, D.C.: Urban Institute, Justice Policy Center. Available at https://www.urban.org/sites/default/files/publication/42841/410974-Returning-Home-Understanding-the-Challenges-of-Prisoner-Reentry.PDF (accessed November 2021).

Notes on the Contributors

Mahuya Bandyopadhyay is Associate Professor, Department of Humanities and Social Sciences, Indian Institute of Technology, Delhi. She is the author of *Everyday Life in a Prison: Surveillance, Confinement, Resistance* (2010) and co-editor of *Towards a New Sociology in India* (2016). Her current interests revolve around unravelling connections between prison and non-prison environments through research in the areas of organisational sociology and prison studies, urban governance and the sociology of crime and violence.

Uma Chakravarti is a feminist historian who has taught at Miranda House College for Women, Delhi University. Among her many publications are *Rewriting History: The Life and Times of Pandita Ramabai* (1998), *Gendering Caste through a Feminist Lens* (2002), and *Thinking Gender, Doing Gender: Feminist Scholarship and Practice Today* (2016). She is closely involved with the women's movement as well as the movement for democratic rights in India. She is also a filmmaker whose latest film, *Yeh Lo Bayaan Humaare*, explores the prison experiences of women during the 1970s in India.

Madhurima Dhanuka is the Programme Head of the Prison Reforms Programme. She is a lawyer with an LL.M. in Criminal Justice from the University of Nottingham, UK. Prior to joining CHRI she practised in the High Court of Madhya Pradesh. She has been associated with CHRI since 2008, and has published numerous studies, reports, and resource materials on issues relating to prisoners and the criminal justice system.

Mangala Honawar is a Social Worker by profession and works with a funding agency for innovative mental health initiatives in India. She has around fifteen years of experience of working on issues of family violence, community policing, mental illness, destitution, criminal and juvenile justice with a Social Work approach. She is also a Trustee of the Malati Vaidya Smriti Trust, focusing on issues concerning women and children.

Upneet Lalli is Head (Training and Research), Institute of Correctional Administration (ICA), Chandigarh. She has trained more than 9,500 police and prison officers in programmes conducted by the ICA. Her publications include *Best Prison Practices in India, Problems of Women Victims of Crime, Child Rights and the Law*. She is closely associated with policymaking on prisons and correctional administration at the state and national levels.

Rimple Mehta is a Lecturer at the School of Social Sciences, Western Sydney University. She has previously worked at the School of Social Work, Tata Institute for Social Sciences, Mumbai and School of Women's Studies, Jadavpur University, Kolkata. Her research and field engagements broadly focus on women in prison, refugee women, and human trafficking. Her paper, 'So Many Ways to Love You / Self: Negotiating Love in a Prison', won the 2013 Enloe Award. She is the author of *Women, Mobility and Incarceration: Love and Recasting of Self across the Bangladesh-India Border* (2018). She has worked with women in prisons in Mumbai, Kolkata, and in detention centres in The Netherlands.

Sadaf Modak is a journalist with *The Indian Express* and writes on issues of prisoners, law, human rights, the criminal justice system, and gender. She completed her Masters degree from the School of Social Work, Tata Institute of Social Sciences, Mumbai.

Sharmila Purkayastha is Associate Professor, Department of English, Miranda House, University of Delhi. She has co-edited *Towards Freedom: Critical Studies on Rabindranath Tagore's Ghare Baire* (2007) and *Bad Women of Bombay Films: Studies in Desire and Anxiety* (2019), and has co-authored articles on the political and cultural practices of literature.

Vijay Raghavan is Professor, Centre for Criminology and Justice (CCJ), School of Social Work, TISS, since 2005. Prior to 2005, he was Project Director, Prayas: Social Work in Criminal Justice, a field action project of the CCJ, engaging with the protection of legal rights and social re-entry of criminal justice clients, with a special focus on women, children and youth. He has written extensively on prison reforms, undertrial prisoners, social re-entry of custodial populations, social work intervention in criminal justice nomadic and denotified tribes, and homelessness and penalisation of poverty.

Shereen Sadiq is Professor, Department of Sociology, Aligarh Muslim University. The focus of her research has been correctional administration and women in prison, and she has contributed to these issues through her research and publications in national and international journals.

Kanupriya Sharma is a doctoral research scholar at the Institute of Criminology, University of Cambridge, UK, and a recipient of the prestigious Gates-Cambridge scholarship. Her research focuses on the intersections of gender identity, cultural agency, familial and community honour in the lives of incarcerated women in India. Kanupriya has previously been a Chief Minister's Urban Leaders Fellow with the Delhi Commission for Women, and has founded the `Cambridge Decolonising Criminology Network' in January 2020.

B. D. Sharma is an IPS Officer of the West Bengal cadre since 1980. He has held a number of important charges in the Police Department, including the charge of Add. S. P. Barrackpore, Superintendent of Police, Murshidabad and South-24 Paraganas Districts, and Dy. Commissioner of Police, before being promoted as D.I.G of Police. He then worked in Border Security Force as DIG at Jaisalmer and IG in Jammu & Kashmir. On his return to West Bengal cadre, he was posted as Inspector General of Correctional Services, West Bengal, and as Head of Prisons of West Bengal State, he introduced a number of pathbreaking initiatives in prisons. He headed the Sashastra Seema Bal (SSB), a Border Guarding Force of India, as its Director General before superannuation in 2016.

Penelope Tong is Fieldwork Supervisor, School of Social Work, Tata Institute of Social Sciences, Mumbai. She has been a senior social worker with Prayas, a field action project of TISS, for seventeen years. She has worked with women prisoners, their children, women and young males released from prison, and victims of violent crimes and their families. Her interests relate to the issues and contexts of persons perpetrating and being victimised by crime, and mental health as a critical factor.

Index